THE NEW TERRORISM:

How to Fight It and Defeat It

by Van Hipp

THE NEW TERRORISM:
How to Fight It and Defeat It

by Van Hipp

Countinghouse Press, Inc.
Bloomfield Hills, Michigan

THE NEW TERRORISM:
How to Fight It and Defeat It.

by Van Hipp.

Countinghouse Press, Inc.
6632 Telegraph Road # 311
Bloomfield Hills, MI 48301
Countinghousepress.com

First Edition: February, 2015

Hardcover: 978-0-9911102 0-9
Paperback: 978-0-9911102 1-6

Cover design: Andy Carpenter Designs
Printed in the United States of America by
Color House Graphics, Grand Rapids, MI

DEDICATION

To the men and women of the nation's armed forces and to our first responders who have kept America and its people safe.

Table of Contents

Acknowledgments

There are many people who have provided invaluable advice, suggestions, and encouragement throughout the process of researching and writing this book. It is impossible to list of all of them, but they have my sincere thanks and appreciation for their help and guidance.

There are several key individuals I would like to especially thank:

Peter Hannaford, who helped convince me of the need to write a book focused on making America's homeland safer and acted as my "quarterback" as we worked our way through the chapters. Research Associate Robert Zapesochny made many valuable suggestions and verified hundreds of facts. Others who have contributed greatly to the research are Rob Cohen, Joshua Paul and Michael Cameron. And my special thanks go to my assistant, Haylee Wilson, for her devotion and tireless energy.

Leonard Charla, my publisher who made this book possible, and Diane Nine, my literary agent, for understanding early the need for a book focused on the changing nature of threats to America's homeland and specific recommendations to make us all safer.

My thanks also go to former Speaker of the House Newt Gingrich for his friendship over the years, and to my friends Spike Karalekas and Marc Rotterman for their advice and recommendations.

I've also been fortunate to receive the advice and encouragement from experts in a number of subject areas: former U.S. Secretary of Energy, Dr. Jim Edwards, for his insight on the beginnings of real missile defense; Dr. Clifton Lacy, Director of the International Institute for Terror Medicine; and General Bo Rybeck for his expertise in biological countermeasures. I've had an especially outstanding team of researchers who have contributed greatly to this book. As a result of the hard work of each of these individuals and others who have requested anonymity, we now have a book focused on the main threats to the security of America's homeland, together with recommendations to make America safer for this and future generations.

Foreword

By Newt Gingrich

As you think about America's future and our country's leadership in the years to come, consider the national security implications of this extraordinary book. The world today is more complex and more threatening than anyone understands. And it is changing much faster than our current systems are capable of dealing with. Very few people have had the courage to look at the full range of threats we face and consider how we must change our thinking and our structures to meet them.

Van Hipp has spent a lifetime studying national security and working on these issues. He has done Americans a great service in these pages.

Far more than most analysts, Van understands that the real danger from the New Terrorism is much greater than a suicide bomber with a body vest or even a hijacked airplane being flown into a building, as horrible as those possibilities might be. He understands that the New Terrorism includes a full range of threats which could lead to disasters that are catastrophic on a scale we have never seen before.

Indeed, some of these are so great that they pose a risk of complete societal collapse. If our enemies get their hands on the capabilities they desire (the technology to launch an electromagnetic pulse attack, for instance), they will seek to destroy entire American cities or even to cripple our entire civilization.

Those are threats worth taking very, very seriously.

Unfortunately, as Van understands, most so-called analysis of our national security is shallow historically, lacking in imagination, and unwilling to confront how big and how real the dangers are.

Van also understands that we have to develop responses commensurate with the scale of the threats. He has the courage to tell the truth both about those who would destroy us and what it will take to keep America and her allies safe. We should measure every potential leader, and especially every potential commander-in-chief, against the Van Hipp standard as we prepare for 2016 and beyond.

And they should all read this book.

Newt Gingrich
Arlington, Virginia

Introduction

In 1986 a delegation of *mujahadeen* fighters from Afghanistan was welcomed to the White House by President Ronald Reagan. Americans were celebrating the tough and resilient guerillas who were using U.S.-made shoulder-fired rocket launchers to shoot down Soviet helicopters.

The project hastened the end of the Soviet occupation of Afghanistan. The *mujahadeen* were routinely described as "freedom fighters." Most were fighting for the freedom of their country.

Some--mostly volunteers from other countries--were fighting for a larger cause: the elimination of all non-Muslim influence in the Muslim world. One of these was Osama bin Laden, a young scion of a prominent Saudi family. Drawn by the gritty success of the Afghan fighters, he fought with them.

When the Russians left, the U.S. mostly abandoned Afghanistan to its own devices and the country fell into internecine battle, led by regional warlords. In time a new contingent joined the fight. They were the *Taliban* (Arabic for "students"), graduates of *madrassas* in Pakistan. In these schools the curriculum consisted largely of rote learning of the Koran and the *hadith*, the writings and sayings of the prophet Mohammed. The students were taught that in its fundamentals, these sources were a guide to every aspect of life. Once their lands had become rid of foreign influences and the historic Caliphate reestablished, the *umma* (all Muslim people) could be united under this banner. Civil, secular governments would not be needed, for the Koran and *hadith* had prescriptions for everything in daily life. Disputes would be settled by clerics. *Sharia* law would prevail (some of its prescriptions antedated Mohammed).

In Afghanistan the Taliban promised clean, uncorrupted rule and an end to seemingly endless battles between warlords. This had an appeal to many in the war-weary country. The Taliban prevailed on the battlefield. Once the central government was theirs, they proceeded to install the most severe version of *Sharia* law imaginable. Executions for minor infractions were frequent. Women could not go to school. Scarcely any form of recreation was permitted.

Osama bin Laden, had gone to Afghanistan to join the *mujaheddin* initially in the fight against the Soviets. He saw victory there as the first step in an Islamist campaign to rid Muslim countries of outside influences. He considered Westerners to be decadent, materialistic and evil. He attracted volunteers. The Taliban in Afghanistan invited him to bring his al Qaeda to build and operate a chain of terrorist training camps from which they could direct attacks against Western interests as part of a holy war. Osama bin Laden found this situation congenial. He dreamt of training an organization of skilled bomb-makers and other operatives who would carry out coordinated attacks on Western targets. The purpose of terror attacks would be to so discourage Western countries that they would withdraw from countries with majority or large Muslim populations. And, he reasoned, if the attacked countries and organizations did not retaliate, he would strike again and again until they finally decided to withdraw from the Muslim world. Making Baghdad once again the seat of the Caliphate was one of his goals. Once there was a vital center, he and his supporters believed, the Muslim world could expand rapidly and continue to consolidate its gains.

For these purposes, Osama bin Laden had founded *al Qaeda*. First, it operated from Sudan. Then, the Taliban cooperated by letting him build his training camps in several locations in Afghanistan. The call went out for like-minded young men to come to the camps to be trained to join the fight against foreign infidels who, Osama was convinced, were corrupting Muslim life.

How and When the World Caught Fire

During the 2008 presidential primaries then-Senator Barack Obama told audiences that the Bush Administration's policies had made us no safer since the events of September 11, 2001. He was mistaken. Had he said, "We are safer, but not safe enough," he would have been correct. And, if he were to say it again today, he would still be right.

Four hijacked airliners and more than 3,000 lives lost--these were the horrendous events that day that jolted the entire nation into awareness of our vulnerability to attack from fanatical and dedicated enemies. The attack had been carried out with careful planning and execution by 19 young Arab men, most of them from Saudi Arabia. These were not the dispossessed of the Middle Eastern "street," but well-educated, middle-class young men who had been radicalized by the likes of Osama bin Laden and his *al-Qaeda.*

We didn't know we were in a war until that terrible day in September 2001. The Nineties dawned with the Soviet Union gone, replaced by a cluster of independent states. All over the world nation after nation was embracing the structure of democratic capitalism. That is, secular, pluralistic democracies combined with market economics. The future looked bright, indeed, after the end of the Cold War.

The West in general and the United States in particular, however, were not paying attention to what was happening in Afghanistan. Once the Taliban had taken over and invited Osama Bin Laden to set up terrorist training camps, he did.

What Osama had in mind was a series of attacks on Western--especially American--targets to probe his enemy's resolve. If the response was weak, he would step up the attacks, with a climax intended to destroy important symbols of America and to cause an American retreat from global engagement.

The first target was the Khobar Towers, an American military high-rise barracks apartment building in the Eastern Province of Saudi Arabia in 1996. This was followed by bombings of the U.S. embassies in Kenya and Tanzania in 1998. That year Osama also issued a "declaration of war" against the U.S. It was not taken seriously. It should have been. In 2000, his forces orchestrated the bombing of the U.S.S. Cole in Yemen's Aden harbor. Earlier, in 1993, terrorists set off a truck bomb in the underground garage of New York's World Trade Center.

The Clinton Administration treated all these events as matters of law enforcement ("bring the perpetrators to justice"), not as the first elements of a *jihad*, or holy war. The only retaliatory action taken was to bomb what turned out to be a pharmaceutical factory in Sudan and an empty al-Qaeda training camp in Afghanistan.

Then, on September 11, 2001, *al-Qaeda* struck, using hijacked airliners and destroying the World Trade Center towers in Manhattan, hitting the Pentagon and barely missing other Washington targets with a third airliner that crashed in a Pennsylvania field (a crash caused by quick-thinking passengers who stormed the terrorist-controlled cockpit).

Osama and his allies underestimated the American response. The nation was jolted into action. In a matter of weeks Afghanistan was swept clean of *al-Qaeda* and the Taliban regime. The process of bringing peace and stability to Afghanistan continues to this day, however, for the Taliban have proved resilient and resourceful. Osama is dead, but his followers and allies are still operating out of remote areas of Pakistan. This is despite our capture of key operatives and killing others by means of drone aircraft. *Al-Qaeda's* inspiration of terrorist activity continues, abetted by affiliates in Yemen, Somalia, the African

Maghreb and elsewhere. Evidence includes the Madrid train bombings of March 11, 2004, the London subway bombings of 2005, and successful attacks (*e.g,* .in Indonesia), along with numerous thwarted or botched ones elsewhere by homegrown cells inspired by *al-Qaeda.*

The Three Hundred Twenty-eight Years' War

It is no coincidence that al-Qaeda struck on September 11. It was the anniversary of the defeat in 1683 of the Ottoman Turks at the gates of Vienna. On that day and the next, a German-Polish-Lithuanian army--under the command of the King of Poland--lifted the second siege of that important trade hub. The effort to take Vienna had been the high-water mark of Muslim expansion into Western Europe. From that time on, the Ottoman Empire began to shrink and lose influence until, at the end of World War I, its lands were carved into French and British spheres of influence. In 1923, Kemal Ataturk ended it formally with the creation of the Republic of Turkey, thus assigning the Ottoman Empire to history.

The loss at Vienna represents one more major "humiliation" in the eyes of today's Islamists. It followed the success of the Spanish Catholic *reconquista* in 1492 when the army of Ferdinand and Isabella overran the last Islamic holdings on the Iberian Peninsula, Andalusia (*al Andalus*), and brought to an end several centuries of rule by the Moors, as they were called.

Gradually, the growth of Western influence throughout the Middle East piled real and imagined humiliations of Islam upon one another, such as the Crusades to take the Holy Land from the Muslims who themselves had been invaders in the 7th and 8th Centuries. Some young Muslims saw the root of their problems today as the willingness of many Muslims to live within the framework of a secular society with a civil government. A collection of Islamic scholars from the 15th Century onward argued that the only way to achieve the kind of near-perfect society they believed had been experienced in the time of the Prophet Mohammed and the first four caliphs after him (the "Right-guided Companions") was to live entirely by the Koran and the *hadith*. If one did that, they contended, there would be no need for a civil government, for the Koran was a guide to every aspect of life. Minor disputes would be settled by learned clerics based at the caliphate in Baghdad. Islamic law would be strictly enforced. Muslims who had been willing to live in secular/civil societies would be required to recant or be subject to extermination.

These scholars believed that gradually the Islamic nation--the *umma*--would spread its influence until the entire world had come under its sway. Infidels would convert or live as second-class persons (in a status called *dhimmitude*), or be eliminated.

Al-Qaeda's radical Islamists and their allies dreamt of a restored Caliphate in Baghdad from which the Muslim world had been ruled for 500 years. A restored Caliphate, in the very center of the Muslim world, would be the hub for training and deploying terrorist cells to wreak continuous destruction on U.S. and European targets until they withdrew entirely from the Middle East, taking the Israelis with them.

Enter George W. Bush with a bold plan: Preempt *al-Qaeda's* goal by overthrowing the dictator Saddam Hussein or establishing a democratically-elected government in Iraq. It was no easy--or widely popular--task; however, it threw a monkey wrench into the plans of *al-Qaeda* and its allies. The reasoning was that if they could be eliminated there as an effective guerilla force—and in Afghanistan—we would have made great progress in the war

Against radical Islamism. The war may continue for another generation, but win it we must--and can.

Throughout the world, the sunny optimism of the early Nineties has given way to uncertainty and anxiety that new wars may flare up any day, as old ones continue to simmer or burn. With the world's economies interconnected, the industrialized nations are subject to economic burps and social stress. Abrupt interruptions in normal life can make investors, markets and governments jittery, whether it be radicals attacking a natural gas plant in Algeria, a suicide bomber in a Baghdad shopping district, North Korea launching more missiles or Iran edging closer to producing nuclear weapons.

While there are millions of moderate Muslims who want nothing more than to live their lives in peace, Islamists with an ideological agenda are not among them. Take the Muslim Brotherhood for example. Founded in 1928 in Egypt by Islamic scholar Hassan al-Banna, it initially concentrated on religious and social service messages, but later on nationalistic fervor. In 1954 it was banned by the Egyptian government.

The anti-Mubarak revolution in 2011 gave it an opportunity to join the ranks of youthful protestors and gain legitimacy again. It won the first free election after the "Arab Spring" through its political arm the Freedom and Justice Party, but its newly elected president soon began to stifle freedoms and sought to rule by decree until the military imprisoned him and again outlawed the Brotherhood.

While the Brotherhood officially eschews violence it has spawned and encouraged a number of violent *jihadist* groups in other countries. The Brotherhood's credo says it all: "Allah is our objective, the Quran is our law, the Prophet is our leader and death for the sake of Allah is the highest of our aspirations."

Over the years the Muslim Brotherhood has been willing to be patient in order to gradually build a large membership, develop an efficient organization and await opportunities to gain power.

Osama bin Laden had no patience for a decades-long campaign to gain public favor. For him, direct and decisive action in the form of terrorist acts was the way to go. Many young men in the countries where *al Qaeda* and its affiliated organizations operate have found his call to action the Siren song that stoked their dreams of glory.

Looking Forward

The United States has done much to increase homeland safety and that of our military and civilian assets overseas. Many radical Islamists, foreign and domestic, have been captured or killed. Our intelligence has improved and there has been no major attack on the United States proper since 2001. That, however, does not mean we are safe enough. In the following pages you will learn what we must do to protect ourselves in an age of continuous attempted assaults by terrorists. It will require determination by our best minds and a great deal of money to defeat the resourceful radical Islamists. Defeat them we must.

Chapter One

Our Missing Homeland Missile Defense

When Kim Jong-un, North Korea's bellicose leader responded to United Nations sanctions after his latest nuclear test, it was in the form of a threat to rain missiles on West Coast cities of the United States. He was immediately countered by President Obama's press secretary who confidently stated that we were prepared to effectively defend against any such attack.[1]

So far as the West Coast is concerned, the press secretary was more-or-less correct. The U.S. does have two missile defense facilities, one in Alaska, the other in California; however, the accuracy is not yet perfect.[2]

As for the East coast and the rest of the country, there is nothing to prevent, say, an Iranian missile from being successfully aimed at a city. That is, if Iran had the capability of delivering a missile at that distance. There is another threat: submarine-launched missiles from off our shores. Such a missile, timed to detonate at a high elevation, could create an Electro-Magnetic Pulse (EMP) which would deliver no radiation to the ground below, but rather a damaging blow to all electric and electronically-powered objects. This could affect a large geographical area. Consider the chaos that could ensue with no power, no water pumping, no refrigeration, rapid reduction of food supplies. No computers, no banking transactions, all retail sales recorded by hand. Even if emergency food supplies could be brought in from other areas, the potential for disruption of daily life would be great.

What is missing in all this is the political will to make homeland missile defense seamless for the entire U.S., then allocation of the funds required to do so. In light of the 2013 "sequester" of billions of dollars of defense funds the possibility of accomplishing this is problematic at best.

Getting to Missile Defense

President Ronald Reagan publicly introduced the intention of developing a national missile defense system in a televised speech from the Oval Office on March 16, 1983. It was no last-minute whim. The idea had been percolating with him for years. In his first year as Governor of California, 1967, he was invited by Dr. Edward Teller, the physicist then in charge of the Lawrence Livermore National Laboratory in Livermore, California to visit the facility and learn about the scientists' work there. He made the trip one day and learned that the focus of their studies was missile defense. That is, creating interceptors to prevent incoming ballistic missiles from afar from hitting U.S. targets.

Twelve years later, in July 1979 (and a private citizen), he was invited to visit the North American Aerospace Defense Command's (NORAD) advanced missile-tracking system deep in a mountain outside Colorado Springs, Colorado. He learned that an intercontinental ballistic missile launched in the Soviet Union could be detected within seconds by this sophisticated system. Yet, the only thing we could do in response was to launch our own ICBMs targeted at the Soviet Union.[3]

There must be a better way, Reagan thought; a way to avoid such a cataclysmic exchange. Later that summer, the Carter Administration completed negotiations with the Soviet side on the Strategic Arms Limitation Treaty, "SALT II." The White House offered to send an expert to Los Angeles to brief Reagan on its contents. He accepted and the briefing took place. Soon after, he called together several independent defense experts to discuss it.

He concluded that he would publicly oppose SALT II because all it would do, as he put it, is "reduce the *rate of increase* of strategic arms, when what is needed is Strategic Arms *Reduction* Talks." toward gradually reducing nuclear arms in the world. One of the unsung heroes of missile defense in the Reagan Administration was President Reagan's first Secretary of Energy, Dr. Jim Edwards. Following President Reagan's inaugural, Dr. Teller was frustrated that he was not able to get to President Reagan to discuss the Strategic Defense Initiative as he was being blocked by then Office of Management and Budget (OMB) Director David Stockman who was concerned with cost issues. Dr. Teller expressed his frustration to Secretary Edwards.

During a series of luncheon meetings, Edwards and Teller discussed the fact that the Department of Energy kept the original letter of Albert Einstein's to President Roosevelt proposing the "Manhattan Project." Edwards felt that SDI could be President Reagan's own Manhattan Project. Accordingly, Edwards obtained a copy of Einstein's letter to Roosevelt, had Dr. Teller prepare his own personal letter to President Reagan, and then put his own letter to the President on top of both letters emphasizing how Dr. Teller's Strategic Defense Initiative could be President Reagan's own Manhattan Project. Edwards then arranged for Dr. Teller to meet personally with President Reagan, bypassing Stockman, and the rest is history.

On March 8, 1983, as president, Reagan addressed the National Association of Evangelicals in Orlando, Florida. The delegates had been debating whether to support a so-called "freeze" in the development and deployment of nuclear weapons by the United States. Reagan urged them to take a moral stand. He said that as long as the Soviet leaders, "preach supremacy of the state, declare its omnipotence over individual man, and predict its eventual domination of all peoples on Earth, they are the focus of evil in the modern world."[4] By calling the USSR and its satellites "an evil empire," he was denounced by the arms control fraternity in Washington.[5]

Over the years, this group had believed that the only effective way to prevent nuclear war between the two "superpowers" was to have Mutually Assured Destruction (MAD). That is, the two sides would have roughly equal abilities to annihilate one another, therefore neither would try. This state of perpetual tension had seemed to work for years, and its U.S. devotees considered anything else provocative and dangerous. Reagan was sure that millions of people in the U.S. and behind the Iron Curtain agreed with him, however, about the "evil empire."

Two weeks later, from the Oval Office, he announced on national television the creation of the Strategic Defense Initiative or SDI. He said the United States was about to "embark on a program to counter the awesome Soviet missile threat with measures that are defensive. Let us turn to the very strengths in technology that spawned our great industrial base and that have given us the quality of life we enjoy today."[6]

He knew from intelligence reports that the USSR was stretching its economy close to the breaking point by increasing conventional arms at a rapid rate and that it could not afford to compete with such a program. And, if the U.S. succeeded, it would render Soviet ICBM's useless. Reagan later seriously offered to share a successful SDI program with the Soviet Union, thus one day eliminating the need for either side to have an ICBM arsenal. They declined the offer.

MAD devotees scoffed at Reagan's SDI proposal, denouncing him as a dangerous warmonger. News media attempted to trivialize the concept by dubbing it "Star Wars." Opponents and skeptics said a missile defense system was impractical, although Lt.

Gen. Daniel Graham (USA Ret.), former head of the Defense Intelligence Agency, insisted some elements of an SDI program were available "off the shelf," while others would have to be developed.

After the collapse of the Soviet Union in 1991, many internal documents came to light that showed just how seriously the men in the Kremlin took Reagan's proposal. One, Gennady Gerasimov, who was the Soviet Foreign Ministry's spokesman in the 1980s, said, "Reagan's SDI was a very successful blackmail. The Soviet Union tried to keep pace with the U.S. military buildup, but the Soviet economy couldn't endure such competition."[7]

A former adviser to Soviet leader Leonid Brezhnev, Genrikh Grofimenko said, "Ninety-nine percent of the Russian people believe that (the United States) won the Cold War because of your president's insistence on SDI."[8]

A Rocky Road

While Reagan pushed missile defense throughout his presidency and progress was made, since then, White House support has waxed and waned. Many Democratic office holders and liberal commentators opposed missile defense from the beginning and continued to do so over the years.

Throughout the thirty years since Ronald Reagan first announced the SDI, remnants of the MAD fraternity continued to express skepticism of SDI's feasibility and, as the Soviet threat declined then disappeared, U.S. skeptics and opponents adopted a "who needs it?" attitude. They found a more sympathetic audience from some members of Democratic White House teams. Nevertheless, over the years the U.S. has spent a total of $157.8 billion on missile defense.[9]

Today's Threat

Ever since Reagan and Mikhail Gorbachev signed the first nuclear arms reduction treaty in 1987 (eliminating an entire class of weapons), the U.S. and Russia have been systematically reducing their nuclear arsenals. Reagan's dream of ending the need for any such arms was not to be realized, however, because new threats have emerged since then.

Both Iran and North Korea represent clear and present dangers to world peace. They are sworn enemies of the West in general and the U.S. in particular. North Korea has systematically developed and tested nuclear weapons and missile technology. Iran, which claims to be pursuing only peaceful uses of nuclear power, shows every sign of developing weapons and has been working steadily on improved missile systems for delivering such weapons.

Unlike Cold War days, the nature of the threat today goes beyond ICBMs to such things as submarine-launched missiles, "dirty" bombs smuggled into U.S. cities, even missiles intended to spread deadly germs. There is also the possibility of radical Islamist gangs of terrorists gaining access to delivery systems. For example, if radicals were to prevail in Pakistan, could they gain access to that country's stockpile of nuclear weapons and its missile delivery systems?

Space-Based Missile Defense

All but the very shortest range ballistic missiles travel through space. Thus, it seems logical that the most capable missile defense system would be one based where the missiles fly--in space.

President George H. W. Bush proposed such a system, called Global Protection Against Limited Strikes (GPALS) in 1990. It included a constellation of space-based interceptors called Brilliant Pebbles. The Clinton Administration cancelled Brilliant Pebbles while separating other components of GPALS.[10] The Brilliant Pebbles technology could be revived, thus ultimately making it possible to deploy space-based interceptors. Experts contend that a space-based system of this type could not stop a fleet of thousands of missiles, but it could stop, say, 15 Iranian or North Korean missiles.

Meanwhile, with the Obama Administration not yet showing an inclination to revive the GPALS or Brilliant Pebbles systems, we must rely on a combination of ground- and ocean-based missile defense systems.

Current U.S. Ground-based Missile Defenses

The nation's ground-based missile defense system can probably effectively protect the West Coast. Until March 2013, the Department of Defense had interceptors in both California and Alaska: 26 at Fort Greely, Alaska, and four at Vandenberg Air Force Base in California. On March 15, Secretary of Defense Chuck Hagel announced that in light of the apparent growth in the range of North Korean missiles, 14 more ground-based intreceptors would be added at Fort Greely.[11]

Commenting on the announcement the same day Adm. James A. Winnefeld, Jr., vice chairman of the Joint Chiefs of Staff, said the U.S. will "put the mechanics in place to deny any potential North Korean objective to launch a missile to the United States, but also to impose costs upon them if they do."[12]

A network of land and ocean-based radar systems support the interceptors. Early Warning radar equipment is being upgraded. This has been done at Beale Air Force Base in California and at Flyingdales in the U.K. Upgrade work is also underway at Thule Air Force Base in Greenland and is scheduled for Clear Air Force

Base, Alaska. The less-powerful west-facing COBRA Dane radar on Shemya Island in the Aleutians off Alaska completed an upgrade in 2010.[13]

Since 1999 when the Pentagon's Missile Defense Agency first tested its Ground-based Midcourse Defense (GMD), interceptors have struck dummy (that is, unarmed) targets in eight of 16 tests. Aegis Ballistic Missile Defense has been more successful with 28 interceptions in 34 attempts from 2002 to 2013. This includes three successful interceptions with the Standard 2 (SM-2) Block IV Interceptors. The remaining tests used SM-3 missiles. Terminal High Altitude Area Defense (THAAD) has been the most successful with a perfect record of 11 successful interceptions since 2006.[14]

Aegis Ballistic Missile Defense Systems

There are, however, no ground-based missile defense facilities to protect the most populous part of the nation, the Eastern one-third. Sea-based Aegis Ballistic Missile Defense systems (BMDs) on U.S. Navy ships can track incoming missiles, but at yet are configured only to intercept short-range missiles (1,000 kilometers) with SM-2 missiles and medium-range missiles (1,000 to 3,000 kilometers) with SM-3 Block IA, not ICBMs (More than 5,500 kilometers).[15]

As of December 2013, the Navy has 30 ships with BMD capability--five Ticonderoga class cruisers and 25 Arleigh Burke class destroyers. Sixteen ships are assigned to the Pacific Fleet and 14 to the Atlantic Fleet. In response to increased demand by combatant commanders, the Missile Defense Agency and Navy are working to increase the number of Aegis BMD-capable ships. Fleet deployments have not been announced as of this writing.[16]

International Missile Defense

The Aegis system is central to the Obama Administration's Phased Adaptive Approach (PAA) to missile defense in Europe. The first deployment of European PAA Phase I capabilities came on March 7, 2011, when an Aegis BMD cruiser, *U.S.S. Monterey*, armed with SM-3 Block IA missiles, was sent to Europe.

The U.S. is on schedule to provide land-based SM-3 Block IB ballistic interceptors to Romania in 2015 and SM-3 Block IIA interceptors to Poland in 2018. These interceptors will be able to counter any Iranian short- or medium-range missiles.[17] In March 2013, however, U.S. Secretary of Defense Hagel announced that the U.S. was intent to "restructure" plans to deploy SM-3 Block IIB against ICBMs in Europe within the coming decade.[18] This was seen by many as a concession in arms control negotiations with Russia. Foregoing this deployment would leave Europe undefended to potential ICBM attacks from Iran in the future.[19]

For the moment, the Iranians do not have ICBMs, but they are determined to get them. In general, defense should be based on our best assessment of how our adversaries will grow in military strength along with their intent. As we have seen over the years, Iran and North Korea are both resolute in improving their missile programs.

Japan is the first ally to purchase Aegis BMDs in part because of the North Korean threat. They are for its four KONGO-class destroyers. The SM-3 Cooperative Development Program is for joint U.S.-Japan development of a 21-inch diameter variant on the SM-3 interceptor (called "Block IIA") to defeat longer-range ballistic missiles. Deployment of these is scheduled to begin in 2018.[20]

Whither the U.S. East Coast?

Despite all these promising developments and the probability that the West coast could be successfully protected in the event that, say, a North Korean ICBM was headed toward it, the East Coast has only the occasional Aegis-capable ship cruising in offshore waters of the Atlantic Ocean and it would not be equipped to counter ICBMs.

A system of radar detection and interceptor installations at key points on the East Coast, as in Alaska and California, would provide a degree of safety not now available. In September 2012 the National Research Council, in a report, recommended installation of an East Coast site to defend against a possible Iranian ICBM attack.[21]

There is in development a new system of detection that could be lower in cost and capable of deployment in far less time than it would take to construct defense systems of the kind we have on the West Coast. It is called the Joint Land Attack Cruise Missile Defense Elevated Netted Sensor System, or "JLENS."

JLENS has been under development since 2005 at a cost of approximately $2 billion thus far. It was in development in response to requests from combatant commanders, especially those in CENTCOM which covers Iran, the Strait of Hormuz and the Persian Gulf. Developed by the U.S. Army, JLENS is the latest and most advanced system to detect, identify and track multiple potentially hostile targets such as low-flying cruise missiles, large-caliber battlefield missiles, air and land delivery vehicles, ships and even small boats.[22]

JLENS is not only a potentially important new system for field commanders, it can also be adapted for homeland defense against cruise missiles launched from surface ships and submarines. It could detect nuclear-tipped missiles and also chemical and biological warheads or Electromagnetic Pulse (EMP) warheads.

The JLENS system is based on twin aerostats (lighter-than-air craft) that amount to "Eyes in the Sky." These would be lifted to an altitude of 10,000 feet or more. One aerostat carries a search radar covering a 400-mile diameter circle. It can detect missiles, ships, aircraft and land vehicles. Its aerostat partner carries a fire-control radar that is integrated with defense missiles such as Patriot, Aegis (on land or sea), the Avenger System and AMRAAM. JLENS can also be linked to fighter aircraft such as F-35s or F-16s or to Unmanned Aerial Vehicles (UAVs) if such drones are in the area that JLENS has under observation. JLENS thus gives these various platforms the ability to engage hostile threats at extended ranges.

JLENS was successfully tested on April 25, 2012 at the Utah Test and Training Range where it destroyed a simulated hostile cruise missile. Congress authorized and appropriated $40.3 million to conduct a second test, requested by field commanders; however, in the face of substantial budget cuts, the Defense Department asked Congress for permission to divert those funds elsewhere.[23]

Lighter-than-air ships proved their worth as long ago as the Civil War when Union spotters telegraphed reports about Confederate troop concentrations from balloons a distance of three miles away.

In World War II, airships were successful in escorting conveys. Out of 89,000 ships covered by airships, only one was sunk. This compares with 532 ships sunk when there was no airship coverage. The airships carried depth charges and homing torpedoes, making the conveys dangerous territory for U-boats.[24]

Airships were so successful because their range was much longer than that of conventional aircraft, they had long endurance on patrol and provided 360-degree defense against the enemy.

Nowadays, The JLENS system would, in many cases, give field commanders more time to react to threats. Most surveillance systems often give the commanders just seconds to respond to an identified target (this is still true in the case of ICBM's or medium range BMs--where Patriot or Aegis missiles must quickly be launched). With other identified threats, JLENS may give the commander perhaps fifteen minutes to assess the exact nature of the threat and take effective action. The extra time may be just enough for the commander to distinguish between a hostile target and one that, on examination, is not.

Cost Effective

Compared to fixed-wing aircraft for detection and fire-control, JLENS is inexpensive. An AWACS or JSTARS can provide coverage similar to that of JLENS, but at a cost as much as 700 percent greater. These fixed-wing systems also required four or five such aircraft to provide 30 days of 24/7 coverage that one JLENS system provides.

Much of the additional cost of fixed-wing aircraft to do this job lies in the price of fuel. JLENS uses just a fraction of the fuel consumed by an AWACS or JSTARS unit. And, it can be manned by five persons versus a crew of 20 on AWACS or JSTARS.

Safety Factors

The JLENS aerostats are filled with non-flammable, low-pressure helium, making them survivable. Flying at 10,000 to 15,000 feet they are beyond the range of rifles, machine guns and rocket-propelled grenades (RPGs). The Army tested man-carried air defense rockets, such as Stingers, against aerostats and found the rockets did not fuse against the fabric. Indeed, they passed right through, leaving only mendable tears in the fabric.

Will high winds buffet the JLENS airships? Army tests showed them surviving 100-knot winds, when they are either airborne or moored. They can withstand both direct and near lightning strikes. The system can fly above overcast weather. It can remain in operation in 60-knot winds, as well as sand and dust storms. Its operational temperature range is -40 degrees Centigrade to +49 degrees Centigrade. In addition to being operational in conditions that would keep conventional aircraft on the ground, JLENS can be transported by road, rail, sea or air with its aerostats ready to fly within 72 hours of arriving at their destination.[25]

Defending the Homeland

JLENS, with its exceptional surveillance capabilities can enhance the defense of the homeland against nuclear missiles, cruise missiles, even weapons smuggled by land or seas.

In 2004, 2008 and 2009, a Congressional commission warned of the potential devastation of an ElectroMagnetic Pulse weapon (EMP). Its members said such a weapon could cover most or all of the country, could destroy the national electrical grid and cause chaos and social breakdown.

Unlike a regular nuclear weapon which leaves great amounts of radiation in its wake, an EMP, launched high enough, produces none. No one on the ground is killed or injured from the blast. Only the electrical grid suffers, but the damage may be 100 percent in the area covered.

Such an attack, by an enemy state or terrorist gangs with the capability, could be delivered by ICBM or a missile fired by a submarine or a surface vessel. If it were detonated over the central U.S., it could cover most of the continent.

A small EMP, delivered by ship or submarine a few miles off the East Coast could knock out power along most of that coast. This is not idle speculation. There have been credible reports of

North Korea making an effort to develop EMP weapons and of test missiles conducted by Iran from barges in the Caspian Sea. The earliest Iran tests date from15 years ago.

The Committee on the Present Danger, in a white paper published in 2012, outlined a plausible scenario. It assumes Iran and/or North Korea completes development of nuclear warheads, but lacks either land or submarine capabilities of launching ICBMs. How would they do it? The CPD says one way would be to buy commercially available cruise missile launchers from a Russian company, *Kontsern-Morinformsistem-Agat.* While the Russian government insists such launchers would never be sold to rogue nations, the history of Russian arms sales to third parties is not reassuring.

Four Russian "Club-K" cruise missiles and a launch control room could be disguised in standard 40-foot shipping containers for loading on the deck of a merchant ship. The missiles could carry EMP weapons.

Add to this the fact that there are not enough U.S. Aegis ships for continuous patrol to intercept missile launches near all U.S. coasts, the lack of Coast Guard ships to inspect merchant vessels and the vast number of containers at sea at any one time and you have the makings of a hard-to-prevent EMP launch.

If it were in place on the East coast, JLENS, with its long-range detection capability, could provide the time needed to get countermeasures actively ready to meet the threat.

Going Forward

Frank Kendall, Under Secretary of Defense (Acquisition, Technology and Logistics), wrote, JLENS is "essential to the national security ... there are no alternatives to the program that will provide acceptable capability to meet the joint military requirement at less cost."[26]

In December 2012, the JLENS was successfully tested and impressed defense analysts.[27] DoD should take immediate action to put the JLENS system into production.

In addition, the Department of Defense should add at least one ground-based missile interceptor installation on the East coast to deter Iran from attempting to send an intercontinental ballistic missile our way.

These actions can provide the Eastern one-third of the nation a missile defense security it does not have. JLENS can of course also help protect our interests and allies in the Middle East and Asia.

Chapter Two

Cyber War: The Final Frontier

For centuries, wars were only fought by land and sea. It was not until the 20th century that we had the technology to fight in the air with fighters, bombers, and intercontinental ballistic missiles. The space race gave the United States another front in military combat. The Persian Gulf War showed the world that the American domination of the air, sea, and land was augmented by our use of satellites gathering intelligence and guiding our troops through the desert. In the 21st century, the threat of terrorism is being rapidly eclipsed by the fifth dimension of warfare, cyber war.

Unlike the other four dimensions of land, sea, air, and space, the cyber dimension is artificial. This makes strategic planning difficult. While the United States military can draw up war plans against a conventional adversary, such as Saddam Hussein's Iraq or North Korea, the geography of this front is in a constant state of flux due to the rapid growth in technology.

In 1965, Stephen Moore, the co-founder of computer chip maker Intel, observed that the number of transistors on integrated circuits doubles every two years. This rule has not only remained constant for decades, but there have been similar rates of remarkable increases in technology. Futurist Ray Kurzweil predicted that we will be able to develop computers more advanced than the human brain. Such rapid increases in technology helps explain why the cyber war is the most complicated national security threat the United States has ever faced. The speed of change in the cyber realm is much faster than the Pentagon's ability to analyze it and adapt. In 2010, then Deputy Secretary of Defense William Lynn highlighted this advantage in an article he wrote in *Foreign Affairs*:

> "On average, it takes the Pentagon 81 months to make a new computer system operational after it is first funded. Taking into the account the growth of computing power suggested by Moore's law, this means that by the time systems are delivered, they are already at least four generations behind the state of the art. By comparison, the iPhone was developed in 24 months. That is less time than it would take the Pentagon to prepare a budget and receive congressional approval for it."[1]

Like the War on Terror, the cyber war has no discernible front. Hackers and terrorists can both be "lone wolves" or supported by a hostile state or criminal syndicate. There will be no clearly defined moment in the cyber war--or the War on Terror--that is equivalent to the surrender ceremony on the USS Missouri in 1945. While there has never been a world without conflict or malcontents, the United States has never been more unprepared for a conflict than it has been against the cyber war. Our enemies are consistently inflicting damage on the American economy. For example, every year we lose more intellectual property on government, university and business networks than all of the intellectual property in the Library of Congress.[2] The Library of Congress and the British Library are by far the two largest libraries in the world with over 150 million items each.

Four Events: 9/11, Katrina, Lehman, and Cyber Command

To fully understand how unprepared our government is against this threat, it is necessary to review four remarkable events, which defined the first decade of the 21st Century and changed the structure of the federal government. Each of these events showed that many institutions within the public sector were grossly incapable of adapting to the new threats facing the United States. It also provides us with some idea of how to fight the cyber war.

In chronological order, the first of the four events was the attack of September 11, 2001. When the 9/11 Commission finished its report, former New Jersey Governor Thomas Kean, co-chairman of the Commission, informed the nation that, "This was a failure of policy, management, capability, and above all a failure of imagination."[3] While our government had the resources to recover after the attack, the lack of imagination to anticipate this crisis is something we cannot afford in the cyber war.

The lack of imagination is remarkable in this instance because, according to the 9/11 Commission Report, "On Friday, December 14, 1998, the CIA included an article in the Presidential Daily Brief describing intelligence received from a friendly government about a threatened hijacking in the United States."[4] Most of the text was declassified and it was entitled, "Subject: Bin Laden Preparing to Hijack U.S. Aircraft and Other Attacks." Although the most famous Presidential Daily Brief (PDB) was the August 6, 2001 article entitled "Bin Laden Determined To Strike In U.S." we now know that for almost three years our government knew of bin Laden's intent to hijack aircraft and attack the United States. We also know that we could have killed him long before 9/11.

According to Michael Scheuer, who was the Chief of the CIA's Bin Laden Issue Station from 1996-1999, and an advisor to the unit from 2001-2004, there were at least eight to ten opportunities where the CIA located and could have killed Osama bin Laden during the Clinton Administration. Although he has been a strong critic of President Bush, Scheuer wrote an op-ed in July, 2006 condemning Richard Clarke's book, *Against All Enemies*, because he believed it provided readers with a false impression that the Clinton administration did everything it could to stop bin Laden.[5] Scheuer would later note that at no point during his tenure as Chief of the Bin Laden Issue Unit were they authorized to kill bin Laden.[6]

Considering how inept our government was before 9/11 to connect the dots, we should understand that the equivalent of 9/11 in the cyber realm has the potential to be even more devastating towards our economy. We cannot wait for our government to respond to the disaster. They must have the authorization to attack known hackers whenever they are located.

Even before 9/11, our nation was attacked by serious cyber-attacks. In May, 2000, the "Love Bug" was caused by a hacker in the Philippines. This virus spread to 50 million computers within days. Our own military was forced to shut down several computers to clean out the virus. The "Love Bug" cost $15 billion dollars of damage. To put that number in perspective, the most expensive natural disaster, before Hurricane Katrina, was Hurricane Andrew, which cost $25 billion dollars in 1992.

While individual hacking can rival the damage caused by natural disasters, this threat has only recently begun to receive any serious news coverage. Hurricane Katrina is the second of the four events that defined the 2000s. It caused $108 billion in damage.[7] According to General Keith Alexander, the former head of both the National Security Agency and the U.S. Cyber Command, American companies lose $250 billion dollars in intellectual property every year. The number of cyber attacks on critical infrastructure in the United States has surged from only nine in 2009 to over one hundred sixty in 2011.[8]

The increase in cyber-attacks is scary enough. The inability of the federal, state and local authorities to work effectively in Katrina should leave us worried because a cyber-attack will hit this nation with less warning than a hurricane. While the state and local authorities generally performed well in over 200 floods, tornados, hurricanes, and other emergencies from 2001 to 2005, the state and local authorities in Louisiana were not able to handle the situation.[9] After years of investigations, we also know that Katrina taught us that Congress did not take the threat seriously enough until it was too late.

From 2001 to 2005, Louisiana received $1.9 billion dollars, more than any other state, in construction projects from the Army Corp of Engineers, which were mostly appropriated to prevent flooding in New Orleans. Yet hundreds of millions of dollars were actually spent on wasteful pork barrel projects.[10]

These wasteful projects included projects named after politicians instead of providing necessary hurricane protection.[11]

We must not also forget that less than a month before Katrina hit, the highway bill was signed. The total bill cost taxpayers over $286 billion dollars to be spent over six years. Although parts of the bill had several important infrastructure provisions, the highway bill alone had 6,371 earmarks worth over $24 billion, which was more than enough to pay for stronger levees.[12] The federal government had to spend $15 billion after Katrina to rebuild the levees in New Orleans.[13]

Considering the rapid advances in technology, the increased number of cyber-attacks and our nation's inability to respond quickly, we need to see any cyber-attack from abroad as an act of war and not just a crime. We cannot wait for a trial. Our technicians must hit back to prevent people from stealing our information and/or causing damage to our networks.

In Article 1, Section 8, of the U.S. Constitution, it was agreed that, "The Congress shall have the power to....raise and support Armies...to provide and maintain a Navy...." Our founding fathers wisely gave the U.S. Congress the power to raise and support the US Military. Note that they expressly did not give this power to the Executive Branch of government. One of the problems in recent years is that Congress in adopting and implementing its "no earmark pledge" has, in the eyes of many, ceded its constitutional responsibility to raise and support the U.S. Military to the Executive Branch of government.

There is no question that the earmark process prior to the congressional ban was greatly abused. Earmarks, however, done the right way did provide for key technologies that were and continue to be helpful in the War on Terror, such as suicide bomber detection technology and unique mine-clearing technology used by the U.S. Military to go through deadly mine fields in the northern part of Afghanistan right after 9/11. An administration not placing a high value on security can create a lot of mischief by gutting important national security programs knowing that Congress' hands are tied as a result of its abdication of its constitutional authority. Thus, it is important that Congress maintain its authority to raise the armies and maintain the Navy, but do so in a way that is fully transparent and ensures close consultation with our military leadership with regard to legitimate unfunded military requirements.

In June 2013, the Senate Appropriations Committee held a hearing on cyber security. This was in part to talk about the cyber threat and to assess President Obama's request for a $13 billion budget for cyber security for fiscal year 2014. Out of $13 billion, approximately $9.2 billion was allocated to the Department of Defense. Of that $9.2 billion, $3.5 billion would be assigned to protect the Pentagon's network, $2.17 billion to the National Security Agency, and $582 million to U.S. Cyber Command. Outside the Defense Department's $9.2 billion budget, almost $1.3 billion would be sent to Homeland Security, $589 million for the Justice Department, $215 million for the Commerce Department, $197 million for the National Science Foundation, $50 million for the General Services Administration, and $37 million for the State Department.[14]

In the cyber war, we are seeing billions of dollars lost every day in stolen data and intellectual property. Considering the necessary secrecy in conducting our national security, it will be difficult to know if this spending will be effective in protecting our networks, financial institutions, or our infrastructure.

What we can say for certain is bad people will be coming after us and that our economy is vulnerable. In no area would hackers cause more damage than within our financial institutions. For this reason, the third event that defined the 2000s was the collapse of Lehman Brothers in 2008. The failure of the bank created a crisis of confidence that nearly brought the collapse of the entire financial system. In any book or chapter on cyber warfare, policymakers have to think where could a state, and/or hacker, inflict the most damage on our nation's economy. For that reason securing our financial system should remain a top priority in the cyber war.

When Lehman collapsed, Congress initially authorized up to $700 billion in the Economic Emergency Stabilization Act (EESA). Of the $422.2 billion that was actually spent from the TARP program, $432.8 billion has been returned to the government. The funds spent on TARP include $245 billion for bank investment programs, $80 billion for the automotive industry, $68 billion to save the American International Group (AIG), and $19 billion for credit market programs.[15] This program was a tactical success through preventing the collapse of the financial system and the auto industry. TARP, along with the Federal Reserve, also provided funds to prevent AIG from failing

TARP stabilized the financial system. Nevertheless, the "too big to fail" banks have become bigger since the crisis. The five biggest banks in the United States possessed $8.5 trillion in combined assets by the end of 2011. These five banks are JPMorgan Chase ($2.3 trillion), Bank of America ($2.1 trillion), Citigroup ($1.9 trillion), Wells Fargo ($1.3 trillion), and Goldman Sachs ($900 billion). These banks have assets equivalent to 56 percent of the America's GDP ($15.1 trillion) at the end of 2011. At the end of 2006, these five banks only had $6 trillion dollars in combined assets. That was equivalent of 43 percent of America's GDP ($13.4 trillion) at the time.[16] Any progress that was made by

TARP could be quickly reversed if any of these financial institutions could be brought down through hacking.

From September 2012 to March 2013, the number and intensity of distributed denial-of-service (DDoS) attacks on our nation's largest bank computer systems have been increasing. The main culprit was a cyber-terrorist organization called Izz Ad-Din Al Qassam. This organization is believed to have ties to Iran.[17]

Russia and China also rely on proxies for cyber-attacks. While both of these countries rely on cyber terrorist groups, the Russians and Chinese limit their espionage to military targets and private companies. Iran is run by a theocracy that is unlikely to be restrained in trying to take down financial institutions.

Today, DDoS attacks can make it difficult to gain access to a website and withdraw money from an account. Should technology continue to advance, the range of nightmare cyber-attack scenarios will increase and our nation's ability to defend itself will continue to diminish.

Even today's technology is dangerous for financial institutions. In 2012, suspects obtained prepaid debit card numbers by hacking into financial institutions. These data were sent to an army of hackers in two dozen countries. The data were encoded onto magnetic strips. People started going to ATMs and withdrawing money until the banks shut down the accounts. On December 21, 2012, the hackers in this scheme stole $5 million. On February 19, 2013, they struck again. Even without the element of surprise in the second attack, the government's ability to improve its defenses was no match for the hackers' ability to improve their offensive capability. In the second attack, they were able to make 36,000 fraudulent withdrawals. They stole $40 million dollars within 10 hours.[18] Replacing the magnetic strips on debit cards with built-in chips would help prevent this type of fraud in the future; however, no strategy can be credible by fighting the last war.

The collapse of Lehman, and the exposure of the European banks to AIG, taught us that systemically important financial institutions in the United States can potentially lead to the collapse of other financial institutions throughout the world. Even if we could resolve the problem of too-big-to-fail in the United States, we may not be able to fix the problem of banks that are too interconnected to fail. For example, after the financial crisis in 2008, the European banks were actually in worse shape in terms of their capital requirements. The average bank in the European Union had enough capital to cover 5.9 percent of outstanding loans in 2007. By 2010, the average amount of capital only increased to cover 6.5 percent of outstanding loans.[19] As the threat grows, we could have thousands of hackers stealing tens of billions of dollars daily. This death by a thousand hackers cutting through the system could eventually collapse one of our major financial institutions.

One of the problems with too-big-to-fail is not just the issue of moral hazard. The risky behavior also stems from the false impression that the government can effectively bail out an institution before it is too late. The speed of a cyber-attack may not give the government enough time to save a financial institution.

In the Cold War, the United States and the former Soviet Union were deterred because such a conflict could only result in the destruction of both countries. This realization, along with the use of the atomic bomb against Japan, ultimately prevented a nuclear exchange. The Cold War deterrence models will not work on radical Islamic terrorists and/or cyber criminals.

Beyond the growing threat of our adversary, the response of the Obama administration has been totally inadequate. For example, in December 2011, an American drone crashed in Iran. The U.S. Government claimed the drone had malfunctioned. The Iranians claimed they had launched a cyber-attack, which brought the drone down. After the incident, President Obama responded to a question on this matter at a news conference. He said, "We've asked for it back. We'll see how the Iranians respond."[20] To even waste time asking the Iranians for the drone back was naïve. It shows how little our government understands the Iranians in particular and the dangers of the cyber war in general.

An inept response to cyber-attacks marks the fourth event that defined the decade of 2001-2010. This event was classified by our military and is still not well known to the general public. Apparently, in 2008, a flash drive was inserted into a laptop at an American military base in the Middle East. Its "malicious code" spread throughout the network and allowed a foreign intelligence service to transfer an enormous amount of data. While the full extent of this damage remains classified, the Pentagon claims that this was the worst breach to our national security in history. In 2009, the creation of the U.S. Cyber Command was a response to this growing threat.[21]

In 2013, the threat continued to grow. There were over 140 attacks on Wall Street from September 2012 to March 2013. In the summer of 2012, Aramco, the national oil company of Saudi Arabia, was attacked in cyber space. While there was no impact on production, approximately 30,000 computers were damaged.

In response to this threat, the U.S. Cyber Command plans to establish 27 teams to work specifically with combat commanders in provide planning and to advise on both defensive and offensive options in any part of the world. The remaining teams will be assigned to protect our nation's military networks. The Pentagon projects that all of the teams will be ready by September 2015.[22]

For now, most of the destructive potential in the cyber war is still in the possession of states with advanced capabilities. While these countries can be deterred, what happens if, unexpectedly, rogue states or cyber-terrorist groups meet the necessary capability to bring about a significant cyber-attack? If technology continues to advance rapidly, it is only a matter of time before such a thing will happen. Richard A. Clarke, who advised three presidents on issues from counterterrorism to cybersecurity, was asked if we would get hit with a massive cyber-attack. Clarke responded:

"I don't know that there ever will be a cyber-Pearl Harbor. What I do know is that we're suffering the death of a thousand cuts in the little Pearl Harbors that are happening every day, where cyberespionage and cybercrime are having a huge cumulative and negative effect. The theft of research and development information, the theft of intellectual property, the theft even of transactional data is giving huge economic advantage to our competitive opponents in other countries."[23]

Possible Showdowns with North Korea and Iran

North Korea: The current North Korean leader has the potential for miscalculation in the cyber war. Kim Jong Un is young and needs to show his generals that he is tough. Without more engagement, the chance of a conflict is more likely. Beyond the fact that this North Korean leader is unpredictable, there is the new South Korean President, Park Geun-hye. She is the eldest daughter of Park Chung-hee and Yuk Young-soo. Her father was

President of South Korea from 1963-1979. The North Koreans tried to kill him at least twice. The first time was in 1968 when Unit 124 of the North Korean Special Operations Forces infiltrated the DMZ and launched an attack on the Blue House (South Korea's equivalent of the White House). The raid was unsuccessful.

In 1974, Mun Se-guang, a Japanese-born Korean, who was sympathetic to the North, tried to assassinate President Park. The assassin missed his intended target, but killed his wife, Yuk Young-soo. The new South Korean President has a career of trying to improve relations with the North, despite her mother's death.[24] When she met with Kim Jong Il in 2002, she admitted that it was tough for her to meet with him. Beyond her personal animus, this new South Korean president, like many elected women leaders, must look tough in front of her own military and political leaders.

Hillary Clinton lost the 2008 Democratic nomination in part because she was seen as too hawkish by the Democratic primary voters.[25] If, however, she went further to the left, some voters in the middle might not have voted for a woman if she wasn't seen as tough on national security. In South Korea, the situation is worse. According to the World Economic Forum, South Korea is ranked 108th in gender equality. It is sandwiched between Kuwait and the United Arab Emirates.[26]

Since both Korean leaders know that a shooting war could be devastating for both sides, a cyber-war could be a useful way for both sides to look tough in front of their constituencies without alienating their allies. In March, 2013, it was reported that North Korea launched a massive cyber-attack on South Korea, shutting down nearly 50,000 computers and servers. These attacks targeted

South Korean banks and broadcasters. The investigators believe that six computers from North Korea were able to gain access to more than 1,000 South Korean electronic addresses. The South Koreans were able to trace some of the attacks to North Korea. They also were able to determine that half of the malware programs were used by the North Koreans in previous attacks.[27]

This situation is tense and is likely to escalate. North Korea has a 1.1 million-man army compared to 640,000 South Korean troops and 28,000 American troops on the peninsula. With 13,000 artillery pieces, and Seoul within 30 miles of the DMZ, hundreds of thousands could be killed before all the artillery pieces were taken out by air power.[28] A Korean conflict in the cyber sphere is one of the few areas that could be less costly than a conventional war. The good news is that people who build statues of themselves are not generally suicidal.

Iran: Islamic fundamentalists are not deterred by rational means. The events of recent years have shown that neither Sunni nor Shia fundamentalists respond rationally to economic pressure. For example Iran cut aid to Hamas in June of 2013 because it supported the Sunni rebels fighting the Assad regime in Syria. When Hamas won the Palestinian elections in 2006, it was estimated that it received £13 to £15 million a month. In Summer 2013, Iran provided only a very small amount and that was more to show its support for the Palestinian cause. Hamas was in no position to turn down the Iranian offer. It was clear that ideology was favored above economic considerations.[29]

Iran is no different from Hamas. The Iranian economy has been severely hit from economic sanctions. The country's crude exports in Spring 2013 dropped 39 percent from 2012 to 1.5 million barrels per day. This is the lowest daily production of exported oil since 1986. Back then, the country was at war with

Iraq.[30] By 2013, Iran was being sanctioned by the world because it is pursuing a nuclear weapons program. There is no need for this nuclear weapons program as much as there was no need for the President of Iran to deny the Holocaust, accuse the United States Government of orchestrating 9/11 and routinely call for the destruction of Israel.

In the cyber war, Iranian attacks on the U.S. are growing in sophistication. Unlike the Chinese or the Russians who steal our secrets because they want our technology, the Iranians are more inclined to engage in sabotage rather than espionage. It was reported in Spring 2013 that the Iranians hacked American oil, gas, and electricity companies.[31] If the United States or Israel is compelled to attack Iran's nuclear facilities, oil prices will likely go up. Sabotaging America's energy companies could be a useful way to raise prices and make an attack even more costly for the United States.

It should be noted that computer viruses were partially responsible for the greatest power outage in American history, which was the Northeast blackout in August, 2003. Over 50 million people in eight U.S. states and Ontario, Canada were without power. This crisis began in Eastern Ohio when three high-voltage transmission lines short-circuited and went off line when they came in contact with trees. Once these lines were inoperative, there was additional stress on the neighboring power lines.[32]

At the worst possible moment a virus caused malfunctions to the alarm system at the power company responsible for the inoperative lines. Because the alarm system could not provide adequate updates, operators did not know what was going on for over an hour. The impact of human errors also played a part in this calamity.[33] Local power outages are routine. Power outages that cascade into a regional blackout are very rare and are now less likely because of the northeast blackout in 2003. Although this blackout was not intended, this is one example of how inadequate computer security can lead to unforeseen risks.

As for the Iranians, they are likely to continue to attack us with increasingly sophisticated cyber tools. We are dangerously unprepared to deal with the threat of such attacks. James Gosler, a cybersecurity expert and veteran of the CIA, National Security Agency and the Department of Energy, said, "You can have vulnerabilities in the fundamentals of the technology, you can have vulnerabilities introduced based on how that technology is implemented, and you can have vulnerabilities introduced through the artificial applications that are built on that fundamental technology."

Gosler believes that only 1,000 people in the United States have the necessary skills to defend the country against the most complex cyber defense tasks. He estimated that at least 20,000 to 30,000 people are needed to meet the challenge of threats to government agencies and the nation's largest corporations.[34]

Recommendation 1: Recruit People at Home and Abroad

To meet the immediate needs of this task, we must recruit an "army" of people trained to defend the nation against this threat. In order to get these new specialists, we will need to recruit at both home and abroad. Providing National Security Scholarships to top computer science majors would be helpful. Students know that joining the military is a great way for people to pay down their student loans. We should also do the same with the cyber war.

The Chinese are experiencing a brain drain and we must exploit it. According to the Chinese Academy of Social Sciences, from 1978 to 2006, 1.06 million Chinese students studied overseas and 275,000 returned. Mandiant, a security firm, issued a report claiming that almost 90 percent of cyber-attacks on the American homeland originate from China.[36]

Attacks are growing more sophisticated. It was estimated by Systemac that the United States lost $338 billion in 2011 when calculating the direct loss of cyber-attacks along with the cost to repair networks that were hacked. Michael Hayden, the former head of NSA and the CIA, believes that this is a trillion dollar problem when you add the loss in intellectual property. Hayden recently pointed out that this is our nation's top threat and could already be the greatest transfer of wealth in human history.[37]

Recommendation 2: Declare PLA Unit 61398 and Its Affiliates to be Terrorist Organizations

The American public needs to have a name by which to personify this threat. I realize that some will say that our two-way trade of over $500 billion dollars makes China too valuable to escalate tensions. Yet the United States cannot compete with China if American companies annually spend millions, and sometimes billions, of dollars in research and development while Chinese continue to steal the resulting technology.

It was estimated that 90 percent of the Chinese espionage is committed by two groups: the Beijing-based Elderwood Group and the Shanghai-based Comment Crew.[38] Comment Crew can be traced to the Unit 61398 of the People's Liberation Army (PLA), while the Elderwood Group is also believed to have significant ties to the Chinese military. In the same way the U.S. Congress declared the Quds Force a terrorist organization, we can go after these groups because the Chinese want to downplay their ties with these organizations along with the twenty other identified cyber espionage groups that operate in China. This can work to our advantage. Instead of declaring a cyberwar on China, or the Chinese military, we are declaring a war officially on these two groups. Declaring these organizations to be cyber terrorist groups, gives the United States military the broad discretionary powers to go on offense. It can give the American people a feeling that this is a threat that is limited to a handful of groups.

Recommendation 3: Set Red Lines For the Cyber War

In the Cold War, the superpowers were encouraged to refrain from first-use of nuclear weapons. In a nation's defense, cyber-attacks can be a powerful way for certain countries to defend themselves against aggression. For example, the United States worked with Israel to launch the Stuxnet virus as a weapon to damage and set back the Iranian nuclear weapons program.

Considering that an American or Israeli air strike could have led to serious repercussions, cyber-attacks allowed us to focus on the problem while defending an ally against an existential threat.

In 2007, Russia attacked Estonia with distributed denial-of-service attacks to the websites of public and private organizations, including the Estonian parliament. It is important to point out that Estonia is a small country of just under 1.3 million people and almost a quarter of its population is composed of ethnic Russians. Russia has a population 143 million people.

There is no reason to suspect that Estonia was or is a threat to Russia. More importantly, this was an unprovoked attack. Its purpose was, apparently, to intimidate the Estonians.

The major powers should eventually adopt a no-first-use policy regarding cyber warfare. We should also recognize that weaker powers will use this technology to offset their weaknesses in conventional warfare. One of the biggest problems with cyber-warfare is that governments will likely require a disaster to produce an atmosphere of cooperation and refrain from the use of this dangerous technology.

In the 1960s, there was an episode on Star Trek entitled, "A Taste of Armageddon." It dealt with the dimensions of cyber warfare. In the episode, the crew of the Enterprise visits a planet that has been in a computer-simulated war with its neighboring planet for five centuries. Sometime before the episode, both sides agreed to a simulated war and have people actually report to a disintegration station to be executed. This way, people will only be killed and neither side will see the destruction of whole cities and other critical infrastructure. This way, people can keep their endless war without losing their civilization in the process.

When Captain Kirk arrives on this planet, he is quickly designated as a casualty in the last simulated attack. Kirk and his entire crew were told to report to a disintegration station or these planets will be forced to fight a real war. Captain Kirk manages to destroy two of these stations and forces the two planets to face the prospect of a real war with the hope that this will frighten them enough to stop. Toward the end of episode, Captain Kirk says:

> "Death... destruction... disease... horror... that's what war is all about, Anan. That's what makes it a thing to be avoided. You've made it neat, and painless. So neat and painless, you've had no reason to stop it. And you've had it for five hundred years. Since it seems to be the only way I can save my crew and my ship... I'm going to end it for you... one way, or another."[39]

Cyber-attacks cannot be regulated as they were in this Star Trek episode. People and their governments may have to feel the consequences of a threat before any swift action can be taken to provide the necessary cooperation among the various governments as well as coordination with the public and private sectors to make serious progress on this issue. That is why the United States has to go after cyber-terroris organizations. At the same time, we must also find a way for governments to understand that these attacks will only escalate in terms of frequency and sophistication.

Recommendation 4: Fight A Preventive War.

There is a big difference between a cyber war that is preventive rather than preemptive. In international law, the Caroline Affair established the standard of what constituted as an acceptable preemptive strike. In 1842, then U.S. Secretary of State, Daniel Webster wrote a letter in response to the incident claiming that preemption can be justified bearing in mind the "necessity that self-defense is instant, overwhelming, and leaving no choice of means, and no moment for deliberation."

By the time our government is fully aware that a government proxy, or sophisticated hacker, has obtained sufficient means to require "no moment for deliberation," they can hack into our networks and steal information that is worth billions of dollars. Since the threat is growing rapidly, along with the advances in technology, we need to fight a preventive war.

Scholars have debated for centuries about when it is appropriate to engage in a legitimate preventive action before a threat fully materializes. One of the best books on the topic of preventive war is Professor Michael Walzer's *Just and Unjust Wars: A Moral Argument with Historical Illustrations*. He points out that in the 1750s, Emmerich de Vattel, a Swiss jurist, suggested an interesting standard regarding a legitimate preventive war. He wrote:

> "Whenever a state has given signs of injustice, rapacity, pride, ambition, or of an imperious thirst of rule, it becomes a suspicious neighbor to be guarded against: and as a juncture when it is on the point of receiving a formidable augmentation of power, securities

> may be asked, and on its making any difficulty to give them, its designs may be prevented by force of arms."[40]

Our intelligence agencies will never know with certainty when cyber terrorist groups will reach a "formidable augmentation of power" to launch crippling cyber attacks. For proxy groups, it can happen very quickly. With a hacker, we have some margin for error. It is clear that the government can be most effective at protecting our networks by going after our enemy before they can cause damage to our economy.

As Vattel was writing about his standard toward preventive war, his analysis was based in reference to the events of 1700 and 1701. It was on the eve of the War of Spanish Succession. At the time, the Spanish king was dying without an heir. The blatantly expansionist desires of Louis XIV brought fear to many states in Europe because of the possibility that the Duke of Anjou, the grandson of Louis XIV, could become the next king of Spain.

A unified Franco-Spanish state was considered by many European states to be a potential future threat that needed to be prevented. Great Britain led an alliance to preclude an unfavorable shift in the balance of power in Europe. In the same spirit, we must stay on offense against any unfavorable balance of power against the United States. Our military remains dominant in conventional warfare; however, in the cyber war, our dominance could diminish if we do not fight a preventive war.

The inconvenient truth is that our government has been luckier over the last decade than many experts care to admit. In George Tenet's memoir, *At the Center of the Storm*, the former Director of Central Intelligence, pointed out that al-Qaeda acquired the services of two distinguished Pakistani scientists. The first was Sultan Bashiruddin Mahmood, who was a former director at the Pakistani Atomic Energy Commission. The second scientist was

Chaudhry Abdul Majeed, who retired from the Pakistani Institute of Nuclear Science and Technology.

Before 9/11, these two scientists formed the Ummah Tameer-e-nau (UTN). Officially, they provided social services to needy people. In reality, this organization was designed to gather the scientific personnel necessary to develop a nuclear bomb. According to Tenet, UTN was supported by scientists sympathetic to bin Laden and senior Pakistani military officials that were opposed to President Musharraf. One of the strongest supporters of UTN was Hamid Gul, who is the former head of Pakistan's Inter-Services Intelligence agency (ISI).

After 9/11, Director Tenet went to Pakistan to secure President Musharraf's support in capturing the UTN leaders Mahmood and Majeed. After Mahmood was captured, he confirmed to an intelligence source that both he and Majeed met with Osama bin Laden and Ayman al-Zawahiri in Afghanistan in August 2001. At that meeting, Mahmood told Osama that the hardest part to developing a nuclear weapon was actually getting the fissile material. According to Mahmood, Osama bin Laden asked him how difficult it would be if they already had the material. Mahmood wasn't sure if Osama was asking a hypothetical question.[41]

Al-Qaeda went to war with the United States before they could develop a nuclear weapon. If 9/11 had not occurred, it is reasonable to assume that the U.S. and its NATO allies would not have attacked al-Qaeda in Afghanistan. With a safe haven in Afghanistan, Osama bin Laden could have waited until Pakistani nuclear scientists helped him develop a nuclear bomb.

We cannot overlook this preventive achievement. I realize that preventive actions often have the potential for abuse though sometimes even legitimate actions are too harshly criticized. Walter Issacson points out in his biography of Einstein how much the famous professor regretted playing a decisive role in persuading Roosevelt to develop an atomic bomb before Nazi Germany. Einstein admitted that if he knew that the Germans would fail to build an atomic bomb, he said, "I never would have lifted a finger."[42]

Since even Einstein had no way of knowing whether the Germans could develop the bomb first, it would have been irresponsible for our government to abandon the Manhattan Project. Just as it would have been irresponsible to assume that al-Qaeda's pursuit of a nuclear weapon would end after American forces entered Afghanistan.

In late 2002 and early 2003, the al-Qaeda chief in Saudi Arabia, Abu Bakr, was in the process of buying three Russian nuclear weapons. According to Tenet's memoirs, Abu Bakr contacted al-Qaeda members Sayf al-Adl and Abdel al-Aziz al-Masri to discuss acquiring these nukes. These two particular terrorists were technically under a loose form of house arrest in Iran. Fortunately, al-Qaeda was foolish enough to launch an attack on Riyadh before it could complete the deal. After the May 12, 2003 bombings, the Saudis launched a significant crackdown of al-Qaeda. The Saudis were able to capture Abu Bakr in June 2003.[43]

As for other forms of WMD from al-Qaeda, the Tenet book provides a great deal of information on the unique threat posed by al-Qaeda. Ayman al-Zawahiri hired Pakistani scientist Dr. Rauf Ahmad to set up a biological weapons facility in Kandahar. Zawahiri was also able to recruit Yazid Sufaat to head al-Qaeda's anthrax program. Rauf Ahmad and Yazid Sufaat were both captured by the end of 2001.

Outside of Afghanistan, according to Tenet, Abu Musab al-Zarqawi of al-Qaeda in Iraq (AQI) had a chemical weapons facility in Khurmal, which is in Northern Iraq. Tenet reports that Zarqawi tested cyanide on one of his subordinates. During the

American invasion of Iraq, this facility was bombed. Intelligence would later confirm that poisons and toxins had been produced there.[44]

The kind of battle that was waged against al-Qaeda a decade ago is the same kind of preventive war that we need to fight against cyber-terrorists. Historically our government cannot take major action unless it is in response to a disaster. We certainly could not re-orient the Cold War era intelligence structure until 9/11 showed us how outdated it had become.

Recommendation 5: Cut Iran's Optical Cables Should Hostilities Escalate

More than half of Iran's population is less than 35 years old. These young people do not remember a world without internet and they openly defy the government's censors. They freely participate in banned websites such as Facebook, Twitter, and YouTube. The government sees the internet as a serious threat to its legitimacy and plans to cut off the country from the rest of the internet. Since 2005, Iran's government has been building a nationwide intranet. The North Koreans have such a system with a limited number of chat rooms and news coverage.[45]

Iranians have grown accustomed to the internet, and they will not give it up without a fight. In some ways, internet is to the Iranians what bread was to the Egyptians. In Egypt, it has been widely reported that the high price of bread led to riots in 1977 that nearly toppled the regime. The increases in bread prices in 2007 and 2008 led to further riots despite Egypt's huge bread subsidies. By the end of 2010, the price of wheat was at an all-time high. This was a critical factor in the fall of Mubarak in January 2011.[46] The Egyptians did not think their government could provide much for them. The one thing that they always expected from their government was bread that was both affordable and readily available to them. In a society such as North Korea, people do not expect the government to do anything and it is unthinkable to demand something. Because Egypt expected more, this led to a revolt. The same thing could occur in Iran.

If the Iranian attacks continue to intensify, we should threaten to sever their optical cables and even interfere with their satellite transponders to cut off their internet access. This could create a backlash strong enough to lead to a more pro-Western and accountable government in Iran.

Recommendation 6: Follow Georgia's Example

Georgia received cyber-attacks from Russia during the 2008 war between the two and over Georgia's breakaway regions of Abkhazia and South Ossetia. Even without the cyber front, the Georgians were greatly outmatched on the battlefield. By 2012, government officials in this former Soviet republic were learning how to fight back. Knowing that Russian hackers would breach the system, the Georgians felt that the battle could be won from within the system. The Georgians set a trap for the hackers and waited for them to open a file with a virus they had planted. When the hacker opened the file, the Georgian program seized control of the hacker's web camera. The Georgians got a picture of this hacker and they also stole his files, which included e-mails from an FSB agent (Russia's intelligence agency).[47] The United States should follow Georgia's example and plant booby traps so that hackers understand we will be willing to match them malware for malware.

Recommendation 7: Cyber War Needs Bipartisanship and Moral Clarity

Nowadays a remarkable number of people will support or critique certain policies depending on whether or not their party is control of the White House. We need to push for two big themes: bipartisanship and moral clarity.

The first is that any policy in the cyber war must maintain some degree of broad-based bipartisan support. This is why both parties need to work together on liability issues. Any bill that tries to create a new regulatory structure to this rapidly changing threat will soon be outdated. We cannot do this without the private sector. With its help, people can learn from each other and adopt "best practices" in the cyber war. In the War on Terror, we have asked very little of the American people. The majority of Americans were not at war--only the military. In cyber war, we must explain to our people that there is not enough space on this Earth to be safe from the cyber war.

There is no room for partisanship when it comes to defending the nation from cyber-attacks. Our politicians can disagree on many things, but this issue should not be one of them.

Bipartisanship is superficial without moral clarity. When cyber warfare was used to set back Iranian mullahs from advancing work on a nuclear bomb, this was not morally the same as Iranians attacking our critical infrastructure. And there is a great moral gulf between effective defense against cyber-attacks and actions such as those of Umar Farouk Abdulmutallab who boarded a Christmas Day 2009 flight from Amsterdam to Detroit, with no luggage or a coat. Rep. Bill Pascrell complained to Administration officials, "He was flying into Detroit without a coat. That's interesting if you've ever been in Detroit in December." This is after the passenger's father had complained to American officials that his son was radicalized.[48]

In the Boston bombings, our government was also warned by Russian officials about one of the Tsarnaev brothers. The FBI even investigated Tamerlan Tsarnaev, but found nothing wrong with him. If our government cannot identify a terrorist when interrogating one, how can they identify a hacker before he or she strikes?

Recommendation 8: Go After Wikileaks and Other Traitors

History will not look kindly on Edward Snowden's betrayal of the NSA or Bradley Manning handing over documents to Wikileaks. Manning has been tried and sentenced. In due course, Snowden should be tried under the Espionage Act of 1917. Looking ahead, our government should be allowed to use all necessary force to prevent any traitor from revealing sensitive information.

Recommendation 9: Never Share Out of Fear, But Don't Fear to Share

Our ability to have any chance to defend the country against this rapidly evolving threat will require the ability of U.S. Cyber Command to coordinate with Homeland Security, the Federal Bureau of Investigation, and most importantly the private sector. Situational awareness during a cyber-attack is impossible without the private sector. We need it to report suspicious activity and sometimes temporarily shut down certain networks. This means the military will have to share sensitive information with companies. Such cooperation will require protecting these companies from liability.

The natural government impulse to create an entirely new regulatory structure is not realistic in this instance. The rapid advances in technology make any regulation obsolete before it can be fully implemented. The U.S. Cyber Command needs allied governments and the private sector to help it report suspicious activity so that we can stay ahead of the hackers.

Recommendation 10: The Cyber War Can Only Be Won With the Expansion of Freedom

Singapore's statesman Lee Kuan Yew argued that one of the main reasons the United States will remain the most important country in the 21st century is that China cannot innovate as the United States does. We have immigrants from all over the world. The Chinese language is difficult to learn and the Chinese cannot quickly assimilate talented immigrants into their country even if that were its intention.[49] At the same time, the Communist system does not encourage innovation, which is one of the reasons why the theft of intellectual property has become essential for China's economic growth.

In their book, *Why Nations Fail*, authors Daron Acemoglu and James Robinson, provide an interesting example of two cities: Nogales, Arizona and Nogales, Sonora in Mexico. They share the same culture and geography, but the differences in politics, economic opportunities, and the rule of law best explains the great wealth disparity among these neighboring cities.[50] The example itself is one of many in this book that places the type of institutions as the lead indicator of a country's success.

The book argues that successful nations form inclusive economic and political institutions. Authoritarian countries form extractive institutions, which concentrates political power and economic power in the hands of parasitic elites. Inclusive societies and their institutions, through the rule of law, provide the opportunity for people to unlock their potential. Without the possibility of failure, there can be no innovation.

The best example of this was the failure of the Soviet experiment. The Soviet economy grew at a pace of six percent a year from 1928 to 1960. The authors explained that there was a great untapped potential for growth. Once peasants from the countryside were forcibly transferred into industry, workers became more productive. With the creation of new tools and factories to industrialize the country, growth slowed once the transition of these workers was complete. Without creative destruction and other incentives to innovate, economic growth was not sustainable.[51] China's economic growth will eventually slow down for the same reasons unless it begins to encourage an environment of innovation.

It was no coincidence that England industrialized faster than Russia during the Industrial Revolution. The English elites invested in the future and not the past. Prior to the Industrial Revolution, the main source of income by 18th century European elites was the land and the trade monopolies granted by monarchs. As nations developed, aristocrats lost their labor surplus to new industries.[52]

More efficient production and new technologies also forced aristocrats to pay their workers more and compete with more efficient businesses. There was eventually a backlash everywhere in Europe. While countries such as Russia and Austria-Hungary had strong monarchs that could keep reforms from continuing, England had a constitutional monarchy and a strong parliament that could let the forces of creative destruction continue.[53] It is for this reason that cooperation in the cyber war will be limited in such countries as China and Russia, unless they see that theft is not an alternative to economic and political reform.

We need a serious preventive strategy to show our rivals that we will not sit back. If we fight back, China and Russia may be deterred enough for us to force them to reform. With Russia and China, we can and will need some plausible distance by officially targeting only their proxies so that we can continue talking and doing business.

The more these two governments deny their links to their proxies, the better it is for the United States. Iran and North Korea have no serious deniability and we will likely require a more open escalation of the cyber conflict. Not all wars end well, but they do eventually end. If creativity is essential in this increasingly complex cyber war, the United States will win this one in the end.

Chapter Three

Securing Our Borders, Harbors & Ports

When television networks and news channels cover stories about undocumented aliens streaming into the United States familiar file footage is usually used, shot from an airplane above while several people below scurry along between scrub bushes looking for a place to hide. In fact, at least 40 percent of illegal immigrants now in the United States may have come as legitimate visa holders and simply failed to leave.[1]

Take the case of Maria (not her real name) from a Central American country. She traveled to California on a tourist visa to visit an aunt. She left behind an ill mother and three siblings who cared for her. She wanted to contribute to her mother's care and decided that getting a job here would be the best way to do it. Using the aunt's Social Security number she applied for a job through a private employment agency. They sent her for an interview to a couple who needed a live-in housekeeper for their large home. She was hired.

At Christmas time that year, when her employers wanted to make a gift to her of a trip home for the holidays, she tearfully confessed that her visa had expired and she had used her aunt's Social Security card. She had been a good worker and they did not want to dismiss her. Several months later the couple planned to move across the country, so her job would end. This was about the time the 1986 Immigration Reform legislation passed. She fell under it, received a work permit, and went into a computer training program with a large bank. She saved and bought a small home, then some rental property and had enough to educate her young son.

Not all expired-visa stories end so happily, but many such immigrants hold responsible positions. While legislation in the

Congress may finally solve the problem of what to do with the approximately 11.7 million undocumented aliens in the U.S., we lack a fully effective method of keeping track of aliens here on visas.[2]

Recommendation 1: Create a Comprehensive Visa Tracking System

The U.S. Government should create a nationwide database of such aliens, with basic data entered at the time they receive their visas. Then, upon arrival in the U.S., obtain the visa holder's current telephone, e-mail and mailing addresses. Also, obtain evidence of departure arrangements such as air tickets. Send him or her 30- and 15-day warnings before the visa expires. If the holder ignores the warnings, we need to be prepared to pick up the person on expiration for deportation proceedings.

At present there is no such comprehensive visa-holder tracking system so it would have to be prospective, covering all new holders from a date certain once the new system is ready to be rolled out.

Let us assume that as a result of Congressional action, work moves forward on completing whatever types of border fences--physical or virtual--are needed by the four states along our border with Mexico: California, Arizona, New Mexico and Texas.

Once this has been accomplished to the satisfaction of the four states' governors and Congress, the expectation is that illegal infiltration of the border will almost completely cease. What a newly-tight border from the Pacific to the Gulf Coast must also do is keep out potential terrorists intent on smuggling in such things as "dirty" nuclear devices, biological or chemical agents that could wreak havoc on urban populations.

Recommendation 2: Congress and the Executive branch should direct the Pentagon to share its sensor research with the CBP, and appropriate funds for adaptation of the Army's new Unattended Ground Sensor (UGS) for use along our borders.

The Customs and Border Protection agency (CBP) is responsible for maintaining 12,800 sensors along the borders that can detect radiation. A 2005 report by the Department of Homeland Security's Inspector General concluded that only four percent of signals picked up by these old border sensors were caused by people who were crossing illegally and the rest were false alarms. These old sensors, for example, cannot distinguish between a person and a cow.[3]

Soldier feedback from the field in Afghanistan is shaping the design of the Army's new Unattended Ground Sensor (UGS) and it holds real promise for border security. The UGS is a device that soldiers place strategically to monitor activity in a given area. They monitor the movement of hostile forces, but it could as easily be used to monitor the entry of occasional illegal border crossers once our new closed border system is in place. The Army has used UGS since 1966. Yet in 2011, our nation's military leaders in Afghanistan issued an "urgent operational needs statement" for better sensors. While there are an estimated 7,500 UGS at the Mexican border, the best sensors have been developed for overseas contingency operations. A next generation of sensors for our border is essential to improving security.[4]

The Army plans to have two types, the Urban-UGS for use in small areas or indoors, and the Tactical-UGS to monitor a wider perimeter. It is the latter that could be used to replace the old and obsolete sensors now in use.

The earlier designs of the T-UGS were bulky and easy to see. One Army press release says they looked like "a pair of soda cans stacked."[5]There may have never been a time when a UGS was as easy to hide and as necessary to deploy.

In recent years more of the cartels have exploited illegal immigrants and used them to carry drugs into the United States.[6] This is often in exchange for having waived the large fee that "coyotes" usually charge to get them over the border. Coyotes are border-crossing specialists who help people get into the United States from providing fake identification to bribing border agents. Whether it is the need to get extra cash or the reasonable concern that the cartels will go after their families, illegal immigrants have little choice but to cooperate and serve as "drug mules."[7] This practice, too, could be stopped by a seamlessly-protected border.

Recommendation 3: Work with the Private Sector to Stop the Drug Tunnels

We are seeing elaborate tunnel systems constructed along our borders to smuggle people and drugs into the United States. Passive seismic monitoring devices, combined with seismic sensors recently developed for the oil and gas industry, offer the best approach to deal with this threat. Here, the Department of Homeland Security needs to reach out to the private sector and leverage this technology for tunnel detection and border security.

On November 30, 2011, agents from the U.S. Immigration & Customs Enforcement (ICE), arrested six men and seized 32 tons of marijuana following the discovery of a smuggling tunnel from a warehouse in Tijuana, Mexico to one at the Otay Mesa Industrial Park near San Diego. This seizure capped a six-month investigation. The nearly half-mile-long tunnel was equipped with lights, electric rail cars, a wooden floor and reinforced walls.[8]

This was the second large-scale drug-smuggling tunnel in the San Diego area within two weeks and the seventh discovered there by U.S. authorities since 2006. All told, federal authorities detected some 75 cross-border smuggling tunnels between 2006 and 2011. Most of these tunnels were in California and Arizona. The total November 2011 seizures deprived drug cartels of sales and revenue from more than 50 tons of marijuana. The Tunnel Task Force worked closely with the Government of Mexico in coordinating the seizures in November 2011.[9]

While the Tunnel Task Force continues to use intelligence-gathering and surveillance to detect new tunnels, our fight with the drug cartels is far from over. In Fiscal Year 2013, federal authorities detected and shutdown six cross-border tunnels in the Nogales area alone.[10]

Recommendation 4: Work with Canada and Mexico to Make Better Use of Mobile RPMS

The U.S.-Canadian border is the longest in the world: 5,525 miles across, touching 13 U.S. states and eight Canadian Provinces. In 2009, U.S-Canada trade amounted to $429 billion. Most of this trade was possible because more than five million trucks crossed the border carrying $247.6 billion of goods. In addition, approximately 300,000 individuals cross the border every day.[11]

Trucks from Mexico present similar problems. In 2012, according to the U.S. Department of Transportation's Bureau of Transportation Statistics' (BTS), 5.1 million trucks crossed our border with Mexico compared to 5.6 million from Canada. While the countries are fairly close in border crossings involving trucks, Mexico leads Canada in border crossings involving personal vehicles (62.7 million to 33.1 million) and buses (212,000 to 108,000).[12] Our economy is dependent on a secure flow of goods crossing these borders.

Customs & Border Patrol (CBP) uses mobile Radiation Portal Monitors (RPMs) at seaports to examine cargo in shipping containers. It can cover a number of containers in a relatively short time.

The RPM technology could be used to detect illicit radiological materials from being smuggled across U.S. border points in trucks. A mobile RPM system, as now used at seaports consists of a truck equipped with two detection panels. This system is equipped with both gamma and neutron sensors, which can detect highly-enriched uranium, plutonium, and "dirty" bombs.[13]

The RPM system can work either as a stationary unit, with traffic going by it or as a mobile "perimeter," traversing several miles of inbound roads to border stations on the Canadian and Mexican sides of the borders. One way to accomplish this would be to seek cooperative agreements with the governments of Canada and Mexico to operate joint mobile RPM trucks on their respective highways leading to border crossings. These would be in a variety of unassuming civilian-type trucks, not marked as to their purpose.

Alternatively, U.S. drones, operating from inside our borders, could detect suspicious shipments and we could send RPM trucks to investigate trucks having just entered U.S soil, but not yet at the actual border station.

Without such a joint patrol agreement, our detection would be limited to either the drones described above or a stationary RPM truck on U.S. soil just short of the border station itself. The danger in either case is that apprehension amidst a packed line of vehicles could give the suspect truck operator an opportunity to trigger an explosion, with considerable loss of innocent lives.

Congress should authorize and appropriate funds to expand the RPM usage to U.S. border stations with Canada and Mexico. The U.S. Government should seek cooperative RPM patrol arrangements with the Canadian and Mexican governments for RPM-equipped trucks to travel several miles on border access roads within those countries in order to detect and investigate possible smuggled nuclear devices.

Recommendation 5: Deploy More Spectrometers on the Border

The U.S. Department of Homeland Security is signing contracts for upgraded technology for detecting the presence of chemical and biological weapons in inbound shipments. In October 2012, the U.S. Army's Contracting Command awarded Hamilton Sundstrand Co. a $49 million contract to build and provide integrated logistics support (ILS) of a Chemical Biological Mass Spectrometer (CMAS).[14] If we can get a cooperative agreement with Canada and Mexico in place with RPM-equipped trucks, we should also equip them with these advanced spectrometers as well.

Recommendation 6: Inspect All Containers for Radioactive Material Before They Enter the Country

There are more than 300 sea and river ports in the United States. There are also over 3,700 terminals for cargo and passengers.[15] In 2009, the top 10 U.S. ports handled approximately 85 percent of the containerized imports.[16]

Since 2007, the amount of cargo scanned with X-rays or gamma rays, has remained at four percent. In Fiscal Year 2012, approximately 11.5 million containers arrived in the United States.[17]

Of the 700 overseas ports that directly trade with the United States, 80 percent of the cargo bound for the U.S. comes from 58 of them.[18] Concentrating on these 58 ports, Customs and Border Protection (CBP) inspected 45,500 suspect containers overseas in 2011. That's awful. If we are only able to scan 45,500 containers in 365 days that means we are averaging just over 124 containers a day. If you divide 124 containers by 58 ports that means, we are only able to scan two containers per day at each overseas port.[19]

Congress passed a law in 2007 specifying that all cargo containers had to be scanned for radioactive material before they enter the United States. Secretary of Homeland Security Janet Napolitano could not meet the 2012 deadline and asked for another two years because it was too costly and difficult to secure the containers coming from all 700 overseas ports that directly send cargo to the United States. Relying on intelligence and risk analysis, we are only able to scan less than one percent of the incoming containers before they enter the country.[20]

The GAO estimates that the damage from a nuclear detonation at a U.S. port could cost anywhere from several billion to $1 trillion. The scale of the danger is large in the absence of full scanning. This is likely the most difficult task in protecting our borders. There are ships that carry up to 3,000 containers of cargo. A standard shipping container is 40 feet long, and eight feet high. The opportunities for hiding explosive devices are many.[21]

There is a better way to detect a hidden nuclear device or a bomb in a container than to scan, as we now do, two containers a day per port and to otherwise rely on intelligence tips. It is designed to detect the substance Krypton-85, which is emitted into the atmosphere from a reprocessing facility. Of the efforts of the International Atomic Energy Agency (IAEA) and the scientific community to verify clandestine nuclear weapons programs, the most promising is the use of atom trap trace analysis (ATTA).[22]

Krypton-85 is a gas that is created along with plutonium by the fission of uranium fuel at a reactor. The detection of Krypton 85 is a reliable sign that plutonium production is occurring even if it is difficult to ascertain the level of production. In 2003, non-proliferation expert Jon Wolfstahl eloquently described the usefulness of Krypton 85. He told *New Scientist*, "It's a red flag, not a yardstick."[23]

While the DHS should seek funds to increase scanning of U.S.-bound containers to begin complying with the 2007 law, use of satellites to detect increased levels of Krypton-85 could pinpoint this material before terrorists can put this material in a cargo container.

Recommendation 7: Do Not Let Budget Cuts Downplay the Growing Threat of Underwater Mines

Another threat that needs more attention than it has received is that of underwater mines planted in our harbors and ports. Under the right circumstances, they might be planted by submarines that then slip away. They might also take the form of Improvised Explosive Devices (IEDs) as insurgents used in Iraq. These could be clandestinely dropped into harbors by agents on land. They need not be large to inflict major damage on large vessels.

The U.S. Navy believes that there are now over 250,000 mines in the world. Our Navy has had a lot of recent experiences in anti-mining activities, especially against Iraq and Iran in the Persian Gulf. Mines are no longer just the spiked iron spheres that float in the ocean. For example, Iran is equipped with a Chinese-built EM-52 mine. This mine can wait at the bottom of the water until it detects a particular ship.[24]

Since World War II, 15 of the 19 U.S. Navy ships that were either destroyed, or seriously damaged, were from sea mines.[25] The U.S. Navy has two mine countermeasure squadrons, a headquarters on the Pacific Coast and forward-deployed ships in Bahrain and Japan. It needs to add units on the Atlantic and Gulf Coasts, as well. As an alternative, the U.S. Coast Guard could also be given mine countermeasures and it might be given the responsibility for the Gulf and Atlantic Coasts.

Given constant pressures on defense spending, one rule of thumb to be applied here is to buy reliable technologies from allied sources, where such exist, rather than inventing new ones of our own.

The Coast Guard or Navy should also conduct periodic surveys of the sea beds of all ports (Q-routes), making use of Autonomous Underwater Vehicles (AUVs) to make sure they are clear of suspicious objects.

Recommendation 8: Both Parties Must Come Together in Order to Produce Sufficient Border Security

Securing the US border with Mexico is one of the most important and significant national security issues of our time. In 2011, FBI Director Robert Mueller told the U.S. House Homeland Security Committee that illegal aliens from countries with ties to Al Qaeda had crossed into the United States from Mexico. FBI Director Mueller also informed us that some of these illegal aliens are people with Middle Eastern names who have adopted Hispanic last names before entering the United States. In 2010, over 59,000 illegal aliens from countries other than Mexico were apprehended while trying to enter the United States. These include individuals from countries such as Syria, Iran, Somalia, Yemen, Pakistan and Sudan.[26]

In 2011, US Border Patrol agents captured the radical Muslim cleric, Said Jaziri, attempting to sneak into the United States across the Mexican border. Jaziri was best known for calling on his followers to execute the Danish cartoonist Kurt Westergaard, who drew pictures of the prophet Mohammed. The Imam was found by U.S. Border Patrol agents hiding in the trunk of a BMW as it attempted to cross the U.S.-Mexican border into California.[27]

When it comes to defending our borders, harbors, and ports, the good news is that we have the technology to vastly improve the situation. The bad news is that there are not enough elected officials who are taking this threat seriously. If there were a real sense of urgency on both sides of the aisle, Congress would have resolved the issues of border security and immigration a long time ago.

Chapter Four

A Forward Strategy That Will Make Our Infrastructure Safe

The purpose of protecting our critical infrastructure is beyond simply providing energy to American homes. The War on Terror has caused more heartbreak than this book has space to recount. Yet there is enough space in this chapter to show readers how to end it. Simply put, we must produce more energy so that the United States can defund Radical Islamists once and for all. This will move us toward safety not only for our homeland, but also for those people everywhere who cherish peace and stability.

Growing and sustaining energy production is the key to a strategy of starving Islamists of funding. Near or actual energy independence of the U.S. will have the effect of bringing energy prices down from their historic highs. For Middle Eastern countries whose economies are dependent upon energy resources, prosperity would continue, but they would no longer be awash in surplus petrodollars. In recent years, some of those petrodollars found themselves directly supporting radical Islamist causes. WikiLeaks made public a December 2009 memo, signed by then Secretary Hillary Clinton, which acknowledged that, "More needs to be done since Saudi Arabia remains a critical financial support base for al-Qaida, the Taliban, LeT and other terrorist groups." Other major sources of financing terrorist groups in Afghanistan and Pakistan include American allies Kuwait, Qatar, and the United Arab Emirates. [1]

The 9/11 Commission Report shows that, in addition to providing direct funds to jihadists, some rich Saudis have played a key role in the creation of *madrassas* in Pakistan. Because of widespread poverty in Pakistan, these religious schools are the only education that is available for millions of children. In Karachi, Pakistan alone, there were 859 *madrassas* educating more than 200,000 young Muslims.[2] That is a lot of people whose minds must be changed lest they become tomorrow's jihadists.

Reduced energy costs will also enable consumer demand to continue to grow in many developing countries. While the demand for gasoline, oil, and electricity will continue to grow at a strong pace, supplies should be great enough worldwide to keep prices from skyrocketing again. A growing economy in a developing country will produce jobs which, in turn, will reduce the number of unemployed and restless young men, susceptible to radical recruiters.

The picture is not as bright for nuclear energy and it must improve. In 2011 there was a dramatic setback: the earthquake/tsunami disaster at Japan's Fukushima Daiichi plant that caused the Japanese and others to reevaluate the potential safety of nuclear power. Fear spread. Germany, for example, bowed to growing demand to phase out all of its nuclear power plants.

In the 14 months following that disaster, Japan shut down all 54 of its nuclear reactors.[3] Before the disaster, the Japanese derived 30 percent of their electricity from nuclear power. Japan has almost no natural resources. Even with these nuclear plants, it had to import 84 percent of its energy needs.[4]

After a few months with no nuclear energy, then-Prime Minister Yoshihiko Noda announced he would reopen two of the

Ohi nuclear reactors to help people suffering from power outages. As for the rest of the power plants, they would remain idle until a two-phase program of stress tests could determine the safety of Japan's nuclear industry.[5] If Japan abandons nuclear power indefinitely, it would have to import even more oil and gas, much of it from the Middle East. This could contribute to rising oil and gas costs and thus set back a strategy to curb radical Islam by means of a growing energy sector.

Even if the U.S. can achieve energy independence by 2020, we will need to continue deriving approximately 20 percent of our energy from nuclear reactors. And, if we were to build 100 new reactors by 2030, most would be used to replace our current reactors. By September 2013 there were 99 plants in operation. Twenty percent of them are over 40 years old; 62 percent are 30 years old and the other 38 percent are 20 years old or older. Only one percent of plants were built in the last 20 years.[6] We must build more reactors and keep the older ones open as long as it is safe to do so.

When Fukushima occurred in 2011, the United States had 104 nuclear reactors in operation. The most politically vulnerable to being shutdown are the 23 boiling water reactors (BWR) with a Mark 1 container system. This is the same model as the Fukushima Daiichi reactor. While a combination of a large earthquake and tsunami is unlikely in the case of the U.S. reactors, the hysteria following the Fukushima disaster has been hard to overcome.

Beyond the fear factor, there are bureaucratic problems. A reactor is given an initial license of 40 years and may apply for a 20-year extension. By the time of Fukushima, 62 U.S. extensions had been accepted, with another 20 pending.[7]

The U.S. Nuclear Regulatory Commission, in accordance with the Atomic Energy Act, has established a license renewal process that can be completed under 30 months. The influence of anti-nuclear groups has grown.[8] In California, 45 anti-nuclear groups protested at Pacific Gas & Electric, the owner of the plant, as well as the Nuclear Regulatory Commission, over the relicensing of the Diablo Canyon nuclear power plant.[9] They didn't succeed with Diablo Canyon, but anti-nuclear protestors have been able to shut down plants in the past. In California, the negative political environment shut down the Rancho Seco Nuclear Power Plant in 1989.[10] The San Onofre Nuclear Power Plant closed in 2013. The closure of that plant led to the loss of more than a thousand jobs.

The shadow of Fukushima created a new pessimistic attitude that has made it difficult for setbacks to be overcome. Any new problem could immediately lead to negative press coverage and, in time, a shutdown.[11]

Even if we cannot extend the plant license beyond 60 years, we need as many of these plants operating as long as possible so that we can keep the price of fuel low enough to pinch the economies of those countries who wish us ill. Some less-than-friendly countries have economies that are dependent on high oil prices. It wouldn't take long for low-priced U.S. competition to seriously hurt them.

The Russian School of Economics, for example, reported in early 2013 that if the price of oil dropped to $60 dollars a barrel for more than one year, Russia's Oil Wealth Fund would be completely depleted. Most OPEC members need the price of oil to be at least $85 dollars to balance their budgets. Iran needs the price to be over $120 dollars.[12] That is why every nuclear reactor built will allow us to export oil elsewhere so that consumers can eventually force these countries to concentrate on keeping their own populations happy and not exporting funds to terrorist groups.

The U.S. Energy Information Administration has estimated that 85 percent of global energy demand from 2010 to 2040 will be generated from developing countries. Global energy consumption could increase 56 percent in this period from 524 quadrillion Btu in 2010 to 820 quadrillion Btu by 2040. While China surpassed the U.S. as the world's largest consumer in 2010, this rising power is projected to consume twice as much energy as the United States by 2040.[13]

Increases in energy consumption do not have to mean increases in oil consumption. Chinese energy consumption is at parity with the U.S., but its *oil* consumption is still much lower than America's. In 2012, the U.S. consumed 18.6 million barrels per day. This was a 16-year low in terms of consumption.[14] It was also considerably less than 2005 when the U.S. consumed 20.8 million barrels a day.[15] At 18.6 million barrels a day, the U.S. was still the world's largest consumer of oil in 2012. China was second at 10.3 million and Japan third with 4.7 million.[16] Of those 18.6 million barrels per day, 7.43 million barrels a day was imported. In 2012, China imported approximately half of its oil while Japan imported nearly all its supply.[17]

As the U.S. moves toward energy independence, it is important for every American to see each nuclear plant and every new barrel of U.S. oil we produce as steps toward making sure we do not have to experience another decade of war against a foe intent upon turning the world into a brutal theocracy.

There often is a direct correlation between aggression in foreign policy and the price of oil when a state has a surplus of petrodollars. For example, the Soviets invaded Afghanistan during the relatively high oil prices of the 1970s. When oil prices dropped from $28 a barrel in 1984 to $14 in 1986, the Kremlin could no longer afford the occupation of Afghanistan. Not long after that,

Gorbachev concluded that the Soviet Union also could no longer afford continuation of the Cold War.[18]

Meanwhile, U.S. dependence on imported oil grew after the 1950s. From 1960 to 1973, it more than doubled, from 16 percent to 35 percent.[19] By 2006, 60 percent of our oil was imported.[20] In recent years the percent edged down, but it was only with technological advances that we have suddenly moved into the position of soon becoming the world's largest producer.

Recommendation 1: Defund terrorist sponsors and build at least 100 Nuclear Power Plants by 2030

The U.S. Energy Information Administration has projected that global energy consumption will increase by 56 percent over the next three decades. In 2010, the global consumption was 524 quadrillion British thermal units. This is expected to grow to 820 quadrillion Btu by 2040. To put this number in perspective, just one quadrillion Btu is the equivalent of 172 million barrels of oil.[21] With more energy production, technological breakthroughs in efficiency, and the growth of nuclear energy, as well as other alternatives, American leverage increases substantially.

Saudi Arabia, like other nations in the Middle East, needs economic reform to meet the needs of a growing population (up from 6 million in 1970 to 28 million in 2012).[22] It cannot continue to provide for an increasing population with oil revenues alone.

It will need international investors to diversify its economy and give its young people the skills to become self-sufficient and rely less on social subsidies. Reduced growth in oil revenues may press the Saudis to focus on doing this.

Energy demands from the developing world will increase and can be met in good part by nuclear power and oil and gas from hydraulic fracturing. To the extent they are it will put downward pressure on oil prices and, indirectly, reduce available funds to help finance the jihadists.

With increasing amounts of oil and natural gas expected from North America, growth in demand for, say, automobiles should be able to occur without big spikes in gasoline prices at the pump.

Vehicle sales are sensitive to price. In the U.S., with rising gasoline prices and a credit crunch, light vehicle sales plunged from 10.4 million in 2007 to 5.6 million in 2009.[23]

Developing countries will surge in vehicle ownership (also appliances and other big-ticket items) once their people have sufficient per capita income to afford these things. With supplies of oil and gas expanding as they have recently, gasoline prices can stay steady or decline some without curbing demand. China, for example, is projected to have 269 vehicles per 1,000 people by 2030. This compares with 16 vehicles per 1,000 people in 2002.[24] India and other nations will experience strong economic growth and thus per capita income growth.

To the extent that oil-producers of the Middle East face steadily increasing competition, this should keep oil prices moderate and no longer produce huge surpluses that could be used to aid ideologically-driven Islamists.

Recommendation 2: Have two permanent repositories for nuclear waste by 2018. One of these should be Yucca Mountain.

While nuclear power is essential, it faces challenges that cannot be ignored. In order to build more nuclear plants, presidential leadership will be needed to make it happen. Building these plants also requires politicians finally to confront the perennial challenge of handling nuclear waste.

From 2010 to 2012, former National Security Advisor Brent Scowcroft and former Representative Lee Hamilton co-chaired a commission to deal with the nuclear waste issue. In 2012, they reported that there were approximately 65,000 metric tons of nuclear waste. Every year our nuclear plants produce another 2,000 metric tons in additional waste. Three quarters of this waste is stored on-site in shielded pools of concrete. The rest is above ground in dry casks.

We need a permanent site to store this spent fuel along with a comprehensive inventory of it made by the Department of Energy. This includes over 3,000 canisters of high-level waste and 90 million gallons of liquids, sludges, and solids from weapons grade production.[25]

Our government has failed to uphold past promises to have a permanent repository for spent nuclear fuel. Instead of Yucca Mountain or some other permanent site, the politicians have ignored these issues.

Ironically, environmentalists who are often the biggest critics of nuclear power, fail to acknowledge that nuclear plants do not emit carbon dioxide, sulfur dioxide, nitrogen oxide or mercury. As for the nuclear waste issues, one reason politicians have ignored this is that storing the fuel on-site and under dry cask storage has been possible. We can keep it safe for years, but not indefinitely. The Nuclear Waste Policy Act of 1982 has provided a blueprint, but it cannot provide politicians with backbone.

As a result, the Hamilton-Scowcroft Commission was designed to find a "consent-based approach" to overcome the "Not in my backyard" (NIMBY) mentality of legislators and voters.

There has been talk about consolidating sites of waste in areas of closed nuclear plants. Even if Yucca Mountain were the final choice, we would very quickly fill it to capacity. Hence, our recommendation is that there must be two repositories for storing nuclear waste. The Hamilton-Scowcroft commission waste management system had eight recommendations.

1. New consent-based approach. Experience in other nations shows that a top-down approach takes longer. We can't force a repository on any state. Spain, Finland, and Sweden provide examples of a successful consent-based approach.

2. The commission recommends creating a new organization to push for waste management. The commission believes that the Department of Energy has not inspired confidence. They recommend a single purpose organization, chartered by Congress, to get this effort on track.

3. Adequate funding to handle nuclear waste. Annual fee revenues to funding nuclear waste of over $700 million dolla rs have been inaccessible to the waste program. Cumulative receipts are over $19 billion, with interest, the fund's balance is now about $27 billion. The commission believes the nuclear waste fee collection process should be reformed so that utilities pay only the amount necessary to pay for the waste, with the rest going to a trust fund for future needs. Finding a permanent repository should be the real goal instead of paying for the waste to remain on site.[26] In a joint op-ed, Co-Chairmen Lee Hamilton and Brent Scowcroft wrote that, ". . . U.S. taxpayers face mounting liabilities from dozens of lawsuits stemming from the U.S. Government's failure to meet its nuclear waste obligations."[27]

4. Prompt efforts to have one or more geological disposal facilities. The U.S. Government set a limit for Yucca Mountain of 70,000 metric tons. The Department of Defense needs to have set aside at least 10 percent, or 7,000 metric tons, for hazard waste as well as nuclear waste from the military. If Yucca is chosen, we will need at least another site because we will have some 65,000 metric tons of waste from the civilian nuclear reactors and only enough room for 63,000 metric tons of waste..

5. Prompt efforts to consolidate facilities. Stranded fuel should be first in line so sites don't continue to be used as waste holders.

6. Prompt efforts to prepare for transportation of spent fuel and nuclear waste. There is a good past record of safety in transferring materials, but we have never transferred nuclear waste on this level.

7. Support for advances in nuclear technology and workforce development. To improve advanced reactor and fuel cycle technologies and existing light water reactor technology.

8. Address safety and nonproliferation concern on a global scale. Strong American leadership is essential.[28]

While the commission's findings are informative, it was created because the Obama Administration stopped nuclear fuel from being sent to Yucca Mountain. Congress and the administration are forgetting what blue-ribbon commissions were designed to do. Sometimes, you find the best and brightest people to study a problem and they provide Congress with a thoughtful report. Much of the time, a blue-ribbon commission is designed by politicians too afraid to tell their constituents the truth. Commissions provide elected officials with the political cover--often for inaction.

Since this commission has not fulfilled its duty by taking a clear position on Yucca Mountain, we should provide a compromise that can satisfy residents of Nevada and other future repository sites. It will be difficult to build a large number of new plants until the government can resolve the waste issue. The Commission's final report pointed out that even a "consent-based" approach would be time-consuming. The Commission estimates it could be as long as 15 to 20 years to find an alternative site to Yucca Mountain and get it licensed. This does not include another five to 10 years for the getting the site ready once permission is obtained to go ahead with the project.[29] In fairness, the current approach provides no end in sight. Conducting a referendum of the people of Nevada might clear the air.

If there is a sense of urgency, the government can resolve this issue much faster than the commission suggests. If the government will not resolve the issue of waste soon, the alternative is for the administration to support nuclear reprocessing.

Recommendation 3: Deplete Niger of its uranium reserves.

Having a nuclear repository is not just to fill it with our uranium. About half the fuel in our nuclear power plants (equal to almost 10 percent of the electricity generated in the United States), is from what were nuclear warheads of the former Soviet arsenal. The highly-enriched uranium from these warheads was diluted to low-enriched uranium. This way the fuel could be used for commercial power.

Approximately 95 percent of the fuel originally targeted has now been transferred to our nuclear power plants. The 1994 agreement that began this arrangement transferred 500 megatons of highly-enriched uranium. This is enough for 20,000 nuclear bombs.[30] This does not include the MOX project in South Carolina's reprocessing plant that is designed to take 34 metric tons of weapons-grade plutonium from Russia and convert into fuel in our nuclear reactors.[31] The constant state of economic crisis in the 1990s gave lawmakers just cause to worry about proliferation of nuclear materials in Russia.

Today, lawmakers should be even more worried about Niger, one of the world's poorest countries with 60 percent of its population living below the poverty line. To make matters worse it also is one of the world's largest sources of uranium.[32]

The war in neighboring Mali, with a rebellion being led by ethnic Tuareg people--and exploited by radical Islamists--has led others to worry that a similar conflict could engulf Niger. In northern Niger and in neighboring Mali, the ethnic Tuareg people in both of these countries have waged multiple rebellions against their governments. The political history of Niger, since its independence from the French in 1960, can be described as one of scandals, military coups and Tuareg rebellions.

The United States has provided economic development and we even have a military base to monitor terrorist groups in West Africa, but this is not enough.[33] We are also going to have to work with China, France, and the government in Niger to push for depleting these uranium reserves so that a potential coup in the future would not lead to a radical Islamist government with large reserves of uranium.

Recommendation 4: Improve the system of employee background checks at our nuclear plants.

Realistically, our nuclear plants are secure from a number of threats. There have been studies that show the thick concrete walls and reinforced steel can survive plane crashes.[34] Since 9/11, the U.S. has increased the security forces at nuclear power plants to over 8,000 well-trained guards. There are physical barriers, surveillance equipment, and technologically advanced equipment that make a break-in very unlikely.[35]

What is more likely is the possibility of an employee who passes a background check and is employed at a plant for several years, but who, long after the background check, is involved in an incident that could lead to blackmail and possibly sabotage or some other form of mischief at the plant. This scenario is unlikely, but possible. This is why there should be a system of roving background checks of the employees at every nuclear power plant. If someone close to an employee has gone to prison or had some misfortune, the employee may be vulnerable to the bribery and/or blackmail leading to a serious breach of our national security.

Recommendation 5: Build more renewable energy plants, more refineries, and excess capacity.

Most of the recommendations in this chapter have concerned nuclear power. If our government was committed to keeping oil prices low, there is no reason to assume that countries that had been used to having surpluses of petrodollars would not resort to countermeasures. Cutting production to keep prices up may not be realistic. Incidents of terrorism, however, could cause uncertainty in the market in order to keep prices high.

If a country were to consider this, the question is where to strike to make the most impact. Hurricane Katrina and Hurricane Rita in 2005 showed us that securing our refineries is crucial. In the aftermath of these two events, 23 percent of our refining capacity was temporarily shut down. It also forced oil companies to temporarily halt offshore oil production by 73 percent and natural gas output by almost half. What is truly extraordinary was that out of a total refinery output of 17.1 million barrels, approximately four million barrels was produced from 18 Texas refineries.[36]

We must build more refineries and make sure that no hurricane in the Gulf of Mexico is going to cause a serious dent in energy prices. Placing new refineries anywhere except the Gulf would provide a best defense against hurricanes.

If we do not build new refineries, increase domestic oil production and build more nuclear plants, buying more Canadian oil will not significantly reduce high gasoline prices. New domestic refineries are crucial to the effort to ease prices.

If you think others aren't fully aware of our predicament, consider this quotation from Prince Bandar bin Sultan of Saudi Arabia. On NBC's *Meet The Press*, Prince Bandar, who was Saudi Ambassador to the U.S., told Tim Russert in 2004 that, "The reason you have high prices in the United States is the refineries are not enough to refine. There is a one-million-barrel shortage of refined products. So even if tomorrow we send you all the oil we have as crude, it will not change the facts here."[37] Almost ten years later this is still the case.

From 1982 to 2013, the number of refineries in the U.S. dropped from 301 to 143.[38] The U.S. Refinery Operable Atmospheric Crude Oil Distillation Capacity reached 17,823,659 barrels per day in 2013. It has not been this high since 1982 when it was 17,889,734 barrels per day.[39] Our refining capacity is getting very close to our annual oil consumption. Until our refining capacity can either match or exceed our oil production, we cannot declare energy independence.

Renewable Energy Sources

Here are some facts: the United States receives approximately 12 percent of its power from renewables. Most of it came from hydroelectric power (56 percent). The rest came from wind power (12 percent), biomass wood (eight percent), biomass waste (four percent), geothermal (three percent), and solar (one percent). The U.S. is second only to China in generating power from renewable power; however, it is the world leader in renewable power outside of hydroelectricity.[40] While renewables are not a large source of power, we must assume that terrorists could try to attack these facilities.

The most attractive targets are hydroelectric power facilities. Beyond the fact that they are the largest source of renewables, they are also the hardest to repair. The most attractive targets would be our dams. The most powerful power station in the United States is the Grand Coulee Dam. This facility produces 6,480 megawatts of power.[41] The biggest power plant in the world, in terms of electricity generation, is the Three Gorges Dam in China with 22,500 megawatts.[42]

The new developments in hydraulic fracturing will cause a revolution in oil prices. It will be in the interests of certain terrorist sponsors to hit our power generation facilities to create uncertainty in order to keep energy prices high. Our strategy must be to build more facilities to prevent any crippling blows that could push up energy prices. This is why we need more facilities spread out geographically-- especially refineries.

When Leslie Stahl asked the former Director of the National Clandestine Service, José Rodriguez, about enhanced interrogation techniques, this former CIA leader said the purpose of those techniques was designed not to hurt the terrorist but to create "a sense of hopelessness and despair in the terrorist, in the detainee, so that he would conclude on his own that he was better off cooperating with us."[43] In short, our energy policy must give us enough power stations spread across the country that even a successful attack will not change the reality that for terrorists and their funders, the days of setting energy prices are over. Instead our new invulnerability will be intended to create in them "a sense of hopelessness and despair."

Recommendation 6: Create a hotline where people can call or text suspicious activity.

We now live in a world where most of our citizens have cell phones with cameras. We must use this to our advantage. We need a phone line where people can report suspicious activity through either phone or text message. Through a text message, they can send a photo of someone near a power plant who appears to be suspicious. In the aftermath of a terrorist bombing, people will likely be able to provide photos from several different angles that might give law enforcement officials additional clues. If it is just "911," we might overwhelm the police with potentially false leads. We need a separate alert number for this purpose.

Conclusion

We live in a world where we will not be able to protect all our facilities all the time. We should not forget how lucky America has been since 9/11. If you look at Israel, since its creation as a nation in 1948, it has lost people to terrorism every year.[44]

Terrorists can only defeat us if they break our spirit. That hasn't happened and won't, but we must not underestimate our ability to win this war. When the Iraq surge was proposed, many thought an influx of troops would only make things worse. This was an odd thought since no war in history was ever lost because the losing side had too many troops. As it turned out, the surge was successful and, in effect, won the war. The same can be said for our production of energy. America cannot lose if we produce "too much" domestic energy at home. With coordination among other top consumer states, we can secure our critical infrastructure and bankrupt the terrorists once and for all.

Chapter Five

Let's Roll: Securing Our Skies

On one Tuesday morning in September, 2001 our nation's confidence in secure skies was shattered. The more our government investigated the 9/11 attacks, the more we realized how it could have been much worse. The fact that more people weren't killed that day is astounding. We will never know precisely how many people were in the buildings that day, but we do know that most of the people below the impact zone of the building were able to escape in time.

According to The 9/11 Commission Report, the National Institute of Standards and Technology estimated that 16,400 to 18,800 people were in the World Trade Center (WTC) when the first plane hit at 8:46 A.M. Of the 2,152 people who died in the WTC who were not police officers, fire fighters, volunteers or first responders, the government was able to identify the workplace of 2,052 victims. What is not surprising is that over 90 percent of the victims were at, or above, the impact zone in either tower.[1]

On that day the heroic resistance of the passengers on Flight 93 prevented either the White House or the Capitol Building from being another target. The people of that flight were forced to take matters into their own hands because our government failed. What is not generally understood is that our government is continuing to fail in securing our skies.

The initial federal response to securing our skies was based on re-playing the events of that day without the flexibility to adapt. For example, when Richard Reid failed to blow up his shoes, in December of 2001, it became evident that people would have to remove their shoes in order to prevent another bomber from trying again. Since shoe-bombs can be made nonmetallic, only x-rays can stop a shoe–bomb from getting past a checkpoint.[2]

While many of these measures were necessary, we should understand that the War on Terror quickly also became the war against frequent fliers. Our government was able to stop a few possible threats at the expense of stifling our ability to disrupt different types of attacks.

As 9/11 fades into a national memory, our bureaucracy will not have the public pressure to be prepared for our current challenges. Only after an incident is there ever any serious discussion. For example, in August 2012, 31-year-old, Daniel Castillo, went out drinking one night with friends in Queens, New York. He decided to go jet-skiing. His craft quit offshore from John F. Kennedy International Airport. Equipped with motion sensors and closed-circuit cameras, this $100 million state-of-the-art security system failed. The airport was easily breached by this young man. All he did was swim to the shore, climb an 8-foot high perimeter fence and walk across two runways to the terminal before anyone noticed he was there.[3] A breach of this magnitude should make us all wonder how many holes exist when it comes to securing our nation's airports.

It is also evident we have been luckier than most of our elected officials would care to admit. Beyond Richard Reid, who could not set his shoes on fire, Faisal Shahzad, the Time Square bomber, could not get gasoline in his car bomb to explode.[4] The plot to bomb Fort Dix was only discovered because the six Islamic terrorists decided to make a video before their attack. Unlike skillful terrorists who send videos on jihadist websites, these idiots decided to convert their video to DVD by dropping it off at a Circuit City store in Mount Laurel, New Jersey. When the clerk saw the video, he immediately alerted the authorities. Chris Christie, who was then U.S. Attorney for the District of New Jersey, admitted that had these terrorists not trusted Circuit City, "I couldn't be sure what would happen."[5]

What is truly frightening is that Nidal Malik Hassan made a more fatal mistake than the "Fort Dix Six", but he was not taken into custody. Apparently, in December, 2008, just 11 months before the Fort Hood shooting, the FBI intercepted 18 e-mails between Hassan and Anwar al-Awlaki.

The fact that it only "sparked concern" that someone in the U.S. Army was e-mailing a high-value target within al-Qaeda should have been sufficient to continue the probe, but political correctness prevailed. The numerous complaints by fellow officers of Hassan making statements sympathetic to Islamic fundamentalism were never taken seriously as well.[6] Once they had the e-mails, they should have confronted Hassan. For those who say that "hindsight is 20/20," I would counter that a clerk at Circuit City should not be more reliable than the FBI investigators, or Army officers, who certainly knew that there was something wrong with Nidal Malik Hassan.

Recommendation 1: Reward Our Sources and Condemn Political Correctness

What is even more frightening is that our "success" in the Fort Dix case was in part because the FBI used a Muslim as a paid informant. Egyptian-born Mahmoud Omar was recruited by the FBI to infiltrate the Fort Dix terrorist cell. Because Mahmoud had been in trouble with the law, he was left with little choice but to cooperate with the FBI. He was also chosen because he managed to identify one of the people in the video.

Once the trial became public, Mahmoud was ostracized from the Muslim community. Since he made a living from an export business shipping cars and equipment to Egypt, Mahmoud was dependent on a network of relatives and friends within the Muslim community to keep his business profitable. Neither his relatives nor his friends wanted anything to do with him after his betrayal became public knowledge.[7]

Informants should always believe that they will be rewarded for their cooperation. If that requires witness protection, and access to new economic opportunities, this can show informants that our government will reward people who provide actionable intelligence.

Radical Islam is a threat and we need moderate Muslims to come forward with information. When they see incidents like Fort Hood or Fort Dix, they must conclude that our government will take action. The case at Fort Dix shows that even when we stop these attacks we do not reward people who helped save American lives.

The gains in the War on Terror can be substantial if we find ways to praise and reward moderate Muslims. To use one prominent example, think of the congregants at the Dar al-Hirjah Mosque in Falls Church, Virginia. Beyond having Anwar al-Awlaki as its Imam in 2001 and 2002, we now know that at least two of the 9/11 hijackers, Nawaf al-Hazmi and Hani Hanjour, attended this mosque. Along with al-Qaeda members, Nidal Malik Hassan was also praying there.

Other notable Imams include Mohammed Adam El-Sheikh who was a member of the Muslim Brotherhood. The founder of the mosque, Ismail Elbarasse, has ties with Hamas. Another congregant and Hamas supporter is Abdurrahman Alamoudi.[8] Alamoudi was sentenced to 23 years in jail in 2004 for participating in a Libyan plot to kill then Crown Prince Abdullah, who is now the King of Saudi Arabia. In his spare time, Alamoudi was the first president of the Islamic Society of Boston, which is the mosque in Cambridge, Massachusetts that was attended by the alleged Boston Bomber Dzhokhar Tsarnaev and his brother Tamerlan.[9]

It would be so much easier to protect our skies if we rewarded moderate Muslims and ended political correctness, which is making it more difficult to fight terrorism. There were plenty of people who knew that Nidal Malik Hassan was a problem and they didn't stop him. There are many people who should have publicly supported Mahmoud Omar for going after the Fort Dix Six. We need to remember that as Americans, we cannot defeat terrorists if only the military is at war. Intelligence is our first line of defense and that is why all of us have to keep our eyes and ears open.

Recommendation 2: Downsize the Transportation Security Administration by at least 10 percent

The Transportation Security Administration (TSA) was created in the response to the events of 9/11. From the beginning, this reactive organization has been plagued with problems. It is, in effect, "fighting the last war" with hardly any flexibility as threats evolve. I have previously provided the example of the shoe bomber Richard Reid. Following that incident, there was a rule of passengers taking off their shoes. In August, 2006, the TSA banned liquids, gels, and certain items of food in response to a failed plot from the United Kingdom.

Beyond its reactive mentality, its personnel costs are bloated. With a budget of over $7 billion, the federal government must make every dollar count in the face of sequestration cuts. Over $3 billion of the TSA's budget goes to personnel costs. Over 47,000 of the 62,000 TSA employees are screeners. The TSA has grown its number of employees irrespective of the fact the recession substantially reduced the number of air passengers. In the private sector, a shrinking customer base would usually trigger downsizing.[10] The public sector must have a staffing model that fits our economic circumstances. The total number of airline passengers of both domestic flights and international flights to and from the United States declined from 838.2 million in 2007 to 769.6 percent in 2009. This is a decline of 8.2 percent.[11] In 2012, the total number of air passengers was only 815.3 million.[12] This is significantly higher than 2009, but not quite the peak of 2007.

With fewer passengers, improvements in screening technology will likely not result in the need to hire more screeners. The popular PreCheck program allows frequent fliers to sign up and receive less scrutiny. From October, 2011 to September, 2013, approximately 15 million passengers signed up for this program.[13] With 1.8 million daily air passengers spread across over 450 airports nationwide, the PreCheck program should be expanded. It speeds up the process by allowing pre-approved passengers to keep their shoes on their feet, belts and other light outwear do not have to be screened, and they can keep a laptop in a bag as well as a 3-1-1 bag for liquids and gels.[14]

In September, 2013, the TSA announced it would expand the PreCheck program from 40 airports to 100. It hoped to have 25 percent of air passengers go through the PreCheck program by the end of 2013.[15] If it comes even close not long after there is no reason why the TSA workforce cannot be reduced by 10 to 20 percent.

Recommendation 3: Eliminate the Baggage Fee

Edmund S. "Kip" Hawley, who was Administrator of the TSA (2005-2009), argued in an article that:“Much of the pain at TSA checkpoints these days can be attributed to passengers overstuffing their carry-on luggage to avoid baggage fees. The airlines had their reasons for implementing these fees, but the

> result has been a checkpoint nightmare. Airlines might increase ticket prices slightly to compensate for the lost revenue, but the main impact would be that checkpoint screening for everybody will be faster and safer."[16]

Obviously without the penalty, passengers will have less incentive to overstuff their bags and cause further delays to the screening process.

Recommendation 4: Defend Commercial Airliners Against MANPADS

From 1975 to 2013, 40 civilian aircraft have been hit by man-carried air-defense systems (MANPADS). More than 800 people have been killed and at least 28 planes have crashed.[17]

When people think of MANPADS, it's hard not to think of the Stingers. In the 1980s, the Reagan Administration sent Stinger missiles to help the Afghan *mujahadeen* in fighting the Soviets. Around the same time, smaller stocks of these weapons were sent to the government of Chad in order to deter Libyan air power. Unita rebels in Angola also received Stingers.[18]

In the case of Afghanistan, the United States Army reported in 1990 that approximately 340 missiles were fired prior to the Soviet withdrawal. With estimates ranging from 900 to 1200 missiles intended for delivery, it has been estimated that the Pakistanis siphoned off at least 200 missiles. The CIA managed to buy back another 60 Stingers. That means that there are approximately 300 to 600 unaccounted for Stingers, which are a serious threat to commercial aircraft.[19]

Some of the Stingers were clearly sold as these weapons were discovered to be used against aircraft in Bosnia and Tajikistan. The Iranians fired a Stinger missile from a boat against a U.S. helicopter in 1987. There have been reports throughout the years that Stingers have been acquired by several terrorist groups.[20] Fortunately, the battery packs on a Stinger missile can only be used for one shot and unused batteries have a shelf life of 4 to 5 years.[21] So the Stingers that were from over 20 years ago are unlikely to be a threat unless an advanced country can supply terrorists with the batteries to fire them.

When U.S. forces initiated Operation Enduring Freedom in 2001 and Operation Iraqi Freedom in 2003, both Afghanistan and Iraq were believed to have the Strela 2 MANPADS. These weapons are better known as the Soviet-made SA-7. In Afghanistan alone, coalition forces were able to capture 5,600 shoulder-fired surface-to-air missiles.[22]

According to the State Department, there have been about 1 million MANPADS produced since 1967. There are several thousand not in the control of governments and likely in the hands of terrorists. From 2003 to 2011, our government has been able to destroy over 32,000 MANPADS from over 30 countries. This includes one of the most successful diplomatic coups of the decade with agreement by the government of Bosnia and Herzegovina to destroy its stockpile of almost 6,000 MANPADS in 2003 and 2004.[23]

While many governments might be willing to destroy their stocks, terrorists are not going to be cajoled into giving up these weapons. We also cannot rely on shelf life to save us because there are sponsors of terrorism that have the capability to produce and distribute MANPADS. Shortly after the 9/11 attacks, it was estimated that the loss of one aircraft could produce $1 billion dollars in direct losses to the economy and another $15 billion in long-term losses.

To install a single laser jammer on 6,800 civilian aircraft would cost $11 billion dollars. After installation, it would cost $2.1 billion a year to maintain such a system.[2] While initial investment may seem costly, it should be noted that terrorism can produce far greater economic losses than expected.

The 9/11 Commission estimated that it cost al-Qaeda about $500,000 dollars to orchestrate 9/11.[25] In response to the attack, the war in Afghanistan alone has cost taxpayers $662.4 billion since 2001.[26] This does not include the actual damage caused by the attack, nor does it include the fact that half of returning veterans will be eligible for some form of disability payment. The future health care costs for these wounded warriors has been estimated at between $600 and $900 billion.[27] Since a terrorist can buy a MANPAD for as little at $5,000, we need to outfit our civilian aircraft with these countermeasures.[28]

Recommendation 5: Cut Off Terrorist Funding and the Drug Cartels

In Chapter 4, it was discussed that our nation must bring down the price of oil to ensure that state sponsors of terrorism will focus more on caring for their own populations and less on funding terrorism abroad. Alas, some terrorism is funded by the drug trade in South America. The U.S. Naval War College estimated in 2004 that Hezbollah made $10 million dollars from the lawless tri-border area of Argentina, Brazil, and Paraguay. In 2009, the Rand Corporation estimated that Hezbollah generated $20 million in that area. Hezbollah clearly needs an independent source of revenue from Iran should sanctions make it impossible for the Iranians to continue funding the organization.[29]

While our veterans and their families have made great sacrifices in this war, it is time we ask more of the American people than going shopping. We need to remind them that part of the revenue from illegal drugs is financing terrorism.

When Nancy Reagan was telling America's youth to "just say no," she made an important speech at the United Nations on this issue. Mrs. Reagan pointed out that we could not solve the drug problem by just pressing foreign governments on the supply of drugs without our government punishing drug offenders and addressing the demand for drugs. She said, "You see the cocaine cartel does not begin in Medellin, Colombia. It begins in the streets of New York, Miami, Los Angeles and every American city where crack is bought and sold."[30]

We need to remind people that our aircraft are shot down by terrorists. If we can significantly reduce their revenue in both oil and drugs, this would make our skies safer. Reforming the TSA and defending against MANPADS will be easier if we can stop the terrorists in their tracks.

The hijackers on Flight 93 were stopped when a group of citizens decided to fight back. For 13 years now our government has been at war, but our citizens have not. We can and must reduce drug use. Many fewer people smoke cigarettes today than before. Successful sustained anti-smoking campaign have highlighted the health danger and changed public opinion about the subject.

Former Secretary of State George Shultz believes the same can be done to combat drug use.[31] In the early 1970s, approximately 40 percent of American adults smoked cigarettes.[32] By 2011, only 19 percent of American adults did. Even after the reduction, cigarettes are still the leading cause of preventable death in the United States with over 440,000 every year.[33]

We need every American to play a part to secure our skies and help defend our nation. There is no time to waste. So in the words of Todd Beamer, "Let's roll!"

Chapter Six

Unleashing Open-source Intelligence (OSINT)

Not long ago a friend of mine who had been an all-state wrestler in high school explained to me how he once lost an important match. He was pinned in a wrestling move called a "cement job." He would finish the story by saying that he didn't think much of this move until it worked on him.

When I try to explain the benefits of open-source intelligence, I am constantly reminded by how many people naturally assume that the most useful information is always classified. It probably comes from the movies and our popular culture. My concern is that our intelligence community will not value the power of OSINT until we receive a cement job.

The terrorists who attacked Mumbai in 2008 used OSINT. On November 26, 2008, ten men used Google Maps to engage in a series of attacks that included the Taj Mahal Palace Hotel and other popular sites. The attacks killed over 100 people and wounded more than 300.[1] As the city was in turmoil, the best information was coming from Mumbai's residents who were using Twitter and Flickrs (a photo-sharing site) to provide the latest coverage to others.[2] In the future, situational awareness during a terrorist attack may require our forces to look at Twitter, and other social media tools, to provide a more complete picture of the tactical situation.

Twitter and Flickr were more effective considering that these terrorists were from Lashkar-e-Taiba (LeT). This terrorist organization has extensive ties with current and former members of Pakistan's Inter-Services Intelligence (agency), ISI. LeT also has ties to al-Qaeda. During these attacks the terrorists in Mumbai were using sophisticated satellite phones that had a Voice-over-Internet Protocol (VoIP). This made the calls difficult to track.[3]

The leaders of LeT in Pakistan were able to communicate with the terrorists in Mumbai with impunity. For this reason, social media suddenly became useful OSINT tools in tracking these killers. The Mumbai case is only one example of the power of OSINT.

Not many people are aware of this, but much of what we know about al-Qaeda was from the communications it provided. Osama bin Laden publicly declared war on the United States twice--in 1996 and 1998--in the form of two *fatwas* that provided great detail as to his motivations for jihad.[4]

One of the ways the U.S. is familiar with Iran's military might is the Iranians' annual parade that shows us how publicly backward their military has become. Every year in April, the Iranian Army shows off its hardware. What has been remarkable is that the Iranians in 2008 were still flying F-4 Phantoms, F-5s, and F-14 Tomcats. These American-made planes were bought when the Shah was in power. The youngest plane was a Soviet MIG 29 from 1992.

Their tanks included Soviet T55's. We can infer from this obsolete weaponry that Iranians are not modernizing their conventional forces. It also provides a clue of how they are relying more on asymmetric warfare to deter their adversaries. This includes funding Hezbollah, as well investing heavily in both nuclear and missile programs.[5]

One of the greatest threats we face is the cooperation between North Korea and Iran in ballistic missile and nuclear technology. North Korea has both nuclear weapons and advanced missile technology. From using open-source intelligence, we can read from Japan's Kyodo agency a report that Iranian technicians have been stationed in North Korea to improve their technological cooperation.[6] In December 2012, I was the first to confirm (on Fox News) that Iranian experts were at North Korea's December

2012 missile launch. While this was reported in non-Western media sources, it was not on any major Western outlets.

The level of cooperation between North Korea and Iran, of course, had been well known for many years. Even without access to their most classified secrets, we can look at Iran's Shahab 3 missile and determine that it is based on the North Korean No Dong missile. The maximum range of a Shahab 3 missile is estimated to be up to 1,300 kilometers.[7] According to Wikileaks, which has unfortunately declassified an enormous amount of material, there was a meeting between American and Russian officials about the threat of North Korea providing Iran with 19 BM-25 missiles. There are two possible models for this missile. The first has a range of 2,500 kilometers, while the other has a range of 3,500 kilometers. If North Korea has delivered these missiles to Iran, every major European capital will be within range of an Iranian missile.

Whether they have a complete BM-25 missile, or simply the parts, is not clear, though Wikileaks shows that the cooperation between the two countries is growing. A country as cash-strapped and isolated as North Korea could use the BM-25 issue to potentially threaten European capitals.[8]

While open-source intelligence has been helpful on gathering intelligence, we should understand that it is not a new concept, but the internet has taken OSINT to a new level. The idea of acquiring information from publicly available sources such as newspapers, radio, and television, actually pre-dates the creation of the Central Intelligence Agency (CIA).

To give you an idea of this new shift from OSINT 1.0 to OSINT 2.0, it's important to quote Bart Geisler. As Executive Director of the Aviation Association of Indiana, Geisler said, "Build one mile of highway, go one mile. Build a mile of runway, go anywhere."[9]

The history of OSINT 1.0 began in 1941 with the Foreign Broadcast Monitoring Service, which analyzed broadcasts from the Axis Powers. Under the National Security Act of 1947, this organization was reconstituted as the Foreign Broadcast Information Service (FBIS). The mission of FBIS was enhanced to monitor all foreign media. By the end of the Cold War, FBIS was regularly translating over 3,000 news outlets from over 60 languages.[10] In OSINT 2.0, there are advanced search engines that can easily provide this type of information.

I have had the great privilege of using some of these advanced search engines. It shows us that OSINT 2.0 requires us to think of new ways of where to find relevant information. For example, if I wanted to read an analysis about the Deputy Secretary General of Hezbollah, Sheikh Naim Qassim, I would not think of looking into a Croatian newspaper.[11] Yet, one day I did find an interesting article from that country. If I want to get an update on the situation in Syria, we can quickly receive reports from newspapers all over the world. Our search engines are much like a highway that is limited when we are staying on the road reading signs in one language. If I decided to switch to a Google advanced search and change the language to search only French websites, I would come up with a completely different list of websites. Imagine an advanced search in dozens of languages and you get an idea of how limited our traditional searches are in finding useful intelligence.

In 2009, John Hagel, John Seely Brown, and Lang Davison wrote a joint article in the *Harvard Business Review* that argued that digital technology and public policy changes have altered the global business environment where "long-term forces of change are undercutting normal sources of economic value." While productivity and the competitive intensity among U.S. companies nearly doubled from 1965 to 2008, the return on assets (ROA) actually declined by 75 percent in the same period.[12] To combat this transformation, their article argued that effective collaboration was essential for companies to remain competitive because there are "far more smart people outside any one organization than inside."[13] The same can be said for Google searches in only one language as opposed to multiple languages, or limiting valued intelligence to only classified information.

According to Lt. Gen. Samuel V. Wilson, former director of the Defense Intelligence Agency, "Ninety percent of intelligence comes from open sources. The other ten percent, the clandestine work, is just the more dramatic. The real intelligence hero is Sherlock Holmes, not James Bond."[14] If 90 percent of our information comes from open sources, we need to focus more of our resources in OSINT for taxpayers to avoid diminishing returns on our intelligence spending.

Recommendation 1: Change the Intelligence Community's Culture so that Sherlock Holmes is Valued More Than James Bond

People who study organizational behavior will eventually come across this quotation:

> "Every organization has a culture; that is, a persistent, patterned way of thinking about the central tasks of human relationships within an organization. Culture is to an organization what personality is to an individual. Like human culture generally, it is passed on from one generation to the next. It changes slowly if at all."[15]

To change the culture within the intelligence community that will value a Sherlock Holmes figure that uses OSINT more than a James Bond figure, who deals with classified information, is a challenge. Both types of information have their place. This chapter simply argues that OSINT is not valued enough. Washington has shown time and again that proposing an idea in a commission will not provide lasting change. As early as 1996, the Aspin-Brown Commission, which was formally known as the Commission on the Roles and Capabilities of the United States Intelligence Community, concluded that:

> "...it is clear that open sources do provide a substantial share of the information used in intelligence analysis. In some areas, such as economic analysis, it is estimated that as much as 95 percent of the information utilized now comes from open sources. With more and more information becoming available by electronic means, its use in intelligence analysis can only grow. Indeed, knowing what is publicly available enables producers and collectors of intelligence to better focus their efforts on that which is not. So crucial is this determination to the overall intelligence process that the Commission finds it surprising that more emphasis has not been given this aspect of the Intelligence Community's operations."[16]

In 2005, nearly a decade later, the Commission on the Intelligence Capabilities of the United States Regarding Weapons of Mass Destruction wrote:

> "Our investigation revealed serious shortcomings; specifically, we found inadequate Intelligence Community collaboration and cooperation, analysts who do not understand collection, too much focus on current intelligence, inadequate systematic use of outside experts and open source information, a shortage of analysts with scientific and technical expertise, and poor capabilities to exploit fully the available data."[17]

The WMD Commission echoed many of the concerns of the Aspin-Brown Commission on OSINT:

> "Clandestine sources, however, constitute only a tiny sliver of the information available on many topics of interest to the Intelligence Community. Other sources, such as traditional media, the Internet, and individuals in academia, non-governmental organizations, and business, offer vast intelligence possibilities. Regrettably, all too frequently these 'non-secret' sources are undervalued and underused by the Intelligence Community."[18]

In a world where analysts are constantly being bombarded by overwhelming amounts of information, the skill of any analyst is to figure out how to sort through it. Sherlock Holmes is a good role model for intelligence analysts not just for his deductive reasoning, but for his instincts for where to find the right information. For example in the "Valley of Fear," Holmes used deductive reasoning in discovering that his copy of Whitaker's Almanac would give him the answer to deciphering a code from one of Professor Moriarty's lieutenants.[19]

Another important quality for OSINT analysis is patience. People who think that most useful information is classified tend to lose sight of the fact that good intelligence is more like solving a mystery. Intelligence is not about "connecting the dots," for the growth in information is so abundant it would be the equivalent to looking at all the different snowflakes during a snowstorm. No individual snowflake has all the facts and actual snowflakes evaporate quickly upon contact--as quickly as intelligence assets. Patience and good instincts are required for effective frequency analysis.

Holmes showed us his talents at frequency analysis during "The Adventure of the Dancing Men." In that adventure Holmes takes on a client, Hilton Cubitt, after his wife Elsie, began receiving disturbing messages containing dancing men. Holmes quickly sees that this is a code. It takes three messages before Holmes is able to read the code and discover that his client is in danger. Although Holmes is unable to reach the house before Hilton Cubitt is killed, London's most famous detective is able to identify the name of the killer: Abe Slaney.

Since the original letters came from the United States, Holmes sent a cable to his friend Wilson Hargreave from the New York Police Bureau. He was able to identify Abe Slaney as a dangerous criminal from Chicago. Holmes eventually learns the dancing men is a code for gangsters and lures Slaney to the Cubitt's residence. When Holmes admits that he wrote the letter in the dancing men code to lure the killer, Slaney points out that, "There was no one on earth outside the Joint who knew the secret of the dancing men. How came you to write it?" Holmes famously replies that, "What one man can invent another can discover."[20]

A third lesson from the adventures of Sherlock Holmes was that we can improve our OSINT when we accept that for every Sherlock Holmes, there is a Mycroft. (Mycroft was Sherlock's older brother.)

Some OSINT analysts will need to go to a Mycroft either inside or outside the government, to provide expertise on certain subjects. Interestingly, we learn later that in the "Adventure of the Bruce-Partington Plans," Holmes in effect admits to Watson that Mycroft is the most important person in the British Government:

"He has the tidiest and most orderly brain, with the greatest capacity for storing facts, of any man living. The same great powers which I have turned to the detection of crime he has used for this particular business. The conclusions of every department are passed to him and he is the central exchange, the clearinghouse, which makes out the balance. All other men are specialists but his specialism is omniscience. We will suppose that ministers need information as to a point which involves the Navy, India, Canada, and the bimetallic question; he could get his separate advices from various departments upon each, but only Mycroft can focus them all, and say offhand how each factor would affect the other."[22]

Today, there is not one individual that could fulfill Mycroft's role in the British Government; however, the FBIS was supplanted by the National Open Source Center (NOSC) in 2005 in order to create a collective worthy of Mycroft.[23]

Recommendation 2: Sustain OSINT Culture through promotion

To form a new culture within the intelligence community that values OSINT more, we have found in the past that the recommendations of bipartisan commissions are not enough. What we need to do is promote this culture by rewarding promotions to people who embrace OSINT.

This point was made clear to me in 2001 as I was watching Brian Lamb of C-SPAN interview the late William Rehnquist,. then Chief Justice of the United States Supreme Court (1986-2005). In the interview, Lamb asked why so few Chief Justices had been Associate Justices as well. Chief Justice Rehnquist pointed out that he was one of a very few Chief Justices who was an Associate Justice at the time of his appointment.

The only other individual that was both an Associate Justice, and later the Chief Justice of the U.S. Supreme Court, was Charles Evans Hughes. He left the court to run for president against Woodrow Wilson in 1916. After losing a close election, he would be appointed to the position of Chief Justice many years later.

The reasons why only a minority of Chief Justices were also Associate Justices are important to understand if we are to create a culture that puts greater value on OSINT. Chief Justice Rehnquist points out that he believes that Presidents, as well as legal scholars, have long been concerned that if it was understood that only an Associate Justice would be considered for the position of Chief Justice then it could poison the collegial atmosphere of the court.[24] The rivalry among the justices could also damage the independence of the judiciary as certain justices could potentially alter their opinions to reflect the President's position in order to curry favor.

If intelligence analysts feel that using OSINT is not as important as classified intelligence, the best people will turn away from it. People respond to incentives and we must give them the right ones.

Recommendation 3: Encourage Open-Source Intelligence Gathering

The intelligence community is today where the news media were about 10 years ago. It was at that time that Dan Rather felt the power of bloggers when Scott Johnson of the blog *Powerline* and Charles Johnson posted on another blog, *Little Green Footballs*, that documents used by "60 Minutes" in reporting on President George W. Bush's Texas Air National Guard service were inaccurate. Johnson explained the power of "open-source intelligence gathering." He was quoted in the *Washington Post*, "We've got a huge pool of highly motivated people who go out there and use the tools to find stuff. We've got an army of citizen journalists out there."[25]

In the case of the discredited documents, there were clearly people who served in the military and who knew an authentic document from the early 1970s when they saw one. In the absence of a Sherlock Holmes, we need to draw from the cumulative knowledge of people. If you take any two people, there is always something that one person knows that the other does not. Depending on the subject, there are now millions of people who can provide a unique perspective on any subject. We must encourage people to speak up. For there are far more people outside of the intelligence community than those who are working in it. Chances are there are many subjects where people from the outside can provide useful information that could help analysts on the inside achieve some breakthroughs.

Recommendation 4: Create in our intelligence community culture a passion for other cultures that rivals that of MacArthur and Yoshida

When we think of the intelligence failures that occurred in Iraq, the biggest was our insufficient understanding of the Iraqi people. This could have been obtained through open sources. When American troops were in Iraq, it was said that the roles of both Americans and Iraqis would be indispensable to ensuring a decent outcome; however, I don't think there was enough discussion on how we could bridge both worlds as we were building a new Iraq together.

In his book *Leaders,* Richard Nixon describes his experiences with Winston Churchill, Charles de Gaulle, Konrad Adenauer, Nikita Khrushchev, Zhou Enlai and many others. With the exception of Douglas MacArthur, the book focused on foreign leaders. In the chapter dealing with MacArthur, the former general shared the chapter with a man named Shigeru Yoshida, and there is a good reason why.

Nixon said that most people remember MacArthur for the role he played in World War II and Korea. Nixon always believed that MacArthur's most lasting contribution was his role in creating modern Japan.[26] MacArthur saw a country that was defeated physically and spiritually, and that was before Hirohito had to renounce his divinity. In what can only be described as a miracle, it recovered to become an economic giant.

When Richard Nixon wrote this book, he tried to clarify that it was not just MacArthur that made all this possible, but the partnership between MacArthur and Shigeru Yoshida. Yoshida was the Japanese prime minister for most of the American occupation of Japan from 1945 to 1951.

Nixon described the importance of the partnership well when he said, "Without MacArthur's vision, the necessary reforms might not have taken place. Without Yoshida's meticulous attention to detail, those reforms might have jarred Japan from confusion into chaos."[27] Nixon believed Yoshida was in many ways an equal to Churchill and de Gaulle, but not many people outside of Japan and academia are even aware of his important role in history.[28]

It was Yoshida who taught us that a postwar occupation by America functions well with strong indigenous leaders that can lead a defeated country from war and devastation to peace and prosperity. Japan's annual GNP growth averaged 10 percent from 1950 to 1973. In 1950, the size of Japan's GNP was only 1/20 of America's GNP. By 1991, Japan shortened the gap by possessing the second largest economy in the world with a GNP that was over half the size of that of the United States[29] Despite two decades of sluggish growth, Japan ($5.9 trillion) still has the third largest economy in the world, after the U.S. ($15.6 trillion) and China ($8.2 trillion).[30]

The success of post-war occupations can sometimes look like miracles in retrospect. It certainly seemed so in the case of Japan. In a way, MacArthur and Yoshida were born to play their respective roles.

In the case of General MacArthur, one cannot understand this complicated man without understanding that his love for Asia was connected to his father. When General Arthur MacArthur died, Douglas said, "My whole world changed that night. Never have I been able to heal the wound in my heart." His father was a man of the frontier and fought in the Civil War, the Spanish-American War, and later the Philippine Insurrection. He then became military governor of the Philippines (1900-1901).[31] Douglas MacArthur saw Asia as the new frontier. In the 20th century, he was simply continuing his father's work to protect our nation. From 1935 to 1951, MacArthur only visited the mainland of the United States once. The rest of his time was spent in the Pacific, mostly in Japan and the Philippines.[32]

As focused as MacArthur was on Asia, Yoshida had a passion for learning about the West. Long before he was prime minister, Yoshida was a diplomat who served as the Japanese Ambassador to the United Kingdom. It was there that he developed a great fondness for the constitutional monarchy that existed in Britain.[33] Both of these men were passionately curious about what they could learn from other cultures. Through their collaboration, they were able to learn from each other.

In OSINT, the whole is truly greater than the sum of its parts. There is simply too much information for tens of thousands of analysts to sort through. In the 1920s, Turkish President Mustafa Kemal Ataturk gave many speeches in favor of women's rights because he believed that, "We shall not catch up with the modern world if we only modernize half the population."[34] The same can be said of our intelligence analysts. We will not improve our intelligence until a far larger percentage of our population joins the effort to help us piece together the vast amounts of information out there. In the end, there are very few secrets that somebody, somewhere does not know. If that somebody talks, we need to use OSINT effectively to make sure that we can hear them. The message to them is: Uncle Sam Needs You!

Chapter Seven

Suicide Bombers: Separating This Cult of Death from The Rest of Islam

Two hundred years before the attacks of 9/11, James Madison wrote in Federalist 41 about the "terrors of conflagration."[1] This particular essay was addressed to the people of New York, a city Madison said was particularly vulnerable to an attack:

"The great emporium of its commerce, the great reservoir of its wealth, lies every moment at the mercy of events, and may almost be regarded as a hostage for ignominious compliances with the dictates of a foreign enemy, or even with the rapacious demands of pirates and barbarians."[2]

After the Revolutionary War, our colonial navy was disbanded. Under British rule, American ships were protected from piracy by the Royal Navy and treaties between England and the Barbary States. As a new independent country, however, we could be attacked by pirates with impunity. This is why President Washington called for the creation of a new navy in 1794 to protect our shipping.[3] Western nations, including the United States, paid tribute to the Barbary pirates who were sanctioned by their government to seize vessels and enslave their crews.

By the time Thomas Jefferson took office, the U.S. had a Navy capable enough to send these pirates a message. In times, the Barbary States, which today are the modern Morocco, Tunisia, Algeria and Libya, stopped harassing us because the United States defeated them.[4]

Much like piracy, the United States can only defeat the threat of suicide bombings when our leaders fully accept the nature of this threat and do what is necessary to end it. Yes, we still have pirates, but their ships are not a serious foe of the U.S. Navy. We can reach a point where suicide bombings are both rare and actually condemned by large parts of the Muslim world.

This chapter is intended to provide a blueprint for such a victory. Any long-term strategy will require broad-based bipartisan support. That will not happen without confronting some of the most persistent myths of the War on Terror. This chapter will also provide historical background on the origins of suicide bombings and some recommendations on how to reduce this threat.

Myth 1: Jihadist groups pervert the teachings of Islam

In 2010, there were 1.6 billion Muslims in the world.[5] We cannot win this war if we lump Islamist jihadists (who want to become martyrs) together with their allies who provide support to them, with the great majority of the world's Muslims who will not support or engage in suicide bombings.

The easiest way to delegitimize al-Qaeda, Hezbollah, Hamas, ISIS and other extremists is to stop calling them Muslims. Apologists for these groups have frequently said that they pervert the teachings of Islam, but somehow are still Muslim. That is not true. To be a Muslim means that one must submit his will to Allah. It is written in Quran 9:51, "Say: 'Nothing will happen to us except what Allah has decreed for us. He is our protector': and on Allah let the believers put their trust."[6] In other words, one who does not follow the path of Allah cannot be called a Muslim.

Either suicide bombers are correctly submitting to Allah's will or they are not Muslims. The rest of the Muslim world must end its timidity and face up to this reality.

Myth 2: People Resort to Terrorism Because of Poverty

Osama bin Laden came from a wealthy family, as did his successor, Ayman al-Zawahiri, a surgeon from a prominent

Egyptian family. Before Mohammed Atta flew the first airliner into the World Trade Center, he was probably conversing with his educated family. Mohammed's father was a lawyer. He also had two educated sisters, one a doctor, the other a professor. Many of al-Qaeda's recruits were middle class and educated.[7] Beheading someone is barbaric, but Ahmed Omar Sheik, who is best known for his role in the kidnapping of journalist Daniel Pearl, actually attended the London School of Economics.

Sub-Saharan Africa seems to present a contradiction. The share of the population living in extreme poverty grew from 11 percent in 1981 to 34 percent in 2010.[8] Yet President George W. Bush became far more popular in Sub-Saharan Africa than in the United States. This is partly a result of the popularity of his administration's Emergency Plan for AIDS Relief.[9] By the time he left office in January 2009, the number of people in Africa receiving anti-retroviral drugs had increased from 50,000 to two million people.[10]

Despite this progress, Sub-Saharan Africa poverty continued to increase during those years. That means 414 million people in Sub-Saharan Africa were living on less than $1.25 dollars a day in 2010.[11]

Nevertheless, I do not fear wholesale suicide bombings from this part of the world because the majority of Sub-Saharan Africa is Christian. The number of Christians living in this region grew from only seven million in 1900 to 470 million in 2010. In the same period the number of Muslims in the area grew from 11 million to 234 million.[12]

Much insurgency in sub-Saharan Africa is tribally based and not related to al-Qaida or its allies. The exception is the Muslim *Boko Haram* movement in northern Nigeria, where the country's Muslims are concentrated, which is waging violent attacks on Christians and the Nigerian government.

The lack of education opportunities should also give us less reason to fear that the vast majority of the Muslims in this area will join the banner of *jihad*. This also leads to the third myth.

Myth 3: There are two types of Muslims: those who are mainstream and a small fraction that are radicalized.

Among both Sunnis and Shia, the "mainstream" includes both "Reform" and "Moderate" Muslims. Then there are Islamists, some of whom favor gradual development of Muslim dominance, on the one hand, and those who become radicalized, on the other. The Muslim Brotherhood, founded in Egypt in the 1920s, has spawned several overt *jihadi* radical groups, but also contents itself with waiting until another movement gains traction, such as the Arab Spring uprising in Egypt, Then it insinuates members into the movement to gain leadership positions.

One of the world's most celebrated Reform Muslims is Irshad Manji. She is a tireless advocate for *ijtihad*, which is an Islamic tradition that involves critical thinking. She is also critical of "Moderate Muslims" who do not criticize the Islamic terrorism that is rooted in parts of the Quran.[13]

Some Moderate Muslims support the grievances, but not the methods, of the jihadists. Reform Muslims understand that suicide bombings are barbaric. Such leaders of the Reform movement as Irshad have the courage to condemn terrorism and seek to reform Islam. Many Moderate Muslims instead are privately critical of radical Islamists, but do not speak out.

Despite the fact few Reform Muslims are following Irshad Manji's lead, the concept of *ijtihad* is alive in the Islamic world. A good way of distinguishing Reform Muslims from either Moderate Muslims, or Islamists, is the poll of whether Sharia can have multiple interpretations versus a single interpretation. There are large majorities in Tunisia (72%) and Morocco (60%) that support multiple interpretations of Sharia. There are also substantial minorities supporting multiple interpretations in Muslim-majority countries such as Iraq (48%), Indonesia (44%), Lebanon (39%), Bangladesh (38%), Kazakhstan (36%), and Malaysia (35%).[14]

This is a good sign. One of the many things that distinguish Islamists from the rest of Islam is the issue of suicide bombings. Contrary to popular belief, the Iraq War did not inflame the Muslim world. In the last decade, support for suicide bombings has actually gone down dramatically throughout Muslim world.

From 2002 to 2013, the percentage of people who thought a suicide bombing was either sometimes or often justified plummeted in Jordan (43% to 12%), Pakistan (33% to 3%), and Lebanon (74% to 33%). Support for suicide bombings in Nigeria dropped from 34 percent in 2010 to eight percent in 2013. (This is in part because Nigeria has lost thousands of its citizens in recent years to *Boko Haram*). A side effect of this campaign is that other terrorist organizations have lost popularity in Nigeria as well. Support for al-Qaeda among Nigerian Muslims dropped from 49 percent in 2010 to nine percent in 2013. In the same period support for Hamas dropped from 49 percent to 25 percent and Hezbollah dropped from 45 percent to 21 percent. *Boko Haram* is the least popular with only two percent of Nigerian Muslims holding a favorable view.[15]

Majorities in most Muslim countries agree that suicide bombings can never be justified. Countries with some of the largest Muslim populations are leaders on this issue. According to Pew, 89 percent of Pakistanis, 81 percent of Indonesians, and 78 percent of Nigerians believe that suicide bombings are never justified.[16]

When terrorists use suicide bombings to kill Muslims, the approval for terrorism declines . Nigeria is a recent case. Note also that in August, 2007, 70 percent of residents in Pakistan's North-West Frontier had a favorable opinion of Osama bin Laden. By January, 2008, shortly after the assassination of Benazir Bhutto, bin Laden's approval rating dropped to four percent. Terrorist organizations, like other movements, cannot survive without support from the populace.[17]

In the long-run, these *jihadis* are wrong, but never in doubt. Either our military or their *hubris* will defeat them. When Hezbollah fought an indecisive war against Israel in 2006, Sheik Hasan Nasrallah, its leader, was the most popular leader in the Arab world. When Nasrallah stopped attacking Israel, and aimed his weapons against Sunni Muslims in Syria, Hezbollah's reputation was tarnished among Sunni Arabs.[18] In 2013, Hezbollah had very unfavorable ratings in Sunni countries such as Egypt (75%), Turkey (73%), and Jordan (72%). Among the Palestinians, the war in Syria helped drop support for Hezbollah from 61 percent in 2011 to 43 percent in 2013.[19]

Islamists who think suicide bombings are justified must be divided into two final categories. One can be best described as the "chicken hawks." These are the Muslims who will knowingly finance terrorism, or provide other levels of support. What they will not do is strap on a belt of explosives. Osama bin Laden encouraged people to be martyrs while he hid from the U.S. military. The other category is composed of people who will happily kill themselves for *jihad.*

Myth 4: Islamic Terrorists Began Suicide Bombings Because of Israel

Before the wars in Afghanistan and Iraq, when Americans thought of suicide bombers, they thought of the Israeli-Palestinian conflict. Former CIA operative Robert Baer provided an informative documentary series, *The Cult of the Suicide Bomber.* Baer, who lost friends to suicide bombings in Lebanon in the 1980s, educated himself to understanding the cult behind suicide bombings.

What he discovered was that modern suicide bombings originated from the Iran-Iraq War. Shortly after the Iranian Revolution, Ayatollah Khomeini reminded people that the war against Iraq was the modern equivalent of the Battle of Karbala (680 AD).[20] The Shite holiday of Ashura commemorates this battle that ended with the defeat of the Shiites, led by Hussein, who was the grandson of the Prophet Muhammad. For the Shiites, Hussein was viewed as a martyr while his Sunni rival, Yazid, and the Umayyad Caliphate, was the personification of evil.[21] It would be equivalent of American soldiers issuing the battle cry to "Remember the Alamo" a thousand years from now.

During the Iran-Iraq War, Khomeini was able to create a culture of suicide bombers. Children were taken out of schools and indoctrinated. As I was watching this documentary, I thought to myself no civilized society encourages their children to volunteer in these "human-wave" attacks. How can parents not cringe at the fact that at least 95,000 Iranian children were killed during this war by literally running towards death?[22]

Young Iranians joined the *Basiji* because of the Battle of Karbala. They wanted to be martyrs and they weren't alone. In November, 1982, 15-year-old Ahmad Qusayr struck Israel with the first Islamic suicide bombing. The Sunni terrorists would eventually follow.[23]

Myth 5: America's foreign policy is hostile to Islam.

America's foreign policy in the last two decades has been pro-Muslim. In fact, n major power can compete with the United

States on this score. Our foreign policy is remarkably more compassionate toward Muslims than are many Muslim-majority countries. No recent example illustrates this point better than the genocide in Darfur.

The politically incorrect way of describing Darfur is that an Islamic government, led by Sudanese President Omar el-Bashir, supported an Islamic militia known as the *Janjaweed* (Arabic for "devils on horseback"). These Arab Muslims have killed 400,000 African Muslims in Darfur and have displaced 2.5 million refugees in the area.[24]

Much as in Kosovo and Iraq, the U.S. was pressing the United Nations Security Council to stand up for human rights in Darfur. Russia and China blocked these efforts. Sudan obtained their votes on the Security Council through buying weapons from Russia and selling oil to China. While the Russians and the Chinese thought they were acting in their strategic interests, I was both stunned and appalled at the lack of outrage from Muslim countries on the Security Council despite the body of evidence against the Sudanese government.

For example, in July, 2004, the Security Council passed Resolution 1556, which warned Sudan to take steps to end the conflict immediately or face possible sanctions. It also established an arms embargo. Out of the 15 Security Council members, 13 voted "yes" while China and Pakistan abstained.[25]

When that failed, the Security Council passed Resolution 1564, which threatened the *possibility* of sanctions if the Sudanese government did not help them end the conflict. Although 11 members were in support, Russia, China, Algeria, and Pakistan abstained.[26]

By early 2005, the United Nations passed Resolution 1591, reaffirming the previous arms embargo along with a travel ban and a freeze in assets. Not surprisingly, Russia, China, and Algeria abstained from this resolution.[27] Darfur put the moral bankruptcy of the United Nations on full display. Anything tougher than that would likely have been vetoed by Russia and China.

With all the Muslim American student organizations on U.S. college campuses, were any of them as passionate about Darfur as they were about the Israeli-Palestinian conflict?

The United States led the fight to help the people of Darfur. We also played a leading role in helping other Muslim countries in times of crisis. A good example was the 2004 *tsunami* that killed some 286,000 people across 14 countries. We should not forget the indispensable role of the United States in the recovery efforts. A majority of these deaths, 221,000 people, were on the Indonesian island of Aceh.[28] The good deeds of the American people helped improve our image in the world's largest Muslim country. America's favorability rating went up from 15 percent in 2003 to 63 percent in 2009.[29]

The United States is not perfect, but our foreign policy has helped more Muslims than the foreign policy of the late Saddam Hussein, Syrian President Bashar al-Assad, the late Libyan leader Muammar al-Gaddaffi, the Iranian mullahs and all the other malcontents in the Middle East.

Myth 6: If we ignore the Middle East, they'll stop trying to kill us.

Over several decades of distinguished scholarship, historian Bernard Lewis came to see that this conflict was based on resentment. It was not a misunderstanding, but rooted among the *jihadis* in the idea that Islam is both a religion and an empire. The theory goes that some of the members of this empire never came to grips with its decline. As a result, Sunni fundamentalists, who helped to spawn al-Qaeda and other groups, saw Britain--and later America--as possessing power that should belong to Islam. Thus, America is not going to win over the hearts and minds of these extremists.[30]

As early as September, 1990, Professor Lewis published these views in great detail. He believes that the majority of Muslims do not reject the West and that Islam has provided an inner peace to millions of its followers. Islam, however, has also inspired a radical segment of people willing to give their lives for jihad.[31]

Lewis points out that the Islamic world, like other civilizations, saw itself as the center of civilization and superior to its neighbors. He believes that the polytheists to the East were never considered a true threat to Islam, but the West was considered a rival from the beginning. Islam was winning this clash for the first few centuries. Even when the Spanish drove the Moors from Spain, the Muslims were able to compensate with gains in Eastern Europe. The Islamic world has been on the defensive ever since the Turks were defeated in Vienna in 1683. The rise of the European colonial powers was not something they were prepared to tolerate.[32]

Lewis would complete this argument by saying that when America became the undisputed leader of Western civilization after the World War II, this made us the most potent symbol of evil to the Islamic fundamentalists. We were the threat to them because American products dominated global markets. This influence of the United States was seen as a threat to the preservation of Islamic culture.[33]

One reactionary "scholar" that Osama bin Laden commonly cites is Sayyid Qutb. Qutb visited America in the 1940s and found America in a state of *jahiliyya,* a religious term for a period of ignorance prior to revelation of Islam. Osama bin Laden agreed with Qutb that a person was either a Muslim or was a nonbeliever. All non-believers had to be fought.[34] These extremists have a way of thinking that is very different from ours.

Along with Bernard Lewis, another great scholar on Islamic fundamentalism and military history is Professor Mary Habeck of the John Hopkins School of Advanced International Studies. In a 2004 lecture, she argued that these Islamic fundamentalists--the *Jihadis*--are not helpless people randomly attacking, but people with a clear intention to restore Islam's dominance.

Various groups attack their enemies, which are Western leaders, apostates that rule in Muslim lands, and any Muslim that does not follow Islam as they do. The difference between these terrorist groups is their strategy. The strategy comes from the Method of Muhammad. It comes from not just the Quran and the Hadith, but the Sirah, which is a biography of Muhammad's life. Habeck argues that Muslims feel that they must emulate Muhammad's miraculous life in order to restore the greatness of Islam.

Professor Habeck points out that once *jihad* begins, the only question is which enemy is the priority. These terrorist groups tend to follow essentially three strategies. *Jihadis* can adopt these policies because Muhammad used all of them. The first is to take on the "near enemy" then the "far enemy." Today the near enemy is in the Islamic world whether they be foreign occupiers or Muslim rulers perceived as traitors to the faith.

The second strategy is to go after the "greater unbelief" and then the "lesser unbelief." Today, that greater unbeliever is interpreted as the United States. The belief is that once America is defeated then the lesser unbelievers will fall in line.

The third strategy is to take on the "apostates," then the other unbelievers. These groups are pretty open about what path they are going to follow, which makes their targets somewhat predictable. The reason *jihadis* attacked Spain in 2004 was not to have an impact in its elections, but because they wanted to take on the near enemy, which, in their eyes, was the Spanish, for occupying land that was once ruled by Islam for eight hundred years.[35]

Osama bin Laden attacked the United States because he believes it is the duty of every Muslim to fight an offensive *jihad* against non-Muslims. One of the best books on al-Qaeda is Raymond Ibrahim's, *The Al-Qaeda Reader*. In it, he translates the statements and writings of Osama bin Laden and his deputy Ayman al-Zawahiri.

What cannot be lost is how bin Laden's official grievances change with his audience. In Western crowds, bin Laden misleads people into believing that he is an unwilling participant in this war and he is waging a defensive *jihad*. In October 2002, bin Laden posted a letter on the Internet addressing his problems with the American people. It was entitled, "Why We Are Fighting You."

In it, he gave the usual grievances including America's support for Israel and secular Arab dictatorships in the Middle East. He also gave reasons that might surprise some people. He listed our failure to ratify the Kyoto Protocol, the inability of the American people to sufficiently condemn Clinton for his immoral acts, allowing usury and gambling to exist, the sexual exploitation of woman, and supporting the separation of religion and politics.[36]

One of the reasons why people should find this hard to believe is because bin Laden altered his message for different audiences. For example, in 2003, al-Jazeera released multiple messages from bin Laden. In one, to Americans, he made it clear he had a right to retaliate against the United States as well other countries that participated in the Iraq War, such as the U.K. and Spain.[37] "Shortly after the 2005 London bombings, 33 percent of British residents polled said that Tony Blair's decision to send British troops into Iraq had "a lot" to do with the attacks. Another 31 percent claimed that Britain's role in Iraq was partly to blame. Only 28 percent of British residents believed, correctly, that there was no link between the London bombers and the Iraq War."[38]

When Osama bin Laden sent messages to Muslims, he advocated an offensive *jihad.* In one public message to Iraqi Muslims through al-Jazeera, bin Laden quotes the Quaran 5:51, "O ye who believe! Take not the Jews and the Christians for your friends and protectors: they are but friends and protectors to each other."[39]

Long before the Iraq War, the creation of Israel, and even the Crusades, Muslims read this Quaran verse 60:4, "We have nothing to do with you and with those whom you worship besides Allah. We have rejected you. Enmity and hatred will separate us forever unless you believe in Allah alone."[40]

The fascist ideology--which al-Qaeda resembles--has the same disregard for the lives of innocent people as the Nazis had. The strategy of placing moral superiority over others was used by Hitler to justify killing non-Germans and by bin Laden for killing infidels. Dr. Joshua Teitelbaum, a Senior Research Fellow at the Dayan Center for Middle East Studies, made connections between the rhetoric of Hitler, bin Laden, and former Iranian President Mahmoud Ahmadinejad. They all seem to stress the moral superiority to justify killing innocent people. Dr. Teitelbaum wrote:

"A common motif of genocide incitement is the dehumanization of the target population. The Nazi weekly *Der Stürmer* portrayed Jews as parasites and locusts. In the early 1990s, Hutu propaganda in Rwanda against the Tutsis described them as 'cockroaches.' Prior to Saddam Hussein's operations against the Iraqi Shiite population in 1991, his Baath Party newspaper characterized them as 'monkey-faced people.' Similarly, President

Ahmadinejad has called Israeli Jews 'cattle,' 'blood thirsty barbarians,' and 'criminals. ' Dehumanization has also appeared in other forms, like demonization, by which the target population is described as 'Satanic'–a theme specifically used by Ahmadinejad."[41]

Recommendation 1: Conservatives Should Collaborate More With 9/11 Liberals

In September, 2012, comedian Bill Maher coined a phrase in American politics called "9/11 liberals." With Salman Rushdie sitting next to him, he described Rushdie, the late Christopher Hitchens, Sam Harris, Ayaan Hirsi Ali and himself as examples of 9/11 liberals. Maher continued, "Let's define where we are different from the mainstream liberals because I have routinely gotten booed here on the show sometimes, on my stand-up act, when I say, and liberals hate to hear this, that all religions are not alike."[42]

In 2003, Bill Maher provided one of the most eloquent liberal arguments against terrorism:

> "The values of Western civilization are not just different, they're *better.* OK? I know a whole generation has been raised on the notion of multiculturalism, that all civilizations are just different. No. Rule of law is *better* than autocracy and theocracy. Equality of the sexes, *better.* Protection of minorities, *better.* Free speech, *better.* Free elections, *better.*"[43]

When Ayatollah Khomeini issued a *fatwa* against Salman Rushdie for the crime of writing a book, Bill Maher and Christopher Hitchens were far better at convincing a liberal audience as to why the War on Terror was not a simple misunderstanding. People in college today are too young to remember the Cold War and the concept of a Scoop Jackson Democrat. For a new generation of liberals, we need spokesmen who can explain this war in their terms.

We need the 9/11 liberals to prevail in the Democratic Party. When Henry Wallace challenged Truman on his "bipartisan reactionary war policy," we should not forget that Wallace opposed the Marshall Plan and blamed Truman for Stalin's 1948 takeover of Czechoslovakia. Thankfully, most New Dealers sided with Truman, and Wallace only had a small following.[44]

While he was not himself a Communist, Henry Wallace believed that American imperialism–not Soviet communism–was the source of the Cold War. In 1947 he said, "The way to handle communism is by what William James called the replacing power of the higher affection. In other words, we give the common man all over the world something better than communism."[45]

This fight continued in the Democratic Party throughout the 1950s and 1960s and reached a boiling point during the peak of America's involvement in the Vietnam War. President Clinton believed that part of the unbridgeable differences about Vietnam among Democrats was in their diverse backgrounds. In his memoir *My Life*, Clinton describes the ongoing struggle between Senator J. William Fulbright, the Chairman of the Senate Foreign Relations Committee (1957-1975) and Secretary of State Dean Rusk (1961-1969) was because they were Rhode Scholars at Oxford at different eras.

Clinton worked for Fulbright and knew that when his mentor entered Oxford in the mid-1920s, the dominant view from students was that the ultra-nationalism in Germany was the result of the punitive measures that the victorious powers put on her following World War I. From that experience, Fulbright tried to find peaceful multilateral solutions and never felt it was productive to demonize adversaries. Dean Rusk came into Oxford in the early 1930s, as the West was allowing Hitler to rearm. Rusk felt that the lesson was that appeasement must never be repeated.[46]

Scoop Jackson's hawkish approach to foreign affairs was crystallized during his visit to Buchenwald on April 22, 1945. It was only 11 days after General Patton's Third Army liberated this death camp. At the time, he said, ". . . how easily it could have happened to us if their program of world conquest had reached our shores."[47]

During the Cold War, these two views were not reconcilable. Senator Fulbright even wrote a book at the height of the Vietnam War called the *Arrogance of Power* to basically blame the United States, and not Communist aggression, for the war. He would keep those views for the rest of his life. In 1989, he even wrote in another book, *The Price of Empire.* He concludes:

> "When you look at Nicaragua and some of Reagan's policies...there is much that we should have learned, above all that we, as a nation, are no more immune than the great powers of the past from the arrogance of power. If we could begin really to appreciate what this means, we might start to turn away from the obsession with Russia and communism that has gripped us for over forty years, and at last confront what the futile quest for primacy has cost us."[48]

Senator Fulbright's blaming America was a far cry from most Democrats prior to 1968. President Kennedy famously reassured Americans in his 1961 Inaugural that: "In the long history of the world, only a few generations have been granted the role of defending freedom in its hour of maximum danger. I do not shrink from this responsibility--I welcome it."[49]

Recommendation 2: Delegitimize Terrorist Leaders Through Smear Campaigns

In 1978, Ion Pacepa became one of the highest defectors of the Eastern Bloc in the entire history of the Cold War.[50] When Nicolai Ceaucescu learned that his top aide, who served as both a presidential advisor and a top intelligence officer, had defected, he was furious. Ceaucescu put a $2 million bounty on Pacepa's head. The Romanian dictator also sent two assassination teams to locate and kill Pacepa. In 1987, Pacepa published a memoir that was so damaging to Ceaucescu's reputation that a second death sentence was placed on him.[51]

It is important to understand that they tried to kill this author to prevent him from revealing his secrets. This is why Pacepa's memoir is worth reading, despite the fact that some of his stories are hard to believe. For example, one of the more interesting ones in Pacepa's memoir, *Red Horizons*, was that Arafat was recorded having sex with his male bodyguard on one of his visits to Bucharest.[52]

If the CIA had access to such a tape, we could have blackmailed Arafat for information. If he refused, or he simply outlived his usefulness, the United States could have discredited the PLO, or Fatah, by releasing this information on their leader. People who seek to be martyrs would be much less likely to follow a discredited leader.

We should remember that even today this would be unacceptable. When Pew polled 39 countries in 2013 on the question of whether society should accept homosexuality, it showed that there was still a much greater acceptance in Western and developed countries than Muslim countries. Majorities in Spain (88%), Germany (87%), France (77%), Britain (76%), and the United States (60%) agreed that society should accept homosexuality. In contrast, overwhelming majorities in such places as Jordan (97%), Egypt (95%), the Palestinian territories (93%), Indonesia (93%), Pakistan (87%), and Turkey (78%) believed that society should not accept homosexuality.[53]

In the Middle East, such a strategy could also keep our less reliable allies in check. For example, in Bob Woodward's book *Shadow*, the veteran journalist reveals how the CIA provided King Hussein with prostitutes when he visited the United States as a young man. To complicate matters, his favorite prostitute was Jewish. This would have caused serious problems for him if it were revealed.[54]

In fighting suicide bombers, nothing can stop a determined man but death. Regarding their allies, we can probably deter, bribe, or blackmail many of them to find another line of work. Blackmail does not have to involve simply personal scandals. For example, in 2004, the French launched a money-laundering probe on Suha Arafat, the widow of Yasser Arafat. Apparently, millions of dollars that were originally intended to help the Palestinian people were siphoned into her bank accounts.[55]

The Palestinian Authority received $5.5 billion in international aid from 1994 to 2003. At the same time, an Israeli intelligence report showed that Arafat was worth $1.3 billion. Whether or not this was true, Azmi Shuaibi , a Palestinian Legislative Council member echoed the sentiments of many Palestinians, in 2003, when he said, "We are afraid if something happens to Arafat, we will not know where all the money is."[56]

Recommendation 3: Assign The Cult of Suicide Bomber Studies to high school seniors

Watching Robert Baer's documentary series on suicide bombers was remarkable. It takes people across Europe and the Middle East. It not only provides a good explanation on how Sunnis and Shia become suicide bombers, but he even interviews failed suicide bombers and the parents of successful suicide bombers. What will shock many Americans is how the parents of suicide bombers are proud of their children.

We need American kids to see such videos because political correctness toward Islam is more entrenched than people think. For example, in Orchard Park, NY, Muzzammil Hassan founded a television station to combat negative stereotypes of Muslims in the United States. Then a week after his wife filed for divorce, Hassan decided to cut off her head.[57] It should be noted that this was Hassan's third wife. The other two wives left him citing domestic violence.[58]

You would think this would be the one time political correctness could be set aside, yet Kim Gandy, who was president of the National Organization of Women (2001-2009), couldn't resist. She wrote in her column:

> "Although the crime was quickly decried by Muslim groups, many talk shows and blogs used the horror of Muzzammil's act to indict an entire community--in a way that they would never have accused the entire Christian religion because a Methodist man murdered his estranged wife in a horrible way. Is a Muslim man in Buffalo more likely to kill his wife than a Catholic man in Buffalo? A Jewish man in Buffalo? "[59]

We need educators to have the courage to call out this moral relativism whenever it emerges. Beyond the known cases of Saudi Arabia where women are fighting for the right to drive a car, Western civilization is far more enlightened when it comes to women's issues. For example, in 2012, 16-year-old Amina Filali committed suicide after the judge ordered her to marry her rapist.[60] Amina would never had to deal with a judge like that in the United States.

Recommendation 4: Target Assassination

In April, 2008, five years of the Iraq War had brought 63 percent of Americans to conclude that this war was a mistake.[61] When Henry Kissinger was asked why he supported the Iraq War, he responded, "Because Afghanistan wasn't enough." He felt that America had to send a message to humiliate radical Islam. Such an action would have to be done, "in order to make a point that we're not going to live in this world they want for us."[62]

As the war was approaching in early 2003, President Bush asked then-Saudi Ambassador Prince Bandar bin Sultan if this would destabilize the region. Prince Bandar said:

> "Mr. President, you're assuming you're attacking Saudi Arabia and trying to capture King Fahd. This is Saddam Hussein. People are not going to shed a tear over Saddam Hussein, but if he's attacked one more time by America and he survives, he will be larger than life. If he survives and stays in power after you've finished this, whatever it is, yes everybody will follow his word. If they say attack the American embassy, they will go and attack it."[63]

Instead of attacking countries, terrorists and their supporters need to know that they will be on targeted assassination lists if they attack the United States. Israel defeated suicide bombings in the Second Intifada by building a security fence. Even before the fence was being built on the West Bank, in response to suicide bombings, similar security fences have been erected along Israel's de facto borders with Lebanon, Syria, Jordan, and the Gaza Strip.

Former Commander of the IDF's Southern Command, Major General Doron Almog (2000-2003), wrote that the success of Gaza Strip's security fence was not due to lack of effort. From 2000 to 2003, there were more than 400 Palestinian attempts to cross the fence and all of them failed.[64] The fence helped stop suicide bombings from a peak of 457 Israeli deaths in 2002 to six in 2009.[65] (This was before the discovery of cross-border tunnels in 2014, of which Israel destroyed more than 30.)

Fences are only part of the solution. Another part is the targeted assassination program.

From September, 2000 to August, 2005, there were 25,000 Palestinian attacks against Israel that resulted in more than a thousand deaths. Of these 25,000 attacks, only 151 were suicide bombings. While suicide bombings were only 0.6 percent of Palestinian attacks in this period, they resulted in 515 deaths. This is almost half of the total fatalities. Hamas was responsible for almost 40 percent of these attacks. The total number of suicide bombings dropped from 55 in 2002 to nine in 2005.[66] The number killed by Hamas in this period dropped from 185 in 2002 to 21 by 2005. When the targeted killing policy on Hamas was instituted in 2002, it was also believed to boost morale as well as kill some of the most capable terrorists within Hamas. Since terrorists and their bomb makers need months if not years of effective training, the policy is effective against the organization.[67]

We can and must do the same to both the *jihadis* and those who support them. Remember to be an old man in a terrorist organization means that the person did not have the religious fanaticism necessary to be a suicide bomber. If they know we're gunning for them, they, or their successors, will eventually get the message.

In the case of Hamas, from when Israel killed Hamas military chief Salah Shahada in July, 2002 to the 2004 deaths of Hamas founder and spiritual leader Sheikh Ahmed Yassin and the de facto leader of Hamas Abdel Aziz al-Rantissi, the organization was set back.

Recommendation 5: Shut down organizations that cannot condemn Hamas and extremists

When SEAL Team Six killed Osama bin Laden in May 2011, Hamas leader Ismail Haniyeh immediately condemned the United States for killing an "Arab holy warrior."[68] Since it's obvious who Hamas is for in this fight, we should be clear that there has to be a zero-tolerance policy. The State Department maintains a list of foreign terrorist organizations. Should a non-profit organization refuse to condemn all of the Islamist organizations on this list, it should be investigated for a possible shut down. We should remember that when Imam Faisal Abdul Rauf refused to condemn Hamas in a 2010 interview, claiming that, "Look I'm not a politician." He claimed that terrorism was a complex question.[69] It was only after several months of political blowback that Rauf was forced to say, "I condemn everyone and anyone who commits acts of terrorism. And Hamas has committed acts of terrorism."[70] We need to find a way to drain the swamp of extremism so that people can get the right answer the first time. Moderate Muslims may not share the zeal of a reformer like Irshad Manj, but they do not want their lives to be in the crossfire. Conservatives must work with 9/11 liberals and Reform Muslims to change parts of Islam and mobilize American morale to invigorate the fight.

As Moderate Muslims can be pushed toward Reform Islam, we can collapse both financial and moral support for suicide bombings. If terrorism is financed by high oil prices, suicide bombings are fueled by fanaticism and the need for irrational men to feel they have made their marks. This is why we need to get Reform and Moderate Muslims to condemn these savages as being part of a cult of death that is separate from Islam.

By delegitimizing their actions more and more people will see them as the savages they are. With intelligence sharing and targeted assassination, we can manage this threat. Some of these terrorist organizations are too well organized to be disbanded anytime soon. Nevertheless, none of them is popular enough to achieve its goals of establishing the caliphate or defeating the United States. Suicide bombings can cause much death and destruction, but they are ultimately self-defeating for the *jihadis*.

Recommendation 6: Defeating ISIS requires a policy of "degrade, destroy, and delegitimize"

As the world watched ISIS behead James Foley and Steven Sotloff, we saw one of the most barbaric, ruthless and savage groups of people that the human race has ever known. Defeating ISIS requires a policy of degrading, destroying, and delegitimizing. We've degraded and largely destroyed Islamic terrorists and their organizations in the past. However, we're done a poor job of delegitimizing them, particularly in the Muslim world. Hence, the ability of an ISIS or a Khorasan Group to emerge and recruit new people to their brand of hate.

With the death of Osama bin Laden and Abu Musab al-Zarqawi, it was natural that al-Qaeda would splinter and metastasize into new groups that would claim to be the successor to bin Laden. ISIS, which has roots in Iraq, was kicked out of al-Qaeda because its leader, Abu Bakr al-Baghdadi, arbitrarily decided that al-Qaeda's branch in Syria, Jabhat al-Nusra, was going to be placed under his command. Nusra's leader, Abu Muhammad al-Jawlani, immediately appealed to Osama's successor, Ayman al-Zawahiri, to officially reject this "merger." When Zawahiri sided with Jawlani, Baghdadi used terror to recruit Nusra fighers and kill whomever defied ISIS. This could be the beginning of other challengers to Zawahiri.

Today, al-Qaeda is more a franchise than a unified organization. Today its leaders in Afghanistan and Pakistan have affiliates that include al-Qaeda in the Arabian Peninsula (AQAP), al-Qaeda in the Islamic Maghreb (AQIM), al-Qaeda in the Indian Subcontinent (AQIS), al-Shabaab in Somalia, and Jabhat al-Nusra in Syria. Until the advent of ISIS, the leaders of these affiliates had the best of both worlds: command over their territories and the respect of potential recruits that came from being affiliated with Osama bin Laden.

Beyond direct affiliates, their allies include the Taliban, the Pakistani Taliban, Laskar-e-Taiba, Jemaah Islamiah in Indonesia, Abu Sayyaf in the Philippines, the Caucasus Emirate, Ansaru, Boko Haram in Nigeria, and a number of other terrorist groups. The al-Qaeda "brand" makes people want to join it or at least have some relationship to it.

To degrade and destroy ISIS, we will need to prevent it from capturing Iraq's vast oil fields and to destroy the few that are now under its control. This task can largely be accomplished through air power. Most of Iraq's oil reserves are in the south and the Iraqi army will likely fight to keep the Shia areas from falling. The Kurdish Peshmerga forces have also proven capable in defending the oil fields around Kirkuk in northern Iraq. Our air cover will only make it that much easier for them.

Bombing the few oil fields that ISIS controls will immediately cripple their finances. As long as there is a demand for cheaper oil, there will always be a supply of smugglers who will transfer the oil and pay off the right people. Any cooperation that we can get from Iraq's neighbors will be limited unless they see we are serious. Also, destroying ISIS's few existing fields would have a negligible effect on world oil prices.

ISIS will compensate for the loss of oil revenues by increasing further kidnappings and extortion among the population in areas they control. This may well get to the point where the Sunni population will clamor for the Iraqi government to return. The new Iraqi government will be more careful than Nouri al-Maliki was. The Obama administration must make it clear to the new government that we are not going to clean up their mess. Without a more inclusive government in Baghdad, ISIS or other killer groups will return in some form.

The late U.S. Army Major General "Sandy" Davidson was one of our best minds in the use of civil affairs and psychological operations in countering and delegitimizing terrorist organizations with their own people. I was with General Davidson and then U.S. Ambassador to Pakistan Ryan Crocker in the fall of 2005 as part of an American relief effort for the Kashmir earthquake that claimed some 75,000 lives. I saw firsthand the impact this effort had in a part of Pakistan not exactly known for its pro-Western views.

General Davidson was also a believer in Alhurra, the then new Arabic TV channel funded by the Broadcasting Board of Governors (BBG), as an effective vehicle in countering the anti-American venom being spewed by Middle East networks. The BBG is a bipartisan U.S. Government independent federal agency. He also saw Alhura as representative of the type of thinking we needed to expose the youth in that part of the world to Western values instead of radical Islam.

In addition, General Davidson was also a big fan of General Lloyd Austin, who he worked for and who later went on to command U.S. Forces-Iraq, serve as Vice Chief of Staff of the U.S. Army and eventually become U.S. CENTCOM Commander.

I remember General Davidson telling me, "Look out for Lloyd Austin—he gets it and is the real deal." Interestingly, in 2010 General Austin advised President Obama to leave a smaller residual force in Iraq to prevent a terrorist resurgence. General Davidson was right—General Austin gets it. If we had listened to him, I firmly believe ISIS, whose predecessor organization had largely been destroyed, would never have taken hold in Iraq—it would have been delegitimized from the start. General Austin understands that at the end of the day, you need "the grunt on the ground" to finish the job.

Following the 9/11 attacks on America, there was a heightened sense of awareness and commitment by all of us. Unfortunately, as ISIS has reminded us, the threats have not subsided. The world is an even more dangerous place today than it was immediately following 9/11. As a people, though, we've let our guard down and taken too much for granted. It's time for us once again to have the same level of commitment for keeping America safe as we did following 9/11.

Chapter Eight

The Threat of Chemical and Biological Weapons: A Moment of Clarity

When the beheading of Nicholas Berg was being circulated on the internet, it provided a rare moment of clarity in the War on Terror. We should not forget that this occurred in the spring of 2004 when the Abu Ghraib scandal on the front pages, the insurgency in Iraq was getting worse, and the failure to find weapons of mass destruction led many to believe that the Iraq War was sold on false premises.

This largely partisan perception has not changed despite the fact that the U.S Senate Select Committee on Intelligence issued a report in 2004 that found no evidence that anyone in the Bush Administration attempted to "coerce, influence or pressure analysts to change their judgments related to Iraq's weapons of mass destruction capabilities."[1]

Some people preferred to believe that Bush lied even after former President Clinton said to interviewer Larry King: "Let me tell you what I know. When I left office, there was a substantial amount of biological and chemical material unaccounted for. That is, at the end of the first Gulf War, we knew what he had. We knew what was destroyed in all the inspection processes and that was a lot. And then we bombed with the British for four days in 1998. We might have gotten it all; we might have gotten half of it; we might have gotten none of it. But we didn't know. So I thought it was prudent for the President to go to the U.N. and for the U.N. to say [to Iraq] you've got to let these inspectors in, and this time if you don't cooperate the penalty could be regime change, not just continued sanctions."[2]

The moment that Nicholas Berg was beheaded in Iraq, it showed a lot of people that we picked the right enemy. Unfortunately, there is still a large segment of society that refuses to acknowledge the severity of the threat of Islamic terrorism and the desire for some people to use weapons of mass destruction. Some are trapped in a bubble and it is remarkable when some facts cannot get through it. For example, when Nicholas Berg's father, Michael Berg, was asked for his reaction to the death of Abu Musab al-Zarqawi, the man who was widely believed to have killed his son, his answer was shocking. He did not contest the fact that Zarqawi was involved, but Michael Berg still said,

"Well, my reaction is I'm sorry whenever any human being dies. Zarqawi is a human being. He has a family who are reacting just as my family reacted when Nick was killed, and I feel bad for that."[3]

While 9/11 was an important event in our nation's history, it did not end fierce partisanship in Washington. Another sad truth is that we were never fully united after 9/11. The myth that Iraq broke our 9/11 unity is not supported by the facts.

In November, 2001 an ABC/*Washington Post* poll asked Republicans and Democrats if they would support sending a large number of ground troops to Afghanistan that resulted in a long war with a significant number of soldiers either killed or wounded. In that poll, 72 percent of Republicans would support a war accepting the costs, but 57 percent of Democrats opposed such an idea only two months after 9/11. As time passed, the divide among the parties widened. By early 2003, a *Washington Post*-ABC News poll found that 57 percent of Democrats opposed going to war with Iraq while 78 percent of Republicans supported it. There was a brief surge of support among Democrats to two-thirds in favor of the invasion during the actual conflict. Clearly, it was a temporary rally-around-the-flag effect. By July, 2003, as the insurgency was in full swing, only 34 percent of Democrats believed it was worth continuing the war effort.[4]

We can be thankful there has been some bipartisanship on the issue of non-proliferation. It is not as strong as it should be, but it does exist. We need leaders in both parties to do a better job of publicly standing by our Presidents in times of trouble. Sometimes our commander-in-chief will have to make a tough decision on issues of non-proliferation.

In other words, we need more leaders like Senators Sam Nunn and Richard Lugar in Washington. As the Soviet Union was collapsing in 1991, we were facing the greatest threat of nuclear proliferation we had ever faced. At the time, the Soviets had a massive arsenal--over 30,000 nuclear weapons.[5] Overnight, there were newly independent countries that suddenly had nuclear weapons on top of massive economic problems: Russia, Ukraine, Belarus, Kazakhstan. On its first day of independence, Ukraine had the largest nuclear arsenal in the world, after the U.S. and Russia. Beyond the threat of loose nukes, there were nightmare scenarios of highly enriched uranium (HEU) falling into the hands of terrorists. Kazakhstan alone had at least 600 kilograms of HEU that was poorly secured. That was enough material to produce twenty nuclear weapons.[6]

The remarkable diplomatic achievement of ending the nuclear programs of Ukraine, Belarus, and Kazakhstan, as well as substantially reducing the Russian arsenal is one of the great bipartisan achievements of modern times. It was not a foregone conclusion.

As Secretary of State James Baker recounts in his memoirs, in Spring, 1992, then Russian Foreign Minister Andrei Kozyrev and Ukrainian Foreign Minister Anatoly Zlenko were unable to come to an agreement that would achieve the Bush Administration's goal of only having one nuclear successor to the former Soviet

Union. President Bush and Secretary Baker worked hard throughout that spring with the presidents of Ukraine, Belarus, and Kazakhstan to address their concerns. Even as the final moments of the Lisbon Protocol was scheduled to be signed by the United States and the four newly independent nuclear states, Secretary Baker talked about how American leadership was crucial in forcing Kozyrev and Zlenko to not leave the room until all of their issues were resolved.[7] Because of the Lisbon Protocol, all five countries were now subject to the START Treaty, which limited the United States and Russia to 6,000 nuclear weapons. Kazakhstan would be nuclear free by 1995 while the last nuclear weapons in Ukraine and Belarus were gone by 1996.[8]

In 20 years, the Nunn-Lugar program has destroyed over 7,600 nuclear weapons, hundreds of air-to-surface, as well as submarine-launched, missiles and 500 nuclear silos.[9] There are now 155 fewer nuclear bombers as well as 33 fewer Russian submarines carrying nuclear weapons.[10] We have never had anywhere near the same type of bipartisan cooperation when it came to the threat of chemical and biological weapons.

While Democrats and Republicans cooperated on the former Soviet arsenal, the passionate debate over the Iraq War led some to spread the lie that the Reagan Administration was complicit in selling Saddam Hussein chemical and biological weapons. The fact is that Iraq developed a chemical weapons program through the help of purchasing chemical precursors from Western firms, especially West German ones. After buying the materials, Saddam was able to build his chemical arsenal.[11] Our experiences in Iraq from the 1980s to the Iraq War (2003-2011) has taught us a great deal about how inadequate our nation is in handling the threat of chemical and biological weapons.

The Republicans are not blameless. When they were out of power, they also should have known better. They should have helped provide political cover for Bill Clinton when he bombed Sudan. To the people who thought it was a factory, my first thought is if you were a businessman would you set up a research facility in Sudan. I did not see the intelligence, but I certainly don't believe my country would do such a thing unless they believed something was there. Mistakes happen in intelligence. When the United States accidentally bombed the Chinese embassy in Belgrade, I certainly believed it was an accident. We need to overcome partisanship when it comes to the use of force and the threat of chemical and biological weapons.

After coalition forces toppled Saddam Hussein's regime, the Iraq Survey Group was formed to find out what happened to Iraq's weapons of mass destruction. The head of the Iraq Survey Group, David Kay, testified before the Senate Armed Services Committee in January, 2004. Kay told them that he believed Iraq had weapons of mass destruction. Kay pointed out that the U.S. had previously underestimated the programs of Iran for 18 years and the sophistication of the Libyan program until it was fully revealed.

The two most important things that David Kay said in his opening statement were that Iraq definitely violated the terms of Security Council Resolution 1441, which Kay saw as Saddam's last chance to cooperate, and that the intelligence was not altered to make the case for war. If the intelligence was altered, it would be easy to explain the failure, but it was not altered and that should concern people. We clearly had to improve our ability to gather and interpret intelligence.

Kay concluded his testimony by saying that because of the looting that occurred immediately following the collapse of the Saddam's regime, the complete picture of Iraq's WMD program may never be known. He declared his confidence that his successor at the Iraq Survey Group, Charlie Duelfer, would give

America the best picture possible. Despite this intelligence failure, David Kay reminded the committee that during the Cuban Missile Crisis, the CIA believed strongly that there were no Soviet warheads in Cuba. The story that Kay believes is not often told was that after the crisis we learned to improve our ability in collecting intelligence data.[12]

Our policy should now be to continue to explore ways of improving our intelligence-gathering abilities. We should also realize that loss of bipartisan cooperation makes it difficult to conduct the War on Terror. Here are some additional recommendations to help us in this fight.

Recommendation 1: Modify Executive Order 12333 on Political Assassinations

According to this Executive Order, "No person employed by or acting on behalf of the United States Government shall engage in, or conspire to engage in, assassination."[13] We must make an exception for not only terrorists, but also the people who support them whether they are private citizens or government officials. This modification should not apply to Americans or government officials of any legitimately elected government. Of course, democracies don't produce governments that should worry us regarding the use of chemical or biological weapons.

Bad people need to know that we will attack them if they use these weapons or give them to terrorists. A policy of assassination can achieve objectives without straining our resources. It can also expand our network of spies by reinforcing the message that we will go to great lengths to protect our interests and reward the people who help us.

When the Syrian government used Sarin on its own people, some of the commentary was predictably partisan and irresponsible. Some anti-war people were happy to repeat lies that the Reagan Administration was supposedly complicit in Iraq's chemical weapons program. We should remember that, beyond the fact that Iraq bought precursors from many countries, nobody had to persuade Saddam to use such weapons. In the case of Sarin, the Iraqi regime produced nearly 800 tons of Sarin from 1984 to 1990.[14] If a person inhales, as little as 200 milligrams of Sarin, he or she would die in minutes.[15]

Promoting a defense *against* an odorless chemical weapon is difficult. When the Duelfer Report was released, the conclusions were startling. On the one hand, they could not find any stockpiles of WMD after more than a year; on the other hand, it was reported that Iraq clearly did not cooperate with the inspectors and there was obvious intent from Saddam to have the option to reconstitute his programs after the sanctions were lifted.[16]

There is no doubt that Iraq violated the terms of the UN resolutions. Tariq Aziz admitted that, in 1999, Saddam believed the long-range missile limits were only prohibited if the missiles were armed with weapons of mass destruction. Aziz countered that he felt it meant all missiles beyond the range of 150 kilometers (approximately 93 miles), in accordance with Security Council Resolution 687, were prohibited. Saddam decided to go ahead despite objections. We also know that several high-level officials of the former regime had reported that Saddam didn't want to admit he did not have stockpiles of WMD because he would lose payments that his neighbors gave him out of fear.[17] Again, this form of bluff was possible in part because our ability to detect these weapons was limited.

The ISG had said that there were undeclared labs that were under the Iraqi security apparatus and were never reported to the

U.N. The report also provided strong evidence that Saddam Hussein had plans to acquire missiles with ranges of at least 1,000 kilometers (620 miles). As previously noted, this is well beyond the limit of 150 kilometers permitted under U.N. sanctions.[18]

Scientists and senior officials captured by coalition forces admitted to Kay and the ISG that Saddam was committed to continuing his programs after the sanctions were removed. Not only did he have facilities and intent, Saddam Hussein kept his nuclear scientists together at the Iraqi Nuclear Energy Commission (IAEC).[19]

As for biological weapons, the Iraqi Intelligence Service (known as the *Mukhabarat*) gave money to graduate students studying biological sciences abroad. As for chemical weapons, Iraqi scientists testified as early as 2000, that Saddam and his sons were pressing them on how long it would take to produce stockpiles of chemical weapons.[20]

I feel it is necessary to explain this recent history because the strong confidence in our intelligence prior to the war was replaced by the opposite extreme of our ability to assume that we would have any idea if Saddam would reconstitute his arsenal if we did not go to war. A targeted assassination program could clarify this dilemma and could provide useful intelligence as well as deterrence. People would feel compelled to give information to the United States if for no other reason to avoid being a target.

Recommendation 2: Implement the Israeli Matzav

After 9/11, President Bush was criticized by asking for people to go shopping. People remember wars when they were asked to actually sacrifice. Keeping in mind that this war is obviously a very different war, we have had some difficulty explaining how other countries have coped with a constant state of war with an enemy that was committed to their destruction.

In effect, the United States is fighting a type of war that is similar to Israel's. While we call this "the War on Terrorism," the

Israelis call this conflict the *matzav*. It translates to "the situation." When Israelis are talking about the situation, they are referring to their ongoing conflict with the Palestinians and generally their other enemies as well.[21]

We must explain to this war-weary public that this conflict is not a sprint, but a marathon. Our country is going to be on this treadmill for a very long time. We have to live our lives even though we are going to use the treadmill every day.

Most of the time, we will have to keep a good pace of vigilance, but in order for the public to avoid being either war-weary or demoralized it is necessary for everyone to maintain clarity about the threat. It will also be necessary for people to see that most of the time this conflict will be a marathon, but occasionally the time will come when we have to turn on the sprint and to go all the way.

To call this a war against a technique is inadequate. It is also inadequate to be unable to name the right mentality for how to cope with this threat. It's not just important to kill terrorists. People need to feel that we are winning in order to keep supporting policies that will ensure victory.

Recommendation 3: Pass "The Enemy Expatriation Act"

Under current law, anyone joining a foreign army can be stripped of his/her citizenship. In 2002, there was a second Patriot Act that was under consideration though ultimately abandoned. One of the ideas included in that law was to extend this concept to American citizens who join terrorist organizations.[22] As Faisal Shahzad, a naturalized U.S. citizen, was caught trying to blow up Times Square, Senator Joseph Lieberman was preparing legislation in the Senate to strip the citizenship of any American who joined a foreign terrorist organization.[23]

The Enemy Expatriation Act, would later be sponsored by Senators Joseph Lieberman (I-CN) and Scott Brown (R-MA) in the Senate and Reps. Charlie Dent (R-PA) and Jason Altamira (D-PA). If the bill were to pass Congress, citizenship could be stripped from "a person who engages in hostilities or purposefully and materially supports hostilities against the United States."[24]

This legislation is needed because most terrorist plots on the American homeland since 9/11 have been homegrown and the number of plots has increased substantially in recent years. According to the Congressional Research Service, there were 50 homegrown terrorist plots from May, 2009 to September, 2013 and three of these plots resulted in successful attacks. All the perpetrators were either American citizens or permanent residents. The first successful attack was in June 2009 when Abdulhakim Muhammad attacked a military recruitment center in Little Rock, Arkansas. The other two attacks were Nidal Malik Hasan's November 2009 attack at Fort Hood and the April 2013 Boston Marathon Bombers. Between 9/11 to May, 2009, there were only 21 plots and all but two were thwarted. The first was Sgt. Hassan Akbar who killed two U.S. Army officers and wounded fourteen others at the U.S. Army Camp Pennsylvania in Kuwait. This occurred in the early days of the Iraq War. The other successful attack was in March, 2006 when Mohammed Reza Taheri-azar used his SUV to hit students at UNC Chapel Hill. No one was killed, but a number of students were injured.[25]

In the case of Sgt. Akbar, he not only shot his fellow soldiers, but he threw four grenades at them.[26] Unlike Sgt. Akbar, most homegrown terrorists do not have access to grenades let alone chemical and biological weapons.

If this threat becomes increasingly homegrown success we must prepare for these militants and yet we are still fighting the last war. For example, after Iraqi forces used chemical and biological weapons in the 1980s, there was outrage throughout the world and 16 countries in 1985 responded by forming the Australia Group. Today there are over 40 members. These members are all signatories of the Chemical Weapons Convention (CWC) and Biological Weapons Convention (BWC). They are working together to provide common export licensing controls.[27] One hopes this will prevent other countries (or advanced terrorist organizations) in the future from repeating the strategy of Saddam Hussein.

While the Australia Group was designed to monitor materials crossing international borders, we do not have an equivalent group for lone-wolf terrorists operating inside the United States.

A central question of our time is, what level of insecurity are we, as a society, willing to tolerate? While homegrown attacks are harder to monitor and generally do not result in 9/11-style casualties, even a crude attack with chemical and biological weapons could result in large number of deaths and cause panic.

On the international front, there have been enormous successes in chemical and biological weapons.

According to the Organization for the Prohibition of Chemical Weapons (OPCW), whose purpose is to implement the provisions of the Chemical Weapons Convention (CWC), almost 82 percent of the world's declared stockpile of chemical weapons has been destroyed. That is 58,172 metric tons of chemical weapons out of a total of 71,196.[28] This does not include Syria's recently declared arsenal of 1,300 metric tons.[29]

The U.S. and Russia have most of what is left. The United States has destroyed 90 percent of its former arsenal of 30,000 metric tons and the Russians have destroyed 75 percent of their arsenal of 40,000 metric tons. For its efforts, the OPCW was awarded the 2013 Nobel Peace Prize to reduce the world's stockpile of chemical weapons.[30] Russia has declared that it will complete the destruction of its remaining chemical weapons by 2015.[31] The United States believes that it will take at least another decade to complete their work.[32]

Beyond Syria, there is the question of how much is left of Iraq's pre-Gulf War arsenal though it has probably degraded to the point where it is no longer a threat. As Democrats and Republicans debate over the motives behind the 2012 attack at our consulate in Benghazi, we should be grateful that by May, 2013, Libya had destroyed 85 percent of its declared arsenal of 22.3 metric tons. The remainder of this arsenal contains primarily mustard gas as well as 846 metric tons of chemical precursors.[33] Along with the chaos in Libya and Syria, there is the North Korean threat. It is estimated to have an even larger arsenal than Syria's. The South Korean Ministry of National Defense believes North Korea has somewhere between 2,500 to 5,000 metric tons.[34] Should the Six-Party talks ever amount to anything, they will have to address North Korea's chemical weapons as well as the nuclear issue.

Even if we destroy all of these weapons, we cannot "uninvent" them. According to the FBI, from January, 2002 to July, 2008, there were at least six known attempts by homegrown terrorists to produce and distribute chemical and biological weapons. Three of these plots involved ricin, two used cyanide, and one involved Sarin. The one successful attack involved ricin. From October, 2003 to February, 2004, three letters were sent by someone, who referred to himself as "Fallen Angel," to a number of government offices. This case remains unsolved.[35] In 2013, the Secret Service confirmed ricin on a letter addressed to the President. There was also another government facility that received a letter containing ricin. It should comfort people to know that there is a process to quickly screen letters for such toxins.[36]

Bad people will always find ways to get around even the best screening process. This is why we must disrupt plots *before* terrorists have a chance to use chemical or biological weapons. If Karl Linnas, the former commandant of a Nazi concentration camp in Estonia, could be deported in 1981, after 30 years in the country, surely people can be stripped of their citizenship due to an ongoing threat of terrorism.[37]

Recommendation 4: Apply Weapons-Choice Theory to Domestic Terrorism

This book has focused on ideologically-driven killers. Following the Boston Marathon bombings, Brian Levin, the Director at the Center for the Study of Hate and Extremism, wrote that there are three categories for explaining why extremists kill: the Ideologically Motivated (Religion, Politics, or both), the Psychologically Dangerous (sociopaths or cognitively impaired persons) and those who killed for either personal benefit or revenge.[38]

Ideologically motivated killings are certainly not limited to Islamist extremists. Nevertheless, I have focused on *jihadis* because I believe they are more dangerous than other ideologically motivated killers. According to the FBI, from 1980 to 2005, 3,178 people were killed and 14,038 people were wounded by terrorist attacks in the United States. Approximately 93.7 percent of the total deaths (2,977) and 85.6 percent of the total wounded (12,017) occurred in September 2001. All but five of those deaths were the result of the 9/11 attacks. The other deaths were the result of anthrax mailings.[39] Our government still does not know the origin of the mailings, but it does know who attacked us on 9/11. Since over 90 percent of the deaths from terrorism are from *jihadis,* it is logical to conclude that *jihadis* are the most dangerous ideologically motivated killers.

As terrorist attacks are more likely to be homegrown, the only way a terrorist could achieve casualties comparable to a 9/11 would most likely be through the use of chemical or biological weapons. While such an attack is unlikely, it not impossible nor is it unprecedented.

To people who would prefer to see terrorism as more of a law enforcement issue than an actual war, it is worth considering that the drop in crime during the 1990s required a similar approach to fighting homegrown terrorists.

While thousands of Americans die in gun violence every year, the tragedy at Sandy Hook Elementary School in Newtown, Connecticut, where twenty elementary school children were murdered, created a new sense of urgency in the country to reduce gun-related violence. The problem was that many liberals tried to compare gun violence in the United States with that of other countries without dividing between determined killers and incidental killers. I first read of the weapons choice theory when I was looking over studies on the restrictions of handguns in Washington, DC. Since then, I have never read a better description of this theory:

"Some are characterized by a sustained, single-minded determination, whereas in others the intention is more episodic and ambivalently motivated. If the resolve is weak or short-lived, the relative frequency with which a particular type of weapon is used will be influenced by availability. The key element in the theory is that firearms are more likely to cause death than other weapons that are likely to be substituted. It follows that even if there is no change in the number of assaults or suicide attempts, a reduction in the availability of guns will result in a reduction in the number of deaths. The theory recognizes that people with more deadly intent may tend to select guns rather than other means, but it assumes that the association is less than perfect."[40]

In other words, the weapon-choice theory argues that some people are determined to kill someone in advance while others kill during confrontations that are not planned. A determined killer will break laws and do whatever it takes over a long period of time to accomplish the task of killing someone. During the crack epidemic, the drug trade motivated people to kill and increased gun-related deaths.

In his book, "The Great American Decline", Dr. Franklin Zimring of the University of California School of Law (Berkeley) points out that the United States and Canada experienced a very similar rate of decline in crime during the 1990s despite the fact that Canada's prison population declined, and their government had reduced the number of police on the streets. The United States took the opposite approach.[41] Both countries' rates declined because the most important factor was the number of determined killers.

We had to take this approach because clearly we had more determined killers. As a result, cities with extensive gun control, such as New York City and Washington, D.C., experienced a drop in violent crime along with cities with less gun restrictions such as Houston, Texas. Violent crimes in 1980s and early 1990s increased due to the crack cocaine epidemic.

By arresting many of these determined killers, we were able to bring crime rates down. Murders peaked in New York City at 2,245 murders in 1990. By 2009, there were 536 murders in the city. Washington, D.C. once had the highest murder rate in the country (per capita) with a peak of 482 murders in 1991.[42] In the last two decades the number of murders has dropped considerably to fewer than 100 in 2012. The last time the capital had below 100 annual murders was in 1963.[43] We need to take a similar approach to terrorism by focusing on determined killers. While crimes do not often take place in front of audiences, the attacks at

Fort Hood and in Boston, have shown that our nation is always forced to read about how people saw strange behavior and refused to act upon it. In a time when people have more friends through social networks, they need to re-establish deeper connections. When we see someone who is odd or struggling, we must all be prepared to help that person and/or take preventive steps.

Recommendation 5: Provide Amnesty To Organized Crime Figures Who Provide Useful Information on Terrorists in the U.S.

Sometimes we can "connect dots" before an attack occurs. At other times, our inability to stop a threat comes from a lack of imagination. A case in point was the death of Alexander Litvinenko. On November 1, 2006, this former FSB agent and critic of Vladimir Putin suddenly fell ill in London. For three weeks, he lay in a hospital. It was only after his death that it was discovered he had been poisoned with a rare substance known as polonium-210. Since polonium emits alpha radiation, it cannot pass through the skin. It can only be inhaled or ingested.[44] The British authorities did not think of scanning for alpha radiation until it was too late.

Since such polonium poisoning had to be within close proximity, this would indicate that agents from Russia were able to strike within close range. Such a scenario does not have to happen in the United States.

We should make it clear to the Kremlin that targeting U.S. citizens or conducting any operations on American soil will not be tolerated. We should be willing to provide something like a witness protection program for Russian gangsters. If the information is good enough, an amnesty for information could create a great deal of information on both Putin's Russia as well as on terrorism. The fear of people turning others in could either cause these gangsters to kill the other gangsters who know what they are doing, or could force the Kremlin to lose potential agents in the U.S.

The end of the Cold War not only led to the rise of the Russian mafia, but also led some people to think that the United States could afford to adopt security policies that reflected short-term political expediency. Many underestimated how dangerous the world remained during the 1990s. An example of this was how we reduced the CIA's human intelligence prior to 9/11. In Bill O'Reilly's book "Who's Looking Out for You," the Torricelli Principle is discussed at length at how it undermined the CIA's human intelligence.

In 1996, then-Rep. Torricelli embarrassed the CIA through the connections of a Guatemalan colonel named Julio Roberto Alpirez. This man ran death camps and was also an informer for the CIA. When this became public, the Clinton Administration responded by enacting the Torricelli Principle. Although the U.S. paid anti-Communist thugs to get information on pro-Communist thugs during the Cold War, many felt the threat was over. As a result, our human intelligence suffered. O'Reilly explains what happened: "Bad people know what other bad people are doing."[45] If you can't work with bad people, your human intelligence will diminish.

In the case of the Torricelli Principle, the United States government went too far. We can stop supporting certain thugs, but we should never hurt our ability to gather intelligence. Due to embarrassment and public pressure, the Torricelli Principle put restrictions on recruiting criminals to be paid informers of the CIA. After 9/11, President Bush was able to sign a law rescinding this principle.[46]

Recommendation 6: Closer Working Relationship with HHS and DoD Is Required from a Training and Fielding Standpoint

The biological threat has been consistently ranked as one of the top two threats to the United States from a homeland security perspective. Several years ago, I did an interview with "Fox and Friends." Senior scientists at the Pentagon, who knew I would be on the show, wanted me to emphasize the severity of the threat as part of an effort to inform the American people. The increased concern is based on several factors: intelligence indicates that less scientific and technological capability is required in order to engineer biological pathogens; increased concern over the possibility of attaching a biological agent to a hemorrhagic fever; biological pathogens can be fairly cheap to make and the length of the incubation period.

From the time a new biological pathogen is discovered until the time we have a countermeasure in place can take many years. The Bush Administration was wise to address this problem through implementation of the Transformational Medical Technology Initiative (TMTI) under the direction of the Defense Threat Reduction Agency (DTRA). The Biomedical Advanced Research and Development Authority (BARDA), which is within the office of the Assistant Secretary for Preparedness and Response in the Department of Health & Human Services, was also established to help develop countermeasures for the civilian population. BARDA, DTRA, and the Department of Defense's Chemical, Biological, Medical Systems Directorate (CBMS) have each done a good job in developing and fielding technologies for diagnostic, treatment, and protection technologies for chemical, biological, and radiological threats.

As we move forward, it is imperative that BARDA be more engaged with DoD, especially with DTR and CMBS from a training and fielding perspective. Military medicine has a great reputation for making things happen and happen quickly. BARDA and the civilian population will benefit greatly from a closer working relationship with the DoD in the event of a chemical, biological, or radiological threat to the homeland.

Recommendation #7: A Prophylactic Radiation Protection Capability Should Be Stockpiled to Counter Radiological/Nuclear Threats

While this chapter focuses on chemical and biological threats, we have discussed EMP and other radiological threats elsewhere in this book. Years ago, the Special Forces medical community realized the need to develop a prophylactic radiation protection capability to give protection to soldiers who may be deployed into a "hot zone" to continue the fight.

Over the years, the Armed Forces Radiobiology Research Institute (AFRRI) has developed a mature prophylactic radiation protection capability. Not only can this countermeasure benefit U.S. soldiers before they deploy into "hot zones," but also holds great promise for the civilians in nuclear, dirty bomb, and other radiological incident scenarios. As the radioactive Japanese wave from Fukushima neared the US, the need for a prophylactic radiation protection capability was underscored. Thanks to AFRRI and "DoD medicine," this capability has been developed. Relevant agencies of the U.S. Government need to work together to ensure that it is stockpiled for not only the American military, but also the American people.

Conclusion

"Just War:" (*Jus Ad Bellum and Jus In Bello.)* This phrase represents two concepts of just war. The first is *jus ad bellum,* which means the right to go to war. The second is *jus in bello,* which refers to the proper conduct during war. I believe we could develop a more bipartisan atmosphere if we were to regularly remind ourselves not to use one to justify the other.

For example, it was justified for the United States to declare war against Japan after Pearl Harbor; however because the war was justified does not mean we should not have a debate about our conduct in the war. One can believe that we had a right to support war against Japan without agreeing to our use of the atomic bomb. I believe it was justifiable because it saved Americans and Japanese lives by forcing a quick surrender though I acknowledge there are many who do not share that view.

Similarly, in the war in Afghanistan, if someone wants to criticize our drone policy, one can do so without delegitimizing the *jus ad bellum.* Regarding our homeland, homegrown terrorists intent on using chemical and biological weapons are going to force us to rethink if we are adapting to this new threat. I don't think we are--as yet-- and should a tragedy occur, it could force us to take very strong measures. In order to maintain unity, we must remember that we can only keep a civil debate if we never let a debate about justifying certain tactics take away from the fact that we all agree that any conflict against *jihadi* terror is just.

Wars are won and lost by timing. There will be moments when engaging the enemy is wise, but that does not traduce the fact that ours is a noble cause.

Chapter 9

How Red Tape Imperils Our National Security: Cutting The Gordian Knot

When politicians run for office, they often talk about how they will go to Washington and "cut the red tape." While slogans win elections, we rarely hold politicians accountable for their lack of progress on this issue. From 1949 to 2005, the number of federal regulations grew by 19,335 pages to 134,261 pages.[1] The Small Business Administration (SBA) issued a study that concluded that regulation compliance cost $1.1 trillion in 2005.[2] In 2012, the cost of federal regulations had grown to over $1.8 trillion while the Code of Federal Regulations grew to 174,545 pages in 2012.[3]

Since all regulations are not created equal, the government distinguishes regulations that cost more than $100 million annually from the other regulations added annually. The growth in major regulations has grown from only 27 per year during the Clinton Administration to 44 per year during the first two years of the Obama Administration.[4]

All this harms our ability to manage our national security. It is not just regulations that directly affect the Departments of Defense or Homeland Security. When we compare the regulations that harm national security directly versus the cumulative impact of unnecessary regulations, I am reminded of something Grover Norquist once wrote:

"As the late Milton Friedman always reminded us, the true cost of government is total government spending, not the deficit. The deficit is visible like the snow-capped part of the iceberg above the water. (Note: the *Titanic* never hit the top of the iceberg.)"[5]

In other words, the *Titanic* felt the power of the entire iceberg and not just the visible part. The same is true of federal regulations. With all those pages of regulations, we must cut the rules that hamper our national security. Since this task will likely take several years, the recommendations in this chapter will focus on what must be done urgently. As Michelangelo understood with his sculptures, some of the marble was necessary. Since he could see the statue inside marble, his purpose was only to get rid of the unneeded pieces for the masterpiece to be complete.[6] The same is true with our task in cutting the unnecessary regulations that harm our national security: cut the unnecessary parts, but keep that which is essential.

Recommendation 1: Congress should pass the SHIELD Act to harden the electric grid for a possible EMP attack.

In Chapter 2, I discuss in detail the threat of a cyber-attack. The other two most catastrophic threats to our homeland involve an electromagnetic pulse (EMP) attack and a geomagnetic storm. While the threat of cyber warfare is an evolving threat, the EMP threat has been known for decades. Such a calamity can be caused by a geomagnetic storm from the Sun or from a nuclear weapon. In the 1990s, Russia was considered the only adversary that could carry out an EMP attack. Rep. Roscoe Bartlett was an early and leading voice about this threat in the mid-1990s. During the 1999 Kosovo War, Rep. Bartlett was present when Russian Duma members Vladimir Lukin and Alexander Shabonov pointed out that if Russia actually wanted to hurt the United States, it could fire a submarine-launched ballistic missile and detonate a nuclear warhead at high altitude.[7]

While Russia, for all its problems, does not seem to be likely to launch such an attack, we should not forget that other countries are also trying to develop this capability. Just because Russia can be deterred, does not mean that North Korea will react the same way.

Kim Jong-Un, its young leader, did not early on have to develop the political skills to fight his way to power, though lately he has demonstrated a streak of ruthlessness. We don't know for sure if he is rational. The young Kim may be a Stalinist in domestic policy, but we should not assume that he will respond to brinksmanship as old Bolsheviks might have in the Kremlin during the Cold War.[8]

The North Koreans do know they cannot defeat the United States and South Korea in a war, but Kim Jong-Un needs to show his military people that he is tough. Provoking the U.S., Japan, and South Korea without causing war is ideal for him and helps his legitimacy. Though, like many ambitious young people, he may not know when to stop. For that reason, things could spiral out of control.

James Woolsey, former U.S. Director of Central Intelligence (1993-1995), and Peter Pry, who was a member of the EMP Commission, wrote an article that argued that all it would take is one ICBM from North Korea to detonate a nuclear warhead over the continental United States and blackout the electric grid for months:

"An EMP attack would collapse the electric grid and other infrastructure that depends on it—communications, transportation, banking and finance, food and water—necessary to sustain modern civilization and the lives of 300 million Americans."[9]

On March 11, 2013, I wrote an article for Fox News which discussed the potential EMP threat from North Korea. In my article, I noted how Dr. Pry and the U.S. Nuclear Strategy Forum had recently made a convincing case that North Korea may already actually possesses an electromagnetic pulse (EMP) nuclear warhead, which would have the ability to take out a national

Power grid and critical infrastructure throughout the United States. Further, I noted how open source intelligence (OSINT) had also suggested that North Korea had obtained proven missile control electronics from Russia and China and that a plan for a high-altitude nuclear burst over the Pacific is on the books.

The Congressionally-mandated EMP Commission has stated that without the power grid, up to two-thirds of our population could be killed within a year. This is partly because American farmers could no longer produce enough food without electricity.

Defending against Iran, North Korea, and terrorist groups from an EMP attack will require support for missile defense. In the event when we may have to deploy Aegis ships to defend the American homeland, I worry that the American people will find it difficult to support this measure.[10]

The majority of Americans do not want another decade of sustained conflict. The best way to prevent war is to have a military that is prepared for war. Countries are not invaded because they are too strong. It is because of our conventional superiority that North Korea and Iran see EMP as the only real chance they have to deter the United States.

The prospect of preemptive attacks on the nuclear and missile programs of either North Korea or Iran, will ultimately force the American people to ask if these threats can be deterred. Are these countries, or even terrorist networks, really crazy enough to bring down the American power grid and possibly bring down the world economy with it?

To a liberal, it should be said that Islamist fanatics, such as the clerical leaders in Iran, are not the Soviet Union. The Communist leaders were secular and could be deterred because they didn't believe in afterlife. People who do believe in an afterlife are seen by some as more dangerous to have the bomb.

Sam Harris has argued for years that some secular liberals are blind to the dangers of Islamist fanaticism because religion plays no role in their own lives. As a result, they cannot comprehend how any individual can actually dedicate his/her life to religion.[11] Sam Harris largely came to this conclusion because he received thousands of letters from people across the political spectrum. This was in response to Harris' controversial book, *The End of Faith.* He came to see that people who were more liberal were far more ignorant to the fact that extremists have a logic that is entirely their own. Harris warned in 2006:

"We are entering an age of unchecked nuclear proliferation and, it seems likely, nuclear terrorism. There is, therefore, no future in which aspiring martyrs will make good neighbors for us. Unless liberals realize that there are tens of millions of people in the Muslim world who are far scarier than Dick Cheney, they will be unable to protect civilization from its genuine enemies."[12]

Even if we can convince some skeptics that Islamist fundamentalism is a threat, people might see an EMP threat as alarmist because they will say that North Korea is Communist.

Our response to these people is for them to read Madeleine Albright's memoirs. In the book, she devotes a chapter to her trip to the Hermit Kingdom in 2000. From reading the book, you will find some predictable exchanges between Secretary Albright and Kim Jong-Il. For example, Albright shows there is a bipartisan understanding that North Korea cannot be permitted to have nuclear weapons and advanced missile systems. At one point she even told the North Koreans that the United States would not tolerate missiles being sold to Iran and Syria.[13]

One of the biggest surprises for her was that North Korea was the first Communist country she visited without any statues to Marx and Lenin, but only statues of Kim Il-Sung and Kim Jong-Il.[14] The cult of personality, along with North Korea's long isolation from the world, makes the behavior of Kim Jong-Un, and his advisors, hard to predict.

As early as 2006, William J. Perry, who was Secretary of Defense under President Clinton, and Ashton B. Carter, who was Deputy Secretary of Defense for President Obama and an assistant Secretary of Defense under President Bill Clinton, wrote an article in 2006 concerning the threat of North Korean ICBMs reaching the United States. These two serious men argued that the Bush administration may have to strike the North Korean missile complex before missile tests improve their capabilities.[15] The mom ent we argue that we cannot take a chance on the North Korean regime, or the Iranian regime, because of an EMP threat, we could lose a large part of the American people who will see this as alarmist. Foreign policy has been polarized and we must find a way to build consensus on the EMP threat.

Fortunately, we have one argument that can bring many of the skeptics on board without causing a debate on missile defense. In order to do this we must talk more about the threat of a geomagnetic storm. The biggest geomagnetic storm in recorded history occurred in 1859. Back then, we didn't have the electrical grid that we have today. That solar storm was called a Carrington Event. It was named after the British astronomer Richard Carrington who discovered the link between solar storms and their effects on Earth.[16]

Bruce Tsurutani at NASA's Jet Propulsion Laboratory in Pasadena, California along with other solar physicists, believes such an event is inevitable in the next 10 to 100 years. At a minimum, any serious solution to the geomagnetic storm will require the government to stockpile transformers to be available should the power grid go down, as well as install dampers, which can perform the role of a lightning rods, to deal with surges in the electric grid.[17]

Remember, a storm must hit at the right time and at the right intensity. It's unclear when it will happen, but we should prepare for this threat. Fortunately, there has been some progress on this front in recent years with the development of "recovery transformers."

The U.S. electric grid is powered by approximately 2,100 high-voltage transformers. A typical transformer weighs over 400,000 lbs. The recovery transformers consist of three-phase units with each unit weighing 125,000 lbs.[18] At this weight, this recovery transformer, which is known as the RecX prototype, can actually be transported by a truck. This prototype was built by Asea Brown Boveri (ABB), a Swiss multinational company.[19] In March, 2012, a RecX was transported from St. Louis to Houston in a drill. In two days, the transformer arrived and it was fully operational in less than a week.[20]

Before the RecX, it would normally take anywhere from nine to 36 months for initial procurement for a transformer. After that, it could take six to nine months to actually design the transformer. Then it could take as much as two months to transport and another month to install it.[21]

Replacing transformers in a timely manner is only one of the biggest problems we face in countering the EMP threat. We must not only replace the transformers, but also SCADA control systems (as well as protective relays which are necessary to operate most of our critical infrastructure).[22] Congress must pass the Secure High-voltage Infrastructure for Electricity from Lethal Damage (SHIELD) Act. This will allow installation of surge protectors that could save the transformers from an EMP attack. The SHIELD Act also encourages the private sector to help develop standards to protect the power grid from the EMP threat.[23]

This SHIELD Act amends Section 215 of the Federal Power Act. Beyond consultation, this bill will give the president, as well as the Federal Energy Regulatory Commission (FERC), more flexibility in implementing emergency measures to protect the power grid during an imminent security threat.[24]

Recommendation 2: Create an independent Commission on Regulation similar to the BRAC Commission

In 2009, Newt Gingrich gave a riveting speech at the Heritage Foundation on how our 20th century bureaucracy is inadequate in dealing with the dangers of the 21st century. The former Speaker of the House argued that America needed a complete reexamination of our strategy. He said:

> "We won the Civil War in four years. We won the Second World War in three years and eight months. It is one of the most amazing achievements in history, from Pearl Harbor on December 7 of 1941 to victory over Japan in August of 1945. We mobilized the nation; built a two-ocean Navy; built the B-24, B-17, B-29; mobilized 15 and one-half million people. We launched American power across North Africa, Sicily, Italy, France, Belgium, and The Netherlands and liberated Germany. At the same time, simultaneously, we went across the Pacific, and the Japanese surrendered in August. 1945--three years and eight months."[25]

He compared the speed of our government in the 1940s with the fact that, "It took us *23 years* to add a fifth runway to the Atlanta Airport."[26] We didn't just win our wars faster in those days, we did everything more quickly.

When we think of Ground Zero, it is worth remembering that we were able to build the Empire State Building in only 14 months.[27] The original World Trade Center (W TC) took over six years to complete. In March, 1966, after the New York State Court of Appeals threw out the final legal challenge, construction began on the WTC. The North Tower was finished by December, 1970. The South Tower was finished two years later.[28] With improvements in technology, we could not offset regulations that produced delays. For that reason, we had a hole in Lower Manhattan for a decade.

In February, 2003, the city decided which design would be used for the new World Trade Center. Because of the national tragedy, many people competed for the building design. In 2003, then-New York Governor George Pataki expected that the Freedom Tower would be built by 2008.[29] Tthis site was not completed until late 2014. The delays in this project were due in part to the complex partnership between the Port Authority of New York and New Jersey, real estate developer Larry Silverstein and several smaller companies.[30] There is no excuse for the project to last this long.

We need an independent commission for regulatory reform that is similar to the BRAC Commission. In 1988, Congress passed the Base Realignment and Closure (BRAC) Act. Its purpose was to cut excess military bases. Before this law was enacted, politicians would rarely vote against military bases because it brought money and jobs to their district/state. BRAC helped secure the principle that a base should be realigned, or closed, unless it was in the national interest to keep it. The way it works is that the Commission sends recommendations to the President. The President cannot change any part of it. If he approves, it goes to the Congress. If Congress does not pass a resolution of disapproval within 60 days, the recommendations are automatically approved.[31] Used by a Commission on Regulations, this procedure would make it possible to dispose of obsolete regulations.

Recommendation 3: Learn from New York City and enact term limits

There is a direct relationship between the amount of money the government takes from taxpayers and those out to get a piece of the action. The more intrusive government is in people's lives, the more incentive many have to make sure that they or their clients are served. In such an environment, the number of regulations will only continue to increase.

The explosion in the number of nonprofits in recent decades has compounded this problem. The growth in regulations, nonprofits, and lobbyists over recent decades has helped produce a dysfunctional budget process. Only a fiscal crisis has been able to begin the process of curbing the growth of government spending. Until recently, a larger budget and more regulation have only continued the cycle of creating more nonprofits for interest groups to grab more federal dollars. In his book *Bowling Alone,* Robert Putnam wrote that the number of national nonprofit organizations in the United States more than doubled from 10,299 in 1968 to 22,901 in 1997.[32]

Despite the routine dysfunction in our annual budget process at the federal and state levels, Fareed Zakaria argued:

> "It's not that our democracy doesn't work; it's that it works only too well. American politics is now hyper-responsive to constituents' interests. And all those interests are dedicated to preserving the past rather than investing for the future."[33]

Organized groups are able to make it politically difficult to cut popula r entitlement programs due to the effective organization of these interest groups. The growth in spending in popular programs has led to a rise in the number of nonprofits organizing to make federal spending grow further. This has resulted in a perpetual causality loop where cause and effect are becoming indistinguishable.

In 2005, over 9 million people were working in the nonprofit sector. While some of these organizations rely mostly on private funds, some have grown due to the increase in government spending since the 1960s. According to the Bureau of Labor Statistics (BLS), private social-service employment rose from 500,000 in 1972 to 3.3 million in 2005.[34]

While the extent of federal aid to nonprofits is not precisely known, the General Accounting Office (GAO) reported that the federal government paid $135 billion to nonprofits for fee-for-servicse in Medicare, another $10 billion in other fee-for-service programs, $25 billion in grants paid direct to nonprofits, $10 billion in contracts, at least $55 billion in federal dollars administered by the states (including Medicaid) and $2.5 billion in loan guarantees in 2006. This also does not include approximately $50 billion in foregone tax revenues that are related to nonprofits.[35]

It is the expansion of government that also allows legislators to reward donors and fuels high reelection rates. George Will's book, *Restoration,* was published in 1992. It is, about term limits. It remains one of the best books on the subject. He writes that in 1991, then Congresswoman Patricia Schroeder, who he described as "intelligent, witty, well-meaning, and warm-hearted" used her position on the House Judiciary Committee to add $3 million to a crime bill to subsidize midnight basketball. George Will saw this as one example of what is wrong with career politicians:

"The mentality of Washington's entrenched incumbents is one of the reasons they are entrenched. They believe–really believe–

that every good idea out there in America should be a federal program. While I am at it, let me stipulate that Schroeder is public-spirited. But she also is, strictly speaking, deranged. (Oxford English Dictionary: 'thrown into confusion.') She has been reduced, as many career legislators like her have been, to constant confusion about what is and is not temperate, restrained, disciplined, discriminating behavior by government. She has been in Washington so long (elected in 1972), she has spent most of her adult life in Congress –she probably cannot fathom how anyone could find anything odd about Washington funding a nice thing like midnight basketball."[36]

In the book, he writes that from 1790 to 1810, reelection rates in the House of Representative were above 90 percent because our country's political system was still in development. When the party system seriously took shape and participation increased, reelection rates only reached 90 percent in four elections from 1810 to 1950; however, from 1950 to 1990, reelection rates have hit 90 percent in 17 out of those 21 Congressional elections. The reelection rates in the other four elections were in the high eighties. The election of 1932 was the last time that less than 70 percent of incumbents seeking re-election were successful. After 1932, there were only two elections where less than 80 percent of House incumbents won re-election: 1938 (79.1%) and 1948 (79.3%).[37] According to Will:

"This has occurred because the modern state, with all its spending, subsidizing, regulating and patronage powers, is a fecund source of support for incumbent seeking to satisfy constituencies."[38]

The Senate has not been much better. The 17th Amendment, which mandated the popular election of Senators, has had little effect on the re-election rates of Senators. Before 1914, the average re-election rates for a Senator was 75 percent; from the elections of 1914 to 1990, the re-election rate was 72 percent.[39]

Re-election rates have only increased since George Will's book was written. In the Senate, reelection from 1992 to 2012 was 86.7 percent. From 1992 to 2012, the House reelection rate averaged 93 percent. This average would be higher if it didn't include the four "wave" elections of 1994 (90%), 2006 (94%), 2008 (94%), and 2010 (85%).[40]

Term limits for members of Congress died a quick death after the Republicans took over in 1994. It will not happen without a constitutional amendment. The Republican takeover of 1994 was meant to change Washington and instead many of those elected were changed by the trappings of power. Without term limits, the growth in red tape will continue. If there is one poster child for how term limits can hold down the nanny state, that person is Michael Bloomberg.

While I think Michael Bloomberg did some good things in office, such as continuing Mayor Giuliani's crime policies and taking on the public sector unions, with each term he supported banning more things. In effect, Mayor Bloomberg was like Rep. Patricia Schroeder. The longer they were in public office, the more they could see the need for a government solution to a problem. I arranged the list in chronological order to show that Bloomberg became more supportive of the "nanny state" over his three terms as mayor of New York.

Mayor Bloomberg's first term began with only modest regulations. In December, 2002, he signed a law that banned smoking in most bars and restaurants. There were few exceptions, which included cigar bars and bars with only one employee. New York had already banned smoking in most restaurants before he was mayor. Smoking was permitted in bars and the bar area inside the restaurant.[41] Obviously, smoking is unhealthy, but the government has no right to outlaw this activity in a restaurant. We can agree that some regulations are necessary, but at some point we must draw a line in the sand. If people don't like it, they can go to places with non-smoking sections. Often, a restaurant would go out of business if it didn't accommodate the majority of people who don't smoke.

When Bloomberg was reelected in 2005, he began to see regulation as the easiest way to solve societal problems. The first sign was in Spring 2006 when the mayor banned cell phones in schools. Technically, the ban on beepers, and other communication devices, occurred in the 1980s, but there was an "out-of-sight-out-of-trouble" mentality. In 2006, Mayor Bloomberg decided to send metal detectors to schools for random searches in order to confiscate cell phones.[42]

Cell phones were not available when I was in high school and I got along just fine. I also think that it is fine for the teacher to demand that they be turned off during class. It is obviously distracting and disrespectful to the teacher for students to text in class, but I don't think government officials have any right to confiscate phones.

In fall 2006, New York City's Board of Health passed a ban on trans fats in restaurants. This ban was more understandable, but when asked if this ban could lead to further bans, Bloomberg responded, "Nobody wants to take away your French fries and hamburgers--I love those things, too."[43]

While it was a few years before the soda ban, it was clear that he just couldn't resist. This well-intentioned Mayor felt that regulations should substitute for the free choices of people who he felt were too stupid to make the "right" choices.

In his second term he increased the pace of regulation with each passing year. In 2007, he proposed a congestion-pricing plan for Manhattan by forcing motorists to pay fines for driving on busier streets,[44] phasing out all of city's 13,000 taxi cabs in favor of hybrid cars,[45] and forcing restaurants with 15 or more outlets to show their calorie counts.[46] As a free-market supporter, I think it is great when information is readily available for consumers to make the right decisions. Nevertheless, I believe this shows that there were at least some city officials who were arrogant enough to believe a calorie count would change people's habits. Do they really think members of the general public are so stupid that they need a chart to show them that a Big Mac is high in calories?

Bloomberg's contempt for the public was clearly on display when he and a majority of City Council changed the two-term limit for New York City Mayor from two terms to three consecutive terms.[47] In a 1993 referendum, a majority of New York City voters supported a limit of two consecutive terms for mayor, comptroller, borough presidents, and members of the city council.[48] With referendums in 1993 and 1996 supporting term limits, Bloomberg decided that his judgment was better. In 2010, almost 74 percent voters supported reinstating the limit of two consecutive terms.[49]

In 2009, Bloomberg was re-elected the same year he added a ban on cars crossing Broadway from 33rd to 35th Street and 42nd to 47th Street.[50] He also set out to ban flavored tobacco products. There was already a federal ban on tobacco-flavored cigarettes. The city went a step further by banning flavored cigars and smokeless tobacco.[51]

Once Bloomberg received a third term, his thirst for regulations increased. In his first term, the mayor was content with banning smoking in bars. In 2011, Bloomberg signed a law that banned smoking in parks, boardwalks, and other public places. Violation of this new law also carried a $50 fine.[52]

Bloomberg was able to get away with acting like a bully because the majority of New Yorkers agreed with him on certain issues, or at least voted for him. Then came 2012 when the Board of Health was scheduled to vote on the "soda ban." Just before the historic vote, only 36 percent of New Yorkers agreed with Bloomberg while 60 percent believed it was not a good idea.[53]

Bloomberg didn't flinch. A state judge found this regulation had exceeded the authority of the health board. The mayor wouldn't give up. He appealed the decision and lost in court. In October 2013, the Court of Appeals, the highest court in New York State, agreed to hear Bloomberg's case.[54] Don't get me wrong, I am not suggesting that drinking 16 ounces of soda is a good idea. I do think that people should be allowed to make their own choices and many liberals and conservatives seem to agree that this regulation smacks of Big-Brother. Even comedian Bill Maher criticized the law:

" I don't know what Mayor Bloomberg has in mind, but there's something wrong about the seventh richest man in the world sitting in bed at night thinking, 'You know what people shouldn't do? Drink too much Sprite. Let's make that a law.' That makes me want to join the Tea Party and marry Ann Coulter, you know, and that's not where I want to be."[55]

While the court battle has not altered Bloomberg's views on soda, the backlash has forced him to adjust his tactics. In 2013, he launched a public campaign about teens experiencing hearing loss. From 1998 to 2006, hearing loss among teens grew by 30 percent. Since some iPods can reach a maximum volume of 115 decibels, this public campaign was timely and appropriate.

Using social media was far less intrusive than banning iPods that have a volume of over 85 decibels, which is a level that doctors consider safe.[56] His strategy for protecting kids from hearing loss, didn't stop the mayor from going on a rampage with attempts at new regulations. For example on smoking, he raised the tobacco-purchasing age from 18 to 21. While other cities and states have raised the age, neighboring New Jersey only raised it to 19.[57]

One of his last bans was the ban on e-cigarettes, which produces neither second-hand nor first-hand smoke.[58] I applaud the fact that the smoking rate among adults in New York City has declined under Mayor Bloomberg's tenure from 21.5 percent in 2002 to 14.8 percent in 2011. Certainly, we don't want teenagers to be addicted to cigarettes.

Yet I prefer public campaigns that can bring awareness rather than a ban in 2013 that included telling convenience stores to actually conceal their tobacco products. We are at a point where the city government not only wants to regulate the size of soda bottles, but also to tell small businesses where the products in the store should be placed.[59]

Events, such as Hurricane Sandy, also produced action for new regulations designed to save lives in Bloomberg's third term. After the hurricane, the Resilient Buildings Task Force was convened by the city and this led to 33 recommendations for the city's building code.[60]

The only places that could limit Bloomberg's desire for more regulation were the courts and that's only when some of his regulations overlapped with others. For example, the courts invalidated Mayor Bloomberg's plan to limit the "Taxi of Tomorrow" to the Nissan NV200. Part of the reason this plan was doomed was that these cabs were not accessible to people in wheelchairs.[61] This takes the "soda ban" to the next level. Instead of just telling people that soda should be limited to 16 ounces, limiting the purchase of taxis to one model is the equivalent of saying you can only buy Coca Cola and absolutely no other soda products. Since Bill de Blasio received more than $350,000 in donations from the taxi industry, during his 2013 campaign for mayor, I doubt he will fight hard for Bloomberg's plan.[62]

It was obvious that the last few months in office for Bloomberg were going to be tough. So many bans to consider and so little time left to implement them. Yet he managed to squeeze four notables through in his last month in office. In October 2013, he expanded "Slow Zones" in 15 neighborhoods. This doubles the number of "Slow Zones" in New York. The program itself was first implemented by Bloomberg in 2011. By reducing the speed limit to 20 mph and including speed bumps and cameras, the hope is that slow zones can reduce speeding and the traffic fatalities that come with them.[63] In December, 2013, Mayor Bloomberg added a regulation that banned mobile and tower cranes over 25 years old. New York City already created more than 25 construction safety laws from 2008 to 2013.[64] He also signed a ban as petty as prohibiting signs on the grass of city-owned areas adjacent to the street.[65]

In December, 2013, the outgoing city council passed 26 laws and resolutions on the last day of its legislative session.[66] One of the bans included food items packaged in foam cups, trays, and containers. The problem with this ban is that the foam cups commonly used for Chinese take-out, or getting coffee at a Dunkin Donuts, cost approximately one-third or less than a biodegradable plastic container, which typically costs between 30 to 40 cents each. If you think of all the coffee cups that are used daily at the city's 480 Dunkin Donuts stores, you can see how this regulation can add up.[67]

Another ban that became a law that day was a regulation where restaurants, grocery stores, and other elements of New York City's food industry were required to separate food that customers didn't eat from the rest of the trash. This wasted food was required to be sent to a food compositor.[68]

I think it's wrong when a government treats its citizens as children. I understand how people develop a dislike for politicians, and bureaucrats, who think they know how to run our lives. For people who think Bloomberg is unique, remember that the San Jose, California, City Council adopted a foam ban in August, 2013. This was months before New York City. By the time San Jose adopted this ban, there were more than 70 cities in California that had already adopted this regulation on polystyrene foam, which is commonly referred to as styrofoam.[69] With the New York City ban in effect, Mayor Vincent Gray of Washington, D.C. as well as Chicago Alderman George Cardena also sponsored bans in their respective cities.[70] People who like to jam more red tape into the system clearly like to talk to each other.

Recommendation 4: Learn from the "Rubber Room" and keep fighting for education reform.

Make no mistake, education is a national security issue. America will need scientists and engineers to keep our technological edge. We will need doctors to treat our growing population, as well as technicians to run our power plants. Today, our schools need to recommit themselves to a classical education system and our country must understand the value to national security of a strong technical college system. In order to get our education system where it needs to be, parents must be given real school choice, thereby promoting competition within education.

There are two areas where Mayor Bloomberg was right and was an effective mayor. In fact, he was right on the two biggest subjects of his tenure, which were crime and education. In the case of crime, he kept Rudy Giuliani's tough policies. When it came to education, he understood that it is the key for upward mobility. For that reason, he bravely chose to confront the public sector unions.

In April, 2010 Mayor Bloomberg, and the Chancellor of the Department o f Education, Joel Klein, signed an agreement with the President of United Federation of Teachers (UFT), Michael Mulgrew, to end the "Rubber Rooms" so named by the public for teachers put on "Temporary Reassignment" because they are surplus and are assigned to these rooms in which they do nothing. At the time of the agreement, Mulgrew praised the cooperation between the UFT and the Department of Education. He also insisted that it was fair that a teacher be given a cap of 60 days of suspension to investigate possible misconduct and 10 days for incompetence. If no wrongdoing could be found, the teacher could return to the classroom.[71]

While the deal increased the number of arbitrators from 23 to 39, there were serious doubts that the backlog could be cleared in under a year's time. The general mood from the Bloomberg Administration and the UFT was that the matter was resolved.[72] Unfortunately, recent findings showed that the deal was actually a partial success at best. It is true that one year after the agreement, only 83 of the 744 teachers in "Rubber Rooms" were still there. As for the remaining 661 teachers that no longer had "reassignment" status, the arbitrators only managed to fire 33. Another 154 teachers were resigned or retired with full pensions. Some even received severance packages. Of the remaining 474 that were "returned to service," 272 were added to the Absent Teachers Reserve (ATR).[73]

As early as 2006, this reserve had over 1,000 teachers. While Chancellor Joel Klein and Dan Weisberg, Mayor Bloomberg's labor relation's chief, were hoping to press this issue with then UFT President Randi Weingarten, they had no chance to end the abuses behind the Absent Teacher Reserve. Mayor Bloomberg, who wanted to run for a third term, informed his negotiators to back down. By the end of 2006, the first contract negotiated since 2002, would take effect in 2007. Under this new contract, the average cost for a teacher, which includes salary and benefits, was $110,551 compared to $63,022 in 2002. This was a 75 percent increase. Also the UFT won a concession that teachers could retire at age 55 and receive full pensions.[74]

Regulations are largely to blame for this problem. Specifically, the Triborough Amendment to New York State's Taylor Law made it possible for the salaries and benefits in any union contract of public employees to continue even after the deal had expired.[75] Even in tough economic times, it is unlikely that labor will lower salaries and benefits for its members, even if these are for people who do not work. Separate from the costs of the Rubber Room, the teachers in the Absent Teacher Reserve cost the taxpayers $100 million in 2010. Unlike the Rubber Room, the teachers in the Absent Teachers Reserve were not there to face any possible charges. Teachers entered the reserve because they were "excessed." The most common reason was that they lost their positions when a school closed or enrollments fell. While they lost their positions, teachers in the ATR still obtain full salaries.[76] The problem was that if budgets ever do get to a point where actual layoffs are necessary, seniority rules may force the city to layoff teachers who are actually working instead of in the reserve.[77]

This teacher reserve is problematic for two reasons. The first is that it is less well known than the Rubber Room, which might give taxpayers a false impression that the problem of paying do-nothing teachers has ended. Secondly, without an arbitration process, these teachers can be in the reserve for years. While some of them have tried to find work quickly, many don't even bother to go to interviews. For example, in May, 2010, approximately 1,000 teachers in the Absent Teachers Reserve (ATR) were invited to a job fair. Only 111 showed up at the event. In June, 2010, over 900 ATRs were invited to another job fair and only 90 came. Since the Department of Education mandates that principals can only hire teachers who are currently in the system, there cannot be a discussion of how to remove these teachers from the reserve.[78]

This is why I feel that the 2010 deal to end the Rubber Rooms was at best a partial success. In the past, the Rubber Room got people to focus on the abuse of tenure. While everyone should be given the presumption of innocence, people understood that there was some disciplinary action pending. The offenses could range from excessive lateness to sexual misconduct. In 2009, the average time for a teacher in the Rubber Room was three years. Until cases could be resolved before an arbitrator, these teachers sat in a room collecting a salary and accruing benefits for doingnothing.[79]

With over 1,700 schools, 75,000 teachers, and 1.1 million students, the New York City School District is the nation's largest.[80] The budget for the Department of Education was $24.8 billion in FY 2014.[81] In 2009, the Rubber Rooms were estimated to cost between $35 to $65 million a year. While the cost varies depending on whether one is just counting salaries or counting both salaries and benefits, what is never counted is the cost of substitute teachers as well and also what else is needed to house and protect these teachers. The city spends at least $500,000 dollars just protecting them from each other.[82]

The problems with the Rubber Room, and the Absent Teacher's Reserve, have shown that there is very little the New York City's government can do without the unions giving into the city's demands. The problem with the unions is that they must defend their members as zealously as a lawyer defends his client. Considering that 1 in 57 doctors loses his/her license and 1 in 97 lawyers lose their license to practice law, it seems probable that the teachers unions are protecting bad teachers when only 1 in 1,000 in most ajor cities has been fired in recent years for performance-related reasons.[83]

While the unions have been defending the status quo of tenure, seven thousand students drop out of high school every day. Most teachers are hardworking, but the current system allows half of our dropouts to be concentrated from just 15 percent of our schools. These schools are referred to as "drop-out factories."[84]

We can learn with the fight over the Rubber Room that the unions are not going quietly. Even when the public is fully outraged, and it looks as if the unions lost, they really didn't. Even when regulations are stacked against us, and the battle is uphill, we must keep fighting for education reform because America cannot remain a superpower if we remain a nation at risk.

Recommendation 5: Learn from New Jersey, 9/11 and Hurricane Sandy.

After Hurricane Sandy, Governor Chris Christie was widely lauded by the people of New Jersey for his response to the disaster. Immediately after it, his job approval jumped from 48 percent to 67 percent.[85] Because of 9/11, and its proximity to New York City, the State of New Jersey had been preparing for disaster response.

A few lessons can be learned from it. The first is that any serious improvements in disaster response may take years. The most important thing is to learn from previous disasters and prepare for the future.

One example is the state communications system. Before 9/11, the State of New Jersey's system was dependent on the antennae of the World Trade Center. During 9/11, these antennae were gone.[86] The state responded with an updated plan to deal with terrorism and other health emergencies. One of the most crucial parts of this plan included 800 MHz two-way radios for each of the state acute-care medical facilities and other relevant government agencies.[87]

Another lesson from Sandy is that bureaucratic delays can be both painful and necessary. In this case, red tape occurred because New Jersey learned from past disasters. Gov. Christie was very critical that it took 92 days for federal aid to reach Sandy victims. To put that number in perspective, it took only 10 days for aid to arrive after Hurricane Katrina. One reason for the delay was the considerable fraud committed regarding Katrina relief.[88]

Preparing regulations for a rapidly changing world is difficult. It is hard to know how the state's workforce will react to a certain scenario when they have never faced a live situation.

We should expect future surprises that could be more difficult than Hurricane Sandy. For example, in 2013, scientists discovered a new form of botulinum toxin. This is the first strand in over 40 years. Because this new toxin cannot be neutralized by any of the anti-botulinum antiserums, there is a very quiet effort to find a solution without giving away too many details.[89]

As scientists try to find a cure, there might be political pressure in support of untested drugs before the FDA can safely approve them. Speeding up the process could allow an unsafe drug to get through that could have adverse effects on the population. Although we wish that more could be done, sometimes that isn't possible during disasters. State governments can learn from the past, but it still remains to be seen how quickly they can adapt to unprecedented scenarios.

Recommendation 6: Constitutional Amendment on Article V conventions

Our Constitution is not perfect. I know there are political junkies with amendments they would like to propose. Of the two methods to amend th e Constitution, only one has been used for all 27 amendments. This method require two-thirds of Congress to vote for an amendment, which is then approved by three-quarters of the state legislatures. The second method has never been used. That method allows two-thirds of the states to call an Article V convention. Any amendments proposed by the convention would then have to be approved by three-quarters of the state legislatures or by state conventions. The main concern about it is that:

> "Some scholars maintain that such attempts violate the very mechanism created by Article V: the text says that upon application of the states Congress 'shall call a Convention for *proposing Amendments*,' not for confirming a particular amendment already written, approved, and proposed by state legislatures (which would effectively turn the convention for *proposing* amendments into a *ratifying* convention). Indeed, it is not at all clear as a matter of constitutional construction (and doubtful in principle) that the power of *two-thirds* of the states to issue applications for a convention restricts, supersedes, or overrides the power of *all* the states assembled in that convention to propose amendments to the Constitution."[90]

If the Constitution can be revamped our entire regulatory structure could be radically changed for better or worse. We need change as well as a stable process for that change. I knew that the prospect for an Article V convention increased when Harvard Law Professor Lawrence Lessig and Mark Meckler, co-founder of Tea Party Patriots, co-hosted an event to discuss whether the country was ready for such a radical change.[91] Such a panel convinced me that we need to preserve the Constitution with an amendment to Article V. Whether it is liberals in academia who believe in the "living" Constitution or activists that want radical change, we need to clear up Article V so that there is no chance that our Constitution is thrown out. It should make clear that a convention will be limited to the amendment proposed and it should also provide a framework for the structure of an Article V convention. For example, how will delegates be chosen or will each state have the same number of delegates? Without an amendment, a convention could potentially spiral out ofcontrol.

Recommendation 7: To make government smaller we must first understand the impact of behavioral economics on regulatory actions.

Three days before the collapse of Lehman Brothers, J.P. Morgan forecast that U.S. GDP would accelerate in the first half of 2009. In early 2009, the Chairman of the President's Council of Economic Advisors predicted that unemployment would fall to 6.5 percent by the end of 2011.[92] The actual number was 8.5 percent. For the last few years, Alan Greenspan has been writing a fascinating book on how the crisis came to be and how economists in both the public and private sector were unable to predict its impact. Without providing a review of the entire book, one of the main points in it was the importance of behavioral economics in forecasting:: "I have come around to the view that there is something more systemic about the way people behave irrationally, especially during periods of extreme economic stress, than I had previously contemplated. In other words, this behavior can be measured and made an integral part of the economic forecasting process and the formulation of economic policy."[93]

Embracing behavioral economics does not invalidate the neoclassical approach to economics.[94] One of the leading behavioral economists, Dr. Dan Ariely of Duke University, points out:

> "We are finally beginning to understand that irrationality is the real invisible hand that drives human

> decision-making. It's been a painful lesson, but the silver lining may be that companies now see how important it is to safeguard against bad assumptions. Armed with the knowledge that human beings are motivated by cognitive biases of which they are largely unaware (a true invisible hand if there ever was one), businesses can start to better defend against foolishness and waste."[95]

As businesses try to better understand cognitive bias, it is only possible for regulations to remain relevant if they reflect how people are motivated by cognitive biases. Ground Zero in this effort will occur in the Office of Information and Regulatory Affairs (OIRA). This position was created by the Paperwork Reduction Act of 1980. This office was strengthened with an executive order from President Reagan, which required all executive-branch agencies to send their proposed regulations to OIRA for review. Jim Tozzi was the driving force of this effort to regulate regulations from the Johnson Administration to the Reagan Administration. As the head of OIRA in the early 1980s, the office functioned with the hope of reducing unnecessary regulatory burdens.[96]

Alas, proponents of the nanny state took over OIRA and are now using behavioral economics to advance their agenda when designing certain regulations. From 2009 to 2012, the head of OIRA was a man named Cass Sunstein. Upon leaving office, this prolific author provided such a vision of using behavioral economics to "nudge" people toward better living. Sunstein continues to push for what he calls "libertarian paternalism."[97] This encourages certain behavior, but does not have a Bloomberg-style regulation that commands a certain response.

Dr. Donald Boudreaux, an economics professor at George Mason University, wrote a fascinating critique of Sunstein's book and explains why this nanny state is a real threat to our country. In the final paragraphs, Boudreaux reaches back and quotes Friedrich Hayek's book "The Road to Serfdom" (1944):

> The political ideals of a people and its attitude toward authority are as much the effect as he cause of the political institutions under which it lives. This means ...that even a strong tradition of political liberty is no safeguard if the danger is precisely that the new institutions and policies will gradually undermine and destroy that spirit."[98]

To safeguard our free spirit, we must realize that behavioral economics does not mean that people are always irrational. Even if they were, as Thomas Jefferson said in his First Inaugural:

> "Sometimes it is said that man cannot be trusted with the government of himself. Can he, then, be trusted with the government of others? Or have we found angels in the forms of kings to govern him? Let history answer this question."[99]

Daniel Kahneman, who won the Nobel Prize in Economics, seems close to the answering this question. In his book, *Thinking: Fast and Slow*, he divides the human thinking as a battle between intuition (fast thinking) and deliberation (slow thinking). As early as the 1970s, Daniel Kahneman, and his late partner, Amos Tversky, tried to learn how decision-making works. There work would not only win Kahneman the Nobel Prize, but it was also used by Cass Sunstein and Richard Thaler in their 2008 book *Nudge*.[100]

While some try to use these methods to push for paternalism, the hopeful message is that the more we understand how our mind works, the more we improve our ability to make rational decisions. Whether it means improving our finances, cutting red tape, or defeating *jihadi* terror, sustaining America's freedoms in this century will require each of us to have a better understanding of how we think fast.

Chapter Ten

Streamlining the Military: Victory without Bankruptcy

In Franklin Roosevelt's first term, Douglas MacArthur was Chief of Staff of the Army. Despite their political differences, MacArthur claimed they were friends long before FDR was elected. Either that, or that FDR considered him invaluable, was the reason he didn't kick MacArthur out of the Army for good. Faced with problems of the Great Depression, FDR proposed cutting the Army's budget by 51 percent to pay for the New Deal. As the conversation became more heated, MacArthur wrote in his memoirs:

"In my emotional exhaustion, I spoke recklessly and said something to the effect that when we lost the next war and an American boy, lying in the mud with an enemy bayonet through his belly and an enemy foot on his dying throat, spat out his last curse, I wanted the name not to be MacArthur, but Roosevelt."[1]

MacArthur quickly apologized for his outburst and offered his resignation. FDR was quick to respond with a joke. "Don't be foolish, Douglas; you and the budget must get together on this."[2]

Today, the American people, regardless of party, must understand we can responsibly cut the defense budget. And in the current economic climate, we will have to cut other areas of the federal budget along with defense.

To be blunt, outside of the interest on the national debt, everything in the federal budget can and should be re-examined. While defense spending must be part of that equation, we cannot hollow out our military and pretend that defense is the biggest part of our spending problem.

As President Roosevelt said in his first inaugural address, "This is preeminently the time to speak the truth, the whole truth, frankly and boldly. Nor need we shrink from honestly facing conditions in our country today."[3]

The truth, "frankly and boldly," is that Democrats usually think that the only part of the federal budget that needs any cuts is defense, while Republicans are conservatives on domestic spending. We must all recognize that in working to solve our fiscal problems, we must also accept the fact our nation is working to win the first war of the 21st century.

While the wars in Afghanistan and Iraq have been costly, they are a small component of federal spending. According to the Congressional Budget Office (CBO), from 2001-2012, the cumulative federal spending in this period was $33.3 trillion. Approximately four percent of that federal spending ($1.4 trillion dollars) was spent on fighting the wars in Afghanistan and Iraq.[4]

In the last 50 years, two great trends have occurred in federal spending: the relative decline of the defense budget and the growth of entitlements. Defense spending declined from 52.2 percent of the federal budget in 1960 to only 20.1 percent in 2010.[5] Entitlement spending has more than doubled from 28 percent of federal budget in 1960 to 66 percent by 2010.[6]

In 2010, the federal government was spending $2.2 trillion on entitlements.[7] The breakdown of this spending in 2010 was 53 percent for the elderly (65 and over), 20 percent for disabled, 18 percent for the working poor, and nine percent for various programs including survivor benefits in Social Security, medical services, and unemployment insurance.[8]

We cannot fully predict how severe the problem will become because the growth in the economy over the next 30 years is harder to predict than demographics. What experts do know is that people are living longer. This is a good thing, but it comes with a cost. If the trends of the last century are an indicator, we may be heading toward a fiscal disaster.

From 1900 to 2000, the population of the United States increased from 76 million to 281 million. The number of Americans, who were 65 and over, increased from 3.1 million in 1900 to 35 million in 2000 while the number of Americans, who were 85 and over, increased from 122,000 to 4.2 million in the same period. So the total population increased about three-and-a-half times while the population 65 and over increased tenfold and the population 85 and over expanded forty-fold.[9]

Before the sixties, our country raised the national debt during wars (from the Revolutionary War to World War II) and in national emergencies such as the Great Depression, but in times of peace, it usually paid down the debt. In 1835, Andrew Jackson actually paid off the entire national debt. This did not last long. In the 1920s, the country was able to pay back about a third of the debt we accumulated to pay for World War I. During the Depression and World War II, the debt rose substantially. The debt was actually falling in constant dollars and percentage of GDP until 1975.[10] Today there is little political will to hold down spending.

Politicians must confront the growing fiscal problem in all areas of the budget. Meanwhile, the purpose of this chapter is to provide recommendations on how to responsibly cut defense spending.

To say that cuts cannot be made, without hollowing the force, is absurd. Gordon England, who was Deputy Secretary of Defense 2006-2009, wrote in an op-ed, that we could cut 100,000 of the 700,000 civilian employees at the Department of Defense without the need for any contractors to replace them. In the same op-ed, England pointed out that the Defense Secretary would require blanket authorization from Congress because civilian employees have union protections and regulations that military employees did not have.[11] I am all for cutting the fat out of the defense budget. I just don't want us to cut the muscle and the bone.

Recommendation 1: Ban Members of Congress from Owning Stocks or Bonds in Companies That Have Defense Department Contracts

Members of Congress have many incentives to keep defense spending high. For example, military bases can bring jobs to a congressional district. Beyond the electoral politics, there are also direct financial gains that should be of concern to American taxpayers. For example, in 2010, it was reported that 19 of the 28 members of the Senate Armed Services Committee held stock/bonds with companies that had contracts with the Pentagon. While committee staffers and key presidential appointees are banned from owning stock, members of Congress are not.[12] This recommendation can begin the conversation about how the purpose of our defense budget should be to provide for the common defense of the nation and its people.

Recommendation 2: Replace Cost-plus Contracting with a Prospective Payment System

In 2010, then-Defense Secretary Robert Gates noted that submarines and amphibious ships were three times more expensive than their 1980s counterparts. "At the end of the day, we have to ask whether the nation can really afford a Navy that relies on $3 billion to $6 billion destroyers, $7 billion submarines, and $11 billion carriers."[13] These types of increases are not limited to the Navy. According to the GAO, from 2001 to 2008, the

Pentagon's major acquisition programs altogether went over $300 billion from their initial estimates.[14]

While we cannot take back the money we have lost, we can stop the bleeding. The problem lies in the "cost-plus" contract system. That is, the Department of Defense provides a contract and pays extra for any overruns. The structure of the contract along with the inherent need for bureaucracies to provide more requirements for weapons systems leads to increased costs.[15] What we need is a prospective payment system in defense contracting.

There is a historical precedent for this idea. In 1983, the Reagan Administration implemented a major reform in Medicare by creating Diagnosis Related Groups (DRGs). DRGs were introduced in the 1980s by Medicare to bring down health care costs through a prospective payment system (PPS).

Before the PPS, Medicare gave hospitals as much money as the hospitals billed following the treatment of patients. Such a system only encouraged hospitals to keep people longer to get more money. A DRG is designed to assess how much should be spent for a patient *before* the money is spent. This way, the hospital has an incentive to get the job done as quickly as possible so that it can spend the money it is given efficiently and make as much of a profit as possible. This is to compensate for people who are either uninsured or people on Medicaid thus forcing hospitals to spend more money than they take in for certain services. Hospitals that succeed in this model are those that promote effectiveness and efficiency.[16] A prospective payment system in defense contracting could be a real "game changer" in terms of reducing costs.

Recommendation 3: End Unnecessary Pentagon Spending Programs

The Pentagon has many examples of programs that no longer have a purpose. For example, earlier I quoted former Deputy Secretary of Defense Gordan England that we could afford to cut 100,000 civilian employees at DoD without having a negative impact on military forces.

In 2010, Secretary Robert Gates proposed efficiency initiatives worth $100 billion. The largest item, which comprises a quarter of these savings, was a proposed 30 percent cut in "service support contractors."[17] This would cut over 30,000 civilian jobs from DoD that can be absorbed through efficiency. The National Commission on Fiscal Responsibility and Reform recommends that we can go further with a cut of over 20 percent. This cut could result in $37.8 billion in savings over the next 10 years.

The National Commission also recommended that we can actually replace 88,000 military personnel who are not performing defense-related activities with 62,000 civilians. This could begin saving $5.4 billion annually by 2015. If this rate can be continued it could produce over $50 billion in savings over the next decade.[18] Advances in information technology have made it possible to cut at least five percent of civilian jobs within the decade. This could save the Department of Defense $22.5 billion.[19]

Now that the United States has withdrawn from Iraq and is likely to withdraw from Afghanistan at the end of 2014, it can seriously reduce its travel budget. In 2008, the federal government spent $13.8 billion on travel for its employees. Approximately two-thirds of that spending ($9.1 billion) was in the Department of Defense.[20] With advances in teleconferencing, as well as fewer soldiers deployed in Iraq and Afghanistan, we could reduce that budget from $9.1 billion and hold spending to $7 billion a year. In addition, promising new technologies from the private sector can reduce paper work and improve efficiencies in travel programs. Over a 30-year period, that could save another $20 billion.

Recommendation 4: Cut the Number of Generals and Flag Officers

A perennial Pentagon problem has been the fact that there are far too many generals and flag officers for a force our size. The U.S. military is almost 30 percent smaller than it was prior to the end of the Cold War, yet the number of three- and four-star generals and admirals has grown by 19 percent in the same period. The base pay of each is over $225,000 dollars a year--not including combat commands. The headquarters' support costs were $459 million in fiscal year 2007 and rose to $1.06 billion in FY 2012. In the same period, support costs for their subordinate commands grew from $395 million to $604 million.[21]

By following Secretary Gates' 2010 recommendation to cut 102 generals and flag officers, we could also cut the bureaucracy that comes with them.[22] So far, the Defense Department has cut 48 one-star generals and six two-star generals, but has cut the number of three- and four-star generals by only three.[23]

Beyond the costs, the officer-to-enlisted personnel ratio can lead to a weaker military. Retired Army Major Donald E. Vandergriff has compared this ratio throughout history. From the data, it is clear that successful militaries have a higher officer to personnel ratio than their enemies. For example in 1806, Prussia had more officers (23,789 to 4,215) and generals (528 to 423) than France. The French Army of 350,000 troops was victorious because the Grand Army was almost twice as large as the Prussian Army.

In 1940, the German Army was able to outperform both the French and the British Armies. While Germany's army (4,555,000) was almost as large as the combined forces of France (3,333,000);

and the United Kingdom (1,615,000), Germany had fewer officers (133,970) than either France (666,600) or the United Kingdom (177,650). Germany's ratio of generals to personnel in 1940 was roughly half that of Britain and France.[24]

At the beginning of 2012, the U.S Navy had more admirals (336) than ships (285).[25] If the sequester on the defense budget is not stopped, the Navy will be reduced from 285 ships in 2012 to 235 commissioned ships by 2021. Our Air Force will be reduced from 1,493 aircraft to 1,157. The U.S. Army will decline from 10 active divisions in 2012 to six in 2021. The top brass cannot be immune to sacrifice. We must address the personnel costs, growing health care costs within the military and inefficient procurement, lest the massive overhead of our military in a decade comes to resemble the hollow post-Vietnam force.[26]

Recommendation 5: Reform Tricare and Transfer It Out of the DoD

TRICARE is the health care program currently run by the Defense Department. With the exception of prescription payments, our active-duty troops and their families essentially have-free health care. In the past decade, they have also increased eligibility for military retirees, which now makes 9.7 million Americans eligible for TRICARE. From 2001 to 2012, the TRICARE budget grew from $19 billion to $52.8 billion. This is almost 10 percent of the Pentagon's budget.[27] This does not include the Department of Veterans Affairs, which proposed $51 billion in spending out of a total budget of a $132 billion for FY 2012.[28] It is understandable why people believe that low health-care costs are a way to honor the sacrifices of our veterans. Even a discussion of the effectiveness of this spending could result in serious political consequences for members of Congress.

Yet, the American people *cannot* ignore this part of the budget. The Defense budget as a whole cannot be treated as a sacred cow. With the exception of the interest on the national debt, every part of the federal budget, including entitlements, must be on the table. Critics of defense spending only talk about total defense spending and rarely take a deep look at what is actually in the budget. If TRICARE remains unaddressed, the defense budget will increase as our military capability degrades. If TRICARE remains in the defense department's budget, it will give the Democrats the best of both worlds. It allows them the ability to criticize the Republicans for defending the total spending of the Pentagon. If the Republicans try to cut it, they will be crucified by veterans and seniors.

This is why TRICARE should be moved out of the Pentagon's budget. It could become a part of the Department of Health and Human Services or the Department of Veteran Affairs. The best option is to make it an independent agency. Either option could make it more likely to consolidate health services among the different branches. Currently the Office of the Assistant Secretary of Defense for Health Affairs along with the Army, Navy and Air Force each has its own headquarters and the bureaucracy that comes with it. According to the General Accounting Office, the savings from consolidation could be at least $200 million annually.[29]

With all the complexities of consolidating services, this is politically much easier than reducing funding for TRICARE. The most cost-effective proposal from the Congressional Budget Office (CBO) would be to limit TRICARE Prime to active duty personnel and their families; military retirees and their dependents would be eligible for TRICARE Standard. This reform could save as much $115 billion.

To be clear, TRICARE Prime has the lowest out-of-pocket costs. If this option were limited to active duty personnel and their families, military retirees would still have access to TRICARE Standard and TRICARE Extra.[30] This option is limited to working-age retirees who are too young to receive Medicare. The savings in this option come from military retirees paying more, and from the fact that three quarters of the retirees are eligible for health insurance from their civilian employers.[31]

Another option in this CBO report talked about providing some out-of-pocket cost-sharing requirements under TRICARE-For-Life for Medicare-eligible retirees. This would save $43 billion over the next decade. Cost-sharing could provide savings in military retirees who are too young for Medicare, ($30 billion) or cost sharing in pharmaceuticals ($26 billion).[32]

While the Veterans Health Administration (VHA) medical care system is technically an issue for the Department of Veteran Affairs, some people could confuse the VA system as a part of the Defense budget.

For this reason, I think we should also propose ending enrollment in the VA medical care for veterans in Priority Groups 7 and 8. This could save at least $30 billion annually. The 1.3 million veterans in these two groups have incomes that exceed the VA threshold. While technically, this option would save $62 billion, half the savings would be offset because some veterans would be eligible for Medicare and Medicaid and they would just charge more spending to those programs.[33]

The retirement of 78 million Baby Boomers will put so much stress on our federal budget that means-testing of entitlement programs becomes inevitable. We can't balance the federal budget on the backs of veterans. We can't even balance the federal budget if all defense spending were cut. Politicians at some point must be honest with the American people.

While there is fat to cut in the defense budget, there is also plenty to cut elsewhere before we talk about increasing taxes or cutting benefits to senior citizens. For example, the number of people receiving disability payments went up from 455,000 people in 1960 to 8.6 million in 2010. Half of these claims are "mood disorders" or back pain (which is difficult to disprove).[34]

I am sure that many of these people have legitimate claims, but such a dramatic increase should make us pause. There are clearly some people who are defrauding the system. If we are going to ask 1.3 million of our richest veterans to accept means-testing, we should also work much harder to means-test entitlements and also go after people who engage in fraud. Recently, physicians have developed promising technology aimed at making disability exams more objective. A pilot program of this technology should be implemented and, if successful, rolled out nationally.

Recommendation 6: Privatize the VA Hospital System

We must address the fact that hospital monopolies are one of the biggest drivers of health care costs. In the case of Massachusetts, even before "Romneycare" took effect, the 1993 merger between Massachusetts General Hospital and Brigham and Women's Hospital allowed the two most powerful hospitals in the state to dictate the cost of care. No insurance provider could afford to leave out either of these two prestigious Harvard-affiliated hospitals in their plans.[35]

Anyone who has read about the scandals in the VA Hospital System and even at the Army's Walter Reed, should reconsider the supposed benefits of any government-run health care.

Furthermore, the monopolies of regional hospitals must be broken up. Privatizing VA hospitals could inject enough supply to keep the demand from spiraling out of control.[36] This could reduce costs and also provide an alternative to cutting veterans' benefits. Under a private system, the hospital would likely improve the quality of its care.

Recommendation 7: Make Maximum Use of the National Guard and Reserve Forces, and Make Certain They're Adequately Equipped

One of the best bargains for the American taxpayer is the use of our National Guard and Reserve Forces. We can train and equip roughly three to four National Guard or Reserve troops for every one active duty soldier; however, when we need them, we must be prepared to use them and make sure they are adequately equipped. The Founding Fathers and the Continental Congress understood the "Citizen Soldier" concept – a vital tradition that made our military unique and has withstood the test of time. We've seen the Guard and the Reserve in action in Afghanistan and Iraq. We've also seen them in action on the home front as first responders.

Because the Pentagon had a history of not properly equipping the National Guard, over 30 years ago Congress wisely established the National Guard and Reserve Component Equipment Account (NGREA) to ensure America's reserve forces had adequate equipment and supplies to respond to national security and homeland needs. The NGREA has been a lifeline for the Guard in recent years. It has enabled them to fight alongside active duty troops at a fraction of the cost and respond quickly to national disasters and homeland security threats.

Unfortunately, in the summer of 2013, some 20 Republicans joined 171 Democrats in supporting the Van Hollen Amendment to the National Defense Authorization Act. It would have severely affected the National Guard's readiness. It specifically included a provision to eliminate $400 million from the NGREA. Fortunately, 22 Democrats joined nearly 90 percent of all House

Republicans in defeating the Van Hollen Amendment by a 232-191 vote. House Armed Services Committee Chairman Buck McKeon and the National Guard Association of the United States (NGAUS) were key players in defeating the amendment and maintaining the readiness of the National Guard. They knew the consequences. Without an adequately equipped National Guard, the nation might eventually be forced to shift this capability to the active force at a cost of many billions of dollars to the taxpayers.

The citizen soldier concept envisioned by our Founding Fathers and Continental Congress continues to make good sense

Recommendation 8: Engage Small Business

Small business is the backbone of the free enterprise system in America. It's also the source of most ingenuity and innovation. The Department of Defense, like other departments and agencies, has a Small and Disadvantaged Business Utilization Office (SADBU), which assists small business in navigating the Pentagon's procurement maze. In addition, there needs to be an active effort on behalf of technology program offices to engage especially the small business community from which so many of our technological advances come.

The Joint IED Defeat Organization (JIEDDO) was established by the Department of Defense to reduce the threat of improvised explosive devices (IEDs) against the U.S. Military. Since its inception in 2006, JIEDDO has spent billions of dollars. Promising technologies to deal with the suicide bomber scenario have been identified, but the problem of the car bomber has been a more difficult challenge. I've seen a number of invitations JIEDDO has sent out over the years advertising industry conferences, but they almost always require a "Secret" clearance in order to attend. The problem is obvious; many small businesses which have the technologies to counter IEDs and the suicide bomber threat don't have a "Secret" clearance to get in the front door to show JIEDDO their capabilities. This is a typical problem throughout the DoD and the homeland security arena. We must do a better job at reaching out to small businesses, many of which have the capabilities we will need to successfully thwart the next terrorist threat.

Recommendation 9: Replicate the Rapid Fielding Directorate Model

The Department of Defense's Rapid Fielding Directorate has had several names since the early 1990s, including the Advanced Concepts Technology Demonstration (ACTD) program and the Joint Concepts Technology Demonstration (JCTD) program. It identifies mature technology capabilities and works with major commands to get their "buy in" on final development, testing and procurement.

By taking this approach it ensures the most efficient use of research and development dollars in acquiring needed technologies. It also works closely with homeland and civil authorities, as well as the intelligence community. Its predecessor, the ACTD program, was best known for bringing the concept of the unmanned aerial vehicle to fruition.

This program has been an effective, efficient use of taxpayer dollars in ensuring that our fighters have the latest technology available. Things happen here and they happen quickly. This model should be replicated throughout each of the military services, as well as the Department of Homeland Security.

Recommendation 10: Return All U.S. Nuclear Weapons Deployed In NATO Countries to the United States

As a holdover from the Cold War, the U.S. has 200 non-strategic nuclear weapons deployed in Germany, Italy, Belgium, the Netherlands, and Turkey.[37] We do not have much reason to keep these weapons in Europe, and Turkey has become a less reliable ally.

Fortunately we have not lost Turkey--yet. For more than a decade, the Turkish government has been ruled by Prime Minister Recep Tayyip Erdoğan and his Justice and Development Party (AKP). The AKP is an Islamist party. In domestic policy, this party has tried to reverse much of the secular legacy of Ataturk.[38]

In foreign affairs, Erdoğan wasn't able to secure support in the Turkish Parliament for the United States to invade Iraq through Turkey. In 2012 its government provided Iran with identities of Iranians who were meeting with Israeli intelligence agents in Turkey. The information was related to Iran's nuclear program.[39]

Although the nuclear weapons in Turkey are under the direct control of the U.S. military, there is no reason to keep them there. With the drift of Turkey away from Western values a chaotic situation could develop in the future. The easiest way to secure these weapons would be to dismantle them. This could also help in our non-proliferation efforts.

Recommendation 11: Ways to contain China

By winning the Cold War, the U.S. was able to responsibly reduce its defense budget. While cutting waste in the budget is important, the best way to reduce the need for defense is by solving problems.

Japan and South Korea need China's help in addressing the North Korean threat. Unlike the former Soviet Union, our strength against Chinese expansion rests on a combination of military and economic power. In terms of the economic interdependence, from 1981 to 2013, U.S.-China trade expanded from $5 billion to an estimated $559 billion.[40] The U.S.-China trade deficit has grown from $83 billion in 2000 to $318 billion in 2013.[41]

How much higher would the trade deficit be if the Yuan was still pegged to the dollar? From 1997 to 2005, China's currency was pegged to the dollar at 8.28 Yuan for every dollar.[42] In 2013, the Yuan appreciated to 6.1 Yuan against the dollar.[43]

The Chinese did not do this because the U.S. Congress complained, or because President Obama gave a convincing speech. The Chinese did this because their economy was overheating. Appreciating their currency was an easy way to tame inflation. Instead of too many dollars chasing too few goods in China, it was easier to send that money abroad. Whether they can successfully transition from an export-led growth model in favor of more consumption, in the face of aging demographics, is an open question.

Our objective must be to press them to curtail their military build-up. Much like the currency issue, they will concede when they see it is in their interest to do so. Our ability to responsibly keep their defense spending low will largely be driven by the decisions in Beijing.

At present, China is simply is not the military threat that the former Soviet Union was during the Cold War. The Soviet Union could attack the United States with 2,500 strategic delivery vehicles. They also had the technology to attack the U.S. with multiple warheads.[44] China by comparison has 50 to 75 ICBMs. It is also developing a sea-based nuclear capability.

The more immediate danger is not an attack to the homeland, but 1,100 short-range ballistic missiles (SRBMs) aimed at Taiwan, as well as China's anti-ship ballistic missiles (ASBMs). The most serious ASBM threat is the DF-21D missile, which is known as "the carrier killer." This missile can hit a ship within a range of 1,500 kilometers.[45] If this anti-ship missile were able to destroy either a Nimitz class or the new Gerald Ford class aircraft carrier, thousands of sailors could be killed in a single attack.[46]

While we can handle any Middle East contingency, including military action against Iran's nuclear facilities, the only country that could genuinely strain our resources is China. Their "official" military budget was $114 billion in 2013. The Pentagon believes that their national security spending is actually somewhere between $135 billion to $214 billion dollars.[47] Despite this massive budget, the Chinese still spend more on domestic security than on any external threats.

We must encourage this internal pressure if we are to avert a serious and unnecessary arms race. China has acknowledged that the number of internal "mass incidents" has increased from 8,700 in 1993 to 90,000 in 2010.[48]

Perhaps a more powerful weapon for freedom than an aircraft carrier is the fact that China has 500 million internet users and more than 100 million bloggers.[49] Even without the internet, Fareed Zakaria points out that the threshold when the middle class grows large enough to push for political reform is when a country reaches middle-income status. This is when per capita annual incomes are between $5,000 to $10,000 dollars. Countries with very different histories, from Spain to South Korea, have proven this rule to have some merit.[50]

China's young bloggers are a problem, but only one of them. China's shift to a middle-class, consumer society will take many more years. The aging of the population presents other problems.

In 2008, with the near collapse of our financial system, there were many who believed that the 21st century would belong to China. Around this time, John Pomfret, who was Beijing bureau chief for the *Washington Post*, provided some sobering statistics:

"Because of the Communist Party's notorious one-child-per-family policy, the average number of children born to a Chinese woman has dropped from 5.8 in the 1970s to 1.8 today -- below the rate of 2.1 that would keep the population stable. Meanwhile, life expectancy has shot up, from just 35 in 1949 to more than 73 today. Economists worry that as the working-age population shrinks, labor costs will rise, significantly eroding one of China's key competitive advantages."[51]

With a birth rate below replacement and people living longer, the demograhic challenges that China faces are similar to those of the developed world, but on a much larger scale.

In 2012, China had 180 million citizens that were over 60 years old. By the middle of the century, that number could approach 500 million people.[52] Short of the Chinese instituting a one-grandparent policy, the financial stress on their budgets could put us in a position to press the Chinese to address their military budget. We can also work with our Asian allies to press the Chinese to prevent any unnecessary incidents from spiraling out of control in the South China Sea.

China's growing internal problems will likely make it impossible for it to mount an offensive policy unless provoked. In order to keep defense spending low, we will have to work with Beijing in pressing it to restrain their military spending. Whether it is too much at stake with trade, or simply because the United States, China, Japan, and other Asian countries must cope with aging populations, it will be in the interest of all involved to learn the lessons from the 20th century.

We must do an effective enough job of averting a massive arms race and still defend our interests. As the Department of Defense approaches the dual task of both responsibly cutting defense and securing our freedom, we should never forget the words of General MacArthur, "There is no substitute for victory."

Chapter 1 End Notes

1 *Fox News.* 8 March 2013. http://www.foxnews.com/politics/2013/03/08/white-house-says-us-can-defend-against-north-korea-attack/. 19 January 2014.

[2] *Missile Defense Agency.* 21 October 2013. http://www.mda.mil/global/documents/pdf/gmdfacts.pdf. 19 January 2014.

[3] Hannaford, Peter. *Washington Times.* 3 March 2009. http://www.washingtontimes.com/news/2009/mar/03/books-the-rebellion-of-ronald-reagan/?page=all. 19 January 2014.

[4] *Reagan Foundation.* n.d. https://www.reaganfoundation.org/pdf/Remarks_Annual_Convention_National_Association_Evangelicals_030883.pdf. 19 January 2014

[5] Warner, Frank. *Morning Call.* 5 March 2000. http://articles.mcall.com/2000-03-05/news/3291248_1_soviet-press-agency-tass-nuclear-war-soviet-union. 19 January 2014.

[6] *Ronald Reagan Presidential Library and Museum.* n.d. http://www.reagan.utexas.edu/archives/speeches/1983/32383d.htm. 19 January 2014.

[7] *NBC News.* 5 June 2004. http://www.nbcnews.com/id/5145921/ns/us_news-the_legacy_of_ronald_reagan/#.UtvAQ_ko6IU. 19 January 2014.

[8] Garvin, Glenn. *Reason.* 1 November 2003. http://reason.com/archives/2003/11/01/the-gipper-and-the-hedgehog. 19 January 2014.

[9] *Missile Defense Agency.* n.d. http://www.mda.mil/global/documents/pdf/histfunds.pdf. 19 January 2014.

[10] Missile Defense Agency. *MDA Interactive Timeline.* n.d. http://www.mda.mil/careers/global/_documents/timeline.txt. 19 January 2014.

[11] Hagel, Chuck. *Department of Defense.* 15 March 2013. http://www.defense.gov/Speeches/Speech.aspx?SpeechID=1759. 19 January 2014.

[12] *Department of Defense.* 15 March 2013. http://www.defense.gov/transcripts/transcript.aspx?transcriptid=5205. 19 January 2014.

[13] Missile Defense Agency. *Missile Defense Agency Sensors.* 2 January 2014. http://www.mda.mil/system/sensors.html. 20 January 2014

[14] Missile Defense Agency. *Ballistic Missile Defense Intercept Flight Test Record* . 4 October 2013. http://www.mda.mil/global/documents/pdf/testrecord.pdf. 19 January 2014.

[15] Gard, Robert G and Kingston Reif. *Arms Control Agency*. July 2012. http://armscontrolcenter.org/issues/missiledefense/articles/fact_sheet_us_ballistic_missile_defense/. 19 January 2014.

[16] Missile Defense Agency. *Aegis Ballistic Missile Defense.* 8 January 2014. http://www.mda.mil/system/aegis_bmd.html. 19 January 2014.

[17] O'Rourke, Ronald. *Congressional Research Service.* 17 October 2013. https://www.fas.org/sgp/crs/weapons/RL33745.pdf. 19 January 2014.

[18] Cohen, Ariel. *Heritage Foundation.* 19 March 2013. http://blog.heritage.org/2013/03/19/how-not-to-negotiate-with-russia-the-missile-defense-fiasco/. 19 January 2014.

[19] Bennett, John T. *Defense News.* 19 March 2013. http://www.defensenews.com/article/20130319/DEFREG02/303190022/Ayotte-Obama-Intends-Cancel-SM-3-IIB-Missile-Program. 19 January 2014.

[20] Missile Defense Agency. *Aegis Ballistic Missile Defense.* 8 January 2014. http://www.mda.mil/system/aegis_bmd.html. 19 January 2014.

[21] Collina, Tom Z. *Arms Control Association.* October 2012. http://www.armscontrol.org/act/2012_10/Report-Critiques-US-Missile-Defense. 19 January 2014.

[22] Nagle, Chet. *Committee on the Present Danger.* August 2012. http://www.committeeonthepresentdanger.org/index.php?option=com_content&view=article&id=2758&catid=4&Itemid=92. 19 January 2014.

[23] Ibid.

[24] Ibid.

[25] Ibid.

[26] Ibid.

[27] Anderson, Edward G., III. *The Hill.* 22 May 2013. http://thehill.com/blogs/congress-blog/homeland-security/301227-north-korea-iran-threats-demand-military-readiness. 19 January 2014.

Chapter Two End Notes:

[1] Lynn, William. "Defending a New Domain: The Pentagon's Cyber Strategy." *Foreign Affairs,* September/October 2010: 97-108.

[2] Nye, Joseph. The Future of Power. New York : Public Affairs, 2011.

[3] Lou Dobbs Tonight. 22 July 2004. 8 June 2013. <http://transcripts.cnn.com/TRANSCRIPTS/0407/22/ldt.00.html>.

[4] U.S. Government Printing Office. July 2004. http://www.gpo.gov/fdsys/pkg/GPO-911REPORT/pdf/GPO-911REPORT.pdf. 27 August 2013.

[5] Scheuer, Michael F. *Washington Times.* 4 July 2006. http://www.washingtontimes.com/news/2006/jul/4/20060704-110004-4280r/. 23 January 2014.

[6] Fox News Sunday With Chris Wallace. 1 October 2006. http://www.foxnews.com/story/2006/10/01/transcript-counterterror-experts-debate-clinton-claims-on-fns/. 8 June 2013.

[7] Blake, Eric S, Christopher W Landsea, and Ethan J. Gibney. "National Hurricane Center." August 2011. 9 June 2013. <http://www.nhc.noaa.gov/pdf/nws-nhc-6.pdf>.

[8] *International Business Times.* 13 July 2012. 9 June 2013. <http://www.ibtimes.com/americas-top-cyberwarrior-says-cyberattacks-cost-250-billion-year-722559>.

[9] Bush, George W., *Decision Points.* New York: Crown Publishers, 2010.

[10] Grunwald, Michael. 8 September 2005. 9 June 2013. <http://www.washingtonpost.com/wp-dyn/content/article/2005/09/07/AR2005090702462.html>.

[11] Grunwald, Michael. 24 November 2010. 9 June 2013. <http://www.time.com/time/specials/packages/article/0,28804,2032304_2032746_2035982-3,00.html>.

[12] Weisman, Jonathan and Jim VandeHei. "Road Bill Reflects The Power of Pork White House Drops Effort to Rein in Hill." *Washington Post,* 11 August 2005.

[13] Bowser, Betty Ann. 26 August 2010. 9 June 2013. <http://www.pbs.org/newshour/rundown/2010/08/five-years-after-katrina-some-question-whether-new-levees-will-protect-the-city-next-time.html>.

[14] C-SPAN. 12 June 2013. http://www.c-spanvideo.org/program/313307-1. 16 June 2013.

[15] U.S. Department of Treasury . *Troubled Asset Relief Program.* 10 January 2014. http://www.treasury.gov/initiatives/financial-stability/reports/Documents/December%202013%20Monthly%20Report%20to%20Congress.pdf. 23 January 2014.

[16] Lynch, David J. *Bloomberg Business Week,* 19 April 2012. 2013 May 17. <http://www.businessweek.com/articles/2012-04-19/big-banks-now-even-too-bigger-to-fail>.

[17] Nakashima, Ellen. *Washington Post,* 21 September 2012. http://articles.washingtonpost.com/2012-09-21/world/35497878_1_web-sites-quds-force-cyberattacks. 9 June 2013.

[18] Santora, Marc. 10 May 2013. 18 June 2013. <http://www.nytimes.com/2013/05/10/nyregion/eight-charged-in-45-million-global-cyber-bank-thefts.html?pagewanted=all>.

[19] Gandel, Stephen and Leo Cendrowicz. "After Three Years and Trillions of Dollars, Our Banks Still Don't Work ," Time (2011): 40-45.

[20] CNN. 13 December 2011. http://edition.cnn.com/2011/12/12/world/meast/iran-us-drone/?hpt=hp_t1. 9 June 2013.

[21] Lynn, William. "Defending a New Domain: The Pentagon's Cyber Strategy." *Foreign Affairs,* September/October 2010: 97-108.

[22] Pellerin, Cheryl. U.S. Department of Defense. 12 March 2013. http://www.defense.gov/news/newsarticle.aspx?id=119506. 28 August 2013.

[23] Censer, Marjorie. *Washington Post.* 6 May 2012. http://www.washingtonpost.com/business/capitalbusiness/richard-clarke-joins-sra-international/2012/05/04/gIQAvGEK6T_story.html.18 January 2014.

[24] Park, Geun-hye. September/October 2011. 17 June 2013. <http://www.foreignaffairs.com/articles/68136/park-geun-hye/a-new-kind-of-korea?page=show>.

[25] Heilemann, John and Mark Halperin. *Game Change*. New York: HarperCollins, 2010.

[26] Brennan, Margaret. CBS News. 7 May 2013. http://www.cbsnews.com/8301-250 162-57583203/south-koreas-first-female-president-takes-hard-line-approach-with-north-korea/. 17 June 2013.

[27] Fox News. 10 April 2013. http://www.foxnews.com/world/2013/04/10/south-korea-says-north-korea-behind-computer-crash-in-march/. 18 June 2013.

[28] Salmon, Andrew. 18 June 2013. 27 March 2013. <http://www.cnn.com/2013/03/27/world/asia/south-north-korea-war-scenario>.

[29] Tait, Robert. 31 May 2013. 17 June 2013. <http://www.telegraph.co.uk/news/worldnews/middleeast/palestinianauthority/10091629/Iran-cuts-Hamas-funding-over-Syria.html>.

[30] Young, Angelo. 29 April 2013. 17 June 2013. <http://www.ibtimes.com/iran-oil-exports-lowest-1986-iran-iraq-war-graphic-1222221#>.

[31] Ynet. 25 May 2013. http://www.ynetnews.com/articles/0,7340,L-4383896,00.html. 18 June 2013.

[32] C-SPAN. 19 November 2003. http://www.c-spanvideo.org/program/179193-1. 18 June 2013.

[33] Perez-Pena, Richard and Matthew L. Wald. 20 November 2003. 2013 June 18. <http://www.nytimes.com/2003/11/20/us/basic-failures-by-ohio-utility-set-off-blackout-report-finds.html?ref=firstenergycorporation>.

[34] Gjelten, Tom. NPR. 19 July 2010. http://www.npr.org/templates/story/story.php?storyId=128574055. 7 March 2013.

[35] *The Guardian*. 1 June 2007. http://www.guardian.co.uk/world/2007/jun/02/internationaleducationnews.highereducation. 8 March 2013.

[36] McCaul, Michael. *Wall Street Journal.* 5 March 2013. http://online.wsj.com/article/SB10001424127887324662404578336862508763442.html. 8 March 2013.

[37] Ackerman, Bob. *Silicon Valley Business Journal.* 28 August 2013. http://www.bizjournals.com/sanjose/news/2013/01/10/allegis-bob-ackerman-sees-growing.html?page=all. 10 January 2013.

[38] Clayton, Mark. *Christian Science Monitor.* 14 September 2012. http://www.csmonitor.com/USA/2012/0914/Stealing-US-business-secrets-Experts-ID-two-huge-cyber-gangs-in-China. 2013 August 28.

[39] Memory Alpha. n.d. http://en.memory-alpha.org/wiki/Eminiar-Vendikar_War. 2013 August 28.

[40] Walzer, Michael. *Just and Unjust Wars: A Moral Argument with Historical Illustrations.* New York: Basic Books, 2000.

[41] Tenet, George. *At the Center of the Storm: My Years at the CIA.* New York: Harper Collins, 2007.

[42] Issacson, Walter. *Einstein: His Life and Universe.* New York: Simon & Schuster, 2007.

[43] Tenet, George. *At the Center of the Storm: My Years at the CIA.* New York: Harper Collins, 2007.

[44] Ibid.

[45] Tajdin, Behrang. 27 April 2013. 19 June 2013. <http://www.bbc.co.uk/news/world-middle-east-22281336>.

[46] Mahr, Krista. *Time* . 31 January 2011. http://science.time.com/2011/01/31/bread-is-life-food-and-protest-in-egypt/. 23 January 2014.

[47] Bucci, Steven P, Paul Rosenzweig and David Inserra. 1 April 2013. Heritage Foundation. 19 June 2013. <http://www.heritage.org/research/reports/2013/04/a-congressional-guide-seven-steps-to-us-security-prosperity-and-freedom-in-cyberspace>.

[48] Hess, Pamela and Ann Sanner. 14 January 2010. 19 June 2013. <http://www.boston.com/news/nation/washington/articles/2010/01/14/bombing_suspect_had_no_coat_luggage/>.

[49] Lee, Kuan Yew. Grand Master's Insights on China, the United States and the World. London: M.I.T. Press, 2013.

[50] Acemoglu, Daron and James A. Robinson. *Why Nations Fail: The Origins of Power, Prosperity and Poverty.* New York: Crown Business, 2012.

51 Ibid.

[53] Ibid.

Chapter 3 End Notes

1 Meckler, Laura. *Wall Street Journal.* 18 February 2003. http://online.wsj.com/news/articles/SB10001424127887323764804578312330678211000. 20 January 2014.

[2] Passel, Jeffrey S, D'Vera Cohn and Ana Gonzalez-Barrera. *Pew Hispanic Center.* 23 September 2013. http://www.pewhispanic.org/2013/09/23/population-decline-of-unauthorized-immigrants-stalls-may-have-reversed/. 20 January 2014.

[3] Beckhusen, Robert. *Wired.* 11 February 2013. http://www.wired.com/dangerroom/2013/02/border-sensors/. 20 January 2014.

[4] Shactman, Noah. *Wired.* 29 May 2012. http://www.wired.com/dangerroom/2012/05/spy-rock/?pid=1206#slideid-1206. 20 January 2014.

[5] *Military Times.* 1 September 2009. http://forums.militarytimes.com/showthread.php?1579761-Unattended-Ground-Sensor-being-designed-tested. 20 January 2014.

[6] National Public Radio (NPR). 4 December 2011. http://www.npr.org/2011/12/04/143025654/migrants-say-theyre-unwilling-mules-for-cartels. 21 January 2014.

[7] Rollins, Jess. *USA Today*, 10 February 2013. http://www.usatoday.com/story/news/nation/2013/02/10/missouri-meth-smuggling-illegal-immigrants/1907003/. 21 January 2014.

[8] *U.S. Immigration and Customs Enforcement.* 30 November 2011. http://www.ice.gov/news/releases/1111/111130sandiego.htm. 21 January 2014.

[9] Ibid.

[10] *U.S. Immigration and Customs Enforcement.* 27 June 2013. https://www.ice.gov/news/releases/1306/130627nogales.htm. 21 January 2014.

[11] *Public Safety Canada.* 2012. http://www.publicsafety.gc.ca/cnt/rsrcs/pblctns/cnsdrtns-ntdstts-cnd/cnsdrtns-ntdstts-cnd-eng.pdf. 21 January 2014.

[12] *U.S. Department of Transportation.* 5 December 2013. http://www.rita.dot.gov/bts/sites/rita.dot.gov.bts/files/bts53_13_0.pdf. 21 January 2014.

[13] GlobalSecurity.org. 13 July 2011. http://www.globalsecurity.org/security/systems/mobile-rpm.htm. 14 January 2014.

[14] *Global Biodefense.* 4 October 2012. http://globalbiodefense.com/2012/10/04/chemical-biological-mass-spectrometer-ii-award-hamilton-sundstrand/. 21 January 2014.

[15] Frittelli, John F. *Congressional Research Service.* 27 March 2005. http://www.fas.org/sgp/crs/homesec/RL31733.pdf. 21 January 2014.

[16] U.S. Department of Transportation. *Research and Innovation Technology Administration.* January 2011. http://www.rita.dot.gov/bts/sites/rita.dot.gov.bts/files/publications/americas_container_ports/2011/pdf/entire.pdf. 21 January 2014.

[17] Donohue, Nathan. *Center for Strategic & International Studies.* 7 September 2012. http://csis.org/blog/inherent-insecurity. 21 January 2014.

[18] Ibid.

[19] Frantz, Douglas. *Washington Post.* 15 July 2012. http://www.washingtonpost.com/world/national-security/port-security-us-fails-to-meet-deadline-for-scanning-of-cargo-containers/2012/07/15/gJQAmgW8mW_story.html. 21 January 2014.

[20] Ibid.

[21] Ibid.

[22] *International Atomic Energy Agency (IAEA).* n.d. http://www.iaea.org/safeguards/Symposium/2010/Documents/PapersRepository/037.pdf. 21 January 2014.

[23] Edwards, Rob. *New Scientist.* 21 July 2003. http://www.newscientist.com/article/dn3960-krypton-clue-to-north-korean-nuclear-progress.html#.Ut7na_ko6IU. 21 January 2014.

[24] *Huffington Post,* 28 February 2012. http://www.huffingtonpost.com/2012/02/27/us-iran-mine-warfare-persian-gulf_n_1304107.html. 21 January 2014.

[25] Rabiroff, Jon. *Stars and Stripes.* 9 May 2011. http://www.stripes.com/news/u-s-military-enters-new-generation-of-sea-mine- warfare-1.143170. 21 January 2014.

[26] Kouri, Jim. *Washington Examiner.* 20 March 2011. http://www.examiner.com/article/illegal-aliens-from-terrorist-sponsoring-nations-revealed-report. 21 January 2014.

[27] Ibid.

Chapter 4 End Notes

1 Walsh, Declan. *The Guardian*, 5 December 2010. http://www.theguardian.com/world/2010/dec/05/wikileaks-cables-saudi-terrorist-funding. 6 October 2013.

[2] U.S. Government Printing Office. July 2004. http://www.gpo.gov/fdsys/pkg/GPO-911REPORT/pdf/GPO-911REPORT.pdf. 27 August 2013.

[3] McCurry, Justin. *The Guardian,* 3 May 2012. http://www.theguardian.com/environment/2012/may/03/japan-nuclear-power-closure. 7 September 2013

[4] 5 August 2013. *World Nuclear Association.* http://www.world-nuclear.org/info/Country-Profiles/Countries-G-N/Japan/#.UiupFfm1EZ4. 7 September 2013.

[5] "World Nuclear News." 18 June 2012. http://www.world-nuclear-news.org/RS-Ohi_reactors_cleared_for_restart-1806124.html. 7 September 2013.

[6] Douglass, Elizabeth. *Inside Climate News.* 24 September 2013. http://insideclimatenews.org/news/20130924/first-us-nuclear-power-closures- 15-years-signal-wider-problems-industry?page=show. 6 October 2013.

[7] Hargreaves, Steve. CNN, 15 March 2011. http://money.cnn.com/2011/03/15/news/economy/nuclear_plants_us/index .htm. 7 September 2013.

[8] *Nuclear Regulatory Commission.* 19 June 2012. http://www.nrc.gov/reading-rm/doc-collections/fact-sheets/fs-reactor-license-renewal.html. 8 September 2013.

[9] Nairn, Carly. *San Francisco Bay Guardian.* 14 April 2011. http://www.sfbg.com/politics/2011/04/14/anti-nuclear-movement-gears. 8 September 2013.

[10] Wald, Matthew. *New York Times.* 8 June 1989. http://www.nytimes.com/1989/06/08/us/voters-in-a-first-shut-down-nuclear-reactor.html. 8 September 2013.

[11] Walker, Mark. *San Diego Union Tribune.* 7 June 2013. http://www.utsandiego.com/news/2013/Jun/07/sanonofre-closure-reaction-edison-nuclear/2/?#article-copy. 8 September 2013.

[12] O'Sullivan, Meghan L. *Bloomberg*. 14 February 2013. http://www.bloomberg.com/news/2013-02-14/-energy-independence-alone-won-t-boost-u-s-power.html. 8 September 2013.

[13] *U.S. Energy Information Administration*. 25 July 2013. http://www.eia.gov/forecasts/ieo/world.cfm. 8 September 2013.

[14] Zhou, Moming. 18 January 2013. *Bloomberg*. http://www.bloomberg.com/news/2013-01-18/u-s-oil-demand-falls-to-16-year-low-api-reports.html. 8 September 2013.

[15] n.d. *Index Mundi*. http://www.indexmundi.com/energy.aspx?country=us&product=oil&graph=consumption. 8 September 2013.

[16] *U.S. Energy Information Administration. n.d.* http://www.eia.gov/countries/index.cfm?view=consumption. 8 September 2013.

[17] *U.S. Energy Information Adiministration*. n.d. http://www.eia.gov/countries/index.cfm?topL=imp. 8 September 2013.

[18] Applebaum, Anne. *Washington Post*. 4 January 2011. http://www.washingtonpost.com/wp-dyn/content/article/2011/01/03/AR2011010304070.html. 8 September 2013.

[19] Remarks by Henry Kissinger at the annual meeting of the National Conference of State Legislators in Detroit, Michigan August 3, 1977.

[20] Friedman, Thomas. *New York Times*. 24 August 2013. http://www.nytimes.com/2013/08/25/opinion/sunday/friedman-foreign-policy-by-whisper-and-nudge.html?ref=thomaslfriedman&_r=0. 8 September 2013.

[21] Zhou, Moming. *Bloomberg*. 25 July 2013. http://www.bloomberg.com/news/2013-07-25/world-to-use-56-more-energy- by-2040-led-by-asia-eia-predicts.html. 6 October 2013.

[22] Sullivan, Kevin. *Washington Post*. 3 December 2012. http://articles.washingtonpost.com/2012-12-03/world/35623000_1_saudi-arabia-poverty-rate-royals. 6 October 2013.

[23] Klier, Thomas H. and Rubenstein, James. "Detroit back from the brink? Auto industry crisis and restructuring, 2008-11." *Economic Perspectives* (2012): 35-54.

[24] Dargay, Joyce, Dermot Gately and Martin Sommer. "Vehicle Ownership and Income Growth, Worldwide: 1960-2030 ." *Energy Journal* (2007): 143-170. http://www.jstor.org/discover/10.2307/41323125?uid=3739832&uid=2&uid=4&uid=3739256&sid=21102595214121. 8 September 2013.

[25] *U.S. Senate Committee on Energy and Natural Resources.* 2 February 2012. http://www.energy.senate.gov/public/index.cfm/files/serve?File_id=d1881c5 3-9805-4cb0-a4c8-b3495f0873f4. 9 September 2013.

[26] Carnesale, Albert. *National Academy of Engineering.* 2012. http://www.nae.edu/Publications/Bridge/59220/59224.aspx. 10 September 2013.

[27] *Oregon Live.* 15 June 2013. U.S. taxpayers face mounting liabilities from dozens of lawsuits stemming from the government's failure to meet its nuclear waste management obligations. 7 October 2013.

[28] *C-SPAN.* 7 June 2012. http://c-spanvideo.org/program/StorageF. 9 September 2013.

[29] *Blue Ribbon Commission on America's Nuclear Future Final Report.* January 2012. http://cybercemetery.unt.edu/archive/brc/20120620220235/http://brc.gov/si tes/default/files/documents/brc_finalreport_jan2012.pdf. 10 September 2013.

[30] McMahon, Jeff. *Forbes.* 30 June 2013. http://www.forbes.com/sites/jeffmcmahon/2013/06/30/u-s-runs-out-of-nuclear-fuel-from-russian-warheads/. 9 September 2013.

[31] Russell, Pam Radtke. *Roll Call.* 5 February 2013. http://www.rollcall.com/news/budget_cutters_eye_nuclear_reprocessing_plan t-222173-1.html?pg=1. 9 September 2013.

[32] Fortin, Jacey. *International Business Times.* 6 February 2013. http://www.ibtimes.com/niger-new-disputes-over-french-uranium-extraction-1064546. 6 October 2013.

[33] Ibid.

[34] *Nuclear Energy Institute.* 23 December 2002. http://www.nei.org/News-Media/Media-Room/News-Releases/Analysis-of-Nuclear-Power-Plants-Shows-Aircraft-Cr. 9 September 2013.

[35] *Nuclear Energy Institute.* August 2011. http://www.nei.org/Master-Document-Folder/Backgrounders/Fact-Sheets/Nuclear-Power-Plant-Security. 9 September 2013.

[36] *New York Times.* 22 September 2005. http://www.nytimes.com/2005/09/22/business/RITA-FACTBOX.html?_r=0. 9 September 2013.

[37] *NBC Meet The Press.* 18 April 2004. http://www.nbcnews.com/id/4829855#.Ui3AXfm1EZ4. 9 September 2013.

[38] *U.S. Energy Information Administration.* 21 June 2013. http://www.eia.gov/dnav/pet/hist/LeafHandler.ashx?n=PET&s=8_NA_8O0 _NUS_C&f=A. 9 September 2013.

[39] *U.S. Energy Information Administration.* 21 June 2013. http://www.eia.gov/dnav/pet/hist/LeafHandler.ashx?n=PET&s=8_NA_8D0_NUS_4&f=A. 9 September 2013

[40] *U.S. Energy Information Administration.* 7 May 2013. http://www.eia.gov/energy_in_brief/article/renewable_electricity.cfm. 10 September 2013.

[41] *power-technology.com.* n.d. http://www.power-technology.com/projects/coulee/. 10 September 2013.

[42] U.S. Geological Survey. 23 May 23. http://ga.water.usgs.gov/edu/hybiggest.html. 10 September 2013.

[43] Davidson, Amy. *The New Yorker.* 30 April 2012. http://www.newyorker.com/online/blogs/closeread/2012/04/jose-rodriguez- 60-minutes-torture.html. 10 September 2013.

[44] *Jewish Virtual Library.* n.d. http://www.jewishvirtuallibrary.org/jsource/Peace/osloterr.html. 10 September 2013.

Chapter 5 End Notes

[1] *U.S. Government Printing Office.* July 2004. http://www.gpo.gov/fdsys/pkg/GPO-911REPORT/pdf/GPO-911REPORT.pdf. 27 August 2013.

[2] Hawley, Kip. *Wall Street Journal.* 15 April 2012. http://online.wsj.com/article/SB10001424052702303815404577335783535660546.html. 14 October 2013.

[3] Messing, Philip. *New York Post.* 12 August 2012. http://nypost.com/2012/08/12/stranded-jet-skier-saunters-through-jfk-safeguards/. 14 October 2013.

[4] Grier, Peter. *Christian Science Monitor.* 10 May 2010. http://www.csmonitor.com/USA/2010/0510/Times-Square-bomb-Did-Pakistan-Taliban-send-its-C-team. 14 October 2013.

[5] Leinwand, Donna. *USA Today.* 9 May 2007. http://usatoday30.usatoday.com/news/nation/2007-05-08-fort-dix-plot_N.htm. 15 October 2013.

[6] Swaine, Jon. *The Telegraph.* 4 August 2013. http://www.telegraph.co.uk/news/worldnews/northamerica/usa/10220449/Fort-Hood-shooter-Nidal-Hasan-left-free-to-kill.html. 15 October 2013.

[7] Anastasia, George. *Philadelphia Inquirer.* 27 June 2010. http://articles.philly.com/2010-06-27/news/24965417_1_muslim-community-fort-dix-informant. 15 October 2013.

[8] McCarthy, Andrew C. *National Review.* 7 August 2010. http://www.nationalreview.com/articles/243635/more-moderate-muslims-andrew-c-mccarthy?splash=. 16 October 2013.

[9] Dorell, Oren. *USA Today.* 25 April 2013. http://www.usatoday.com/story/news/nation/2013/04/23/boston-mosque-radicals/2101411/. 16 October 2013.

[10] Subcommittee on Transportation Security . *Rebuilding TSA into a Smarter, Leaner Organization.* Majority Staff Report. Washington, DC, 2012. http://homeland.house.gov/sites/homeland.house.gov/files/092012_TSA_Reform_Report.pdf.

Swaine, Jon. *The Telegraph.* 4 August 2013.

[1] Reed, Dan. *USA Today.* 30 March 2010. http://usatoday30.usatoday.com/travel/flights/2010-03-29-airline-passengers-revenue-decline_N.htm. 17 October 2013.

[2] U.S. Department of Transportation. *Bureau of Transportation Statistics (BTS).* 4 April 2013. http://www.rita.dot.gov/bts/press_releases/bts016_13. 17 October 2013.

[3] Johanson, Mark. *International Business Times.* 4 September 2013. http://www.ibtimes.com/7-questions-about-tsas-precheck-program-answered-1402795. 17 October 2013.

[4] U.S. Department of Transportation. *Bureau of Transportation Statistics (BTS).* 4 April 2013. http://www.rita.dot.gov/bts/press_releases/bts016_13. 17 October 2013.

[5] Jansen, Bart. *USA Today.* 4 September 2013. http://www.usatoday.com/story/travel/flights/2013/09/04/tsa-pre-check-airports/2763495/. 17 October 2013.

[6] Hawley, Kip. *Wall Street Journal.* 15 April 2012. http://online.wsj.com/article/SB10001424052702303815404577335783535660546.html. 14 October 2013.

[7] *Associated Press.* 2013 June 11. http://news.yahoo.com/news-summary-civilian-planes-shot-down-manpads-153105655.html. 17 October 2013.

[8] Cushman Jr, John H. *New York Times.* 17 January 1988. http://www.nytimes.com/1988/01/17/weekinreview/the-world-the-stinger-missile-helping-to-change-the-course-of-a-war.html. 19 October 2013.

[9] Kuperman, Alan J. "The Stinger Missile and U.S. Intervention in Afghanistan." *Political Science Quarterly,* (1999): 219-263.

[20] Ibid.

[2] White, Jeremy. *Huffington Post.* 28 July 2010. http://www.huffingtonpost.com/jeremy-white/taliban-missiles-likely-s_b_662812.html. 19 October 2013.

[22] Tucker-Jones, Anthony. *Homeland1.* 9 September 2010. http://www.homeland1.com/air-traffic/articles/879393-Successful-surface-to- air-missile-attack-shows-threat-to-airliners/. 19 October 2013.

[23] U.S. State Department. 27 July 2011. http://www.state.gov/t/pm/rls/fs/169139.htm. 19 October 2013.

[24] Magnusun, Stew. *National Defense Magazine.* April 2006. http://www.nationaldefensemagazine.org/archive/2006/April/Pages/aircraft2990.aspx. 19 October 2013.

[25] CNN. 17 June 2004. http://www.cnn.com/2004/ALLPOLITICS/06/16/911.commission/. 19 October 2013.

[26] *National Priorities Project.* 27 August 2013. http://nationalpriorities.org/cost-of/notes-sources/. 19 October 2013.

[27] Stiglitz, Joseph E. *Slate.* 1 September 2011. http://www.slate.com/articles/business/project_syndicate/2011/09/the_true_cost_of_911.html. 19 October 2013.

[28] Pena, Charles. *CATO Institute.* 19 April 2005. http://www.cato.org/sites/cato.org/files/pubs/pdf/pa541.pdf. 19 October 2013.

[29] Brice, Arthur. CNN. 3 June 2013. http://www.cnn.com/2013/06/03/world/americas/iran-latin-america/. 19 October 2013.

[30] Lewis, Paul. *New York Times.* 26 October 1988. http://www.nytimes.com/1988/10/26/world/nancy-reagan-at-un-says-us-must-do-more-to-combat-drugs.html. 19 October 2013.

[3] Heyl, Eric. *Trib Live.* 24 August 2013. http://triblive.com/opinion/qanda/4569182-74/drugs-drug-think#axzz2iCznrfBO. 19 October 2013.

[32] Saad, Lydia. *Gallup.* 24 July 2008. http://www.gallup.com/poll/109048/us-smoking-rate-still-coming-down.aspx. 19 October 2013.

[33] *Centers for Disease Control and Drug Prevention.* 5 June 2013. http://www.cdc.gov/tobacco/data_statistics/fact_sheets/adult_data/cig_smoking/ 19 October 2013.

Chapter 6 End Notes

1 Garner, Dwight. *New York Times.* 29 October 2013. http://www.nytimes.com/2013/10/30/books/the-siege-describes-the-attack-on-the-taj-hotel-in-mumbai.html. 20 December 2013.

[2] Arthur, Charles. *The Guardian.* 27 November 2008. http://www.theguardian.com/technology/2008/nov/27/mumbai-terror-attacks-twitter-flickr. 20 December 2013.

[3] Woodward, Bob. *Obama's Wars.* New York : Simon & Schuster, 2010.

[4] Heritage Foundation. *Al-Qaeda: Declarations & Acts of War.* n.d. http://www.heritage.org/research/projects/enemy-detention/al-qaeda-declarations. 20 December 2013.

[5] Rubin, Uzi. *Jerusalem Center for Public Affairs.* 25 August 2009. http://jcpa.org/article/new-developments-in-irans-missile-capabilities-implications-beyond-the-middle-east/. 20 December 2013.

[6] Hipp, Van. Fox News. 26 January 2013. http://www.foxnews.com/opinion/2013/01/26/time-to-get-tough-with-north-korea-and-iran-as-imminent-nuclear-bomb-test-looms/. 20 December 2013.

[7] Cordesman, Anthony H and Bryan Gold. *Center for Strategic & International Studies (CSIS).* 9 December 2013. http://csis.org/files/publication/131207_gulf_military_balance.pdf. 20 December 2013.

[8] Broad, William J, James Glanz and David E. Sanger. *New York Times.* 28 November 2010. http://www.nytimes.com/2010/11/29/world/middleeast/29missiles.html. 20 December 2013.

[9] *Yumpu.* n.d. http://www.yumpu.com/en/document/view/3516145/growing-your-way-south-bend-airport. 15 December 2013.

[10] Riddel, J. Niles. *Federation of American Scientists.* 2 December 1992. http://www.fas.org/irp/fbis/riddel.html. 20 December 2013.

[11] *Advance HR.* 9 December 2013. http://www.advance.hr/vijesti/intervju-drugi-covjek-hezbollaha-sheikh-naim-qassem-o-siriji-i-drugim-temama-sad-i-zaljevske-zemlje-se-osjecaju-ugrozeno-znaju-da-ce-na-kraju-morati-ponovno-uspostaviti-odnose-s-assadom/. 24 December 2013.

[12] John Hagel III, John Seely Brown and Lang Davison. "Harvard Business Review." 19 June 2009. http://blogs.hbr.org/2009/06/measuring-the-big-shift/. 20 December 2013.
<http://blogs.hbr.org/bigshift/2009/06/measuring-the-big-shift.html>.

[13] Friedman, Thomas. *New York Times.* 19 January 2010.
http://www.nytimes.com/2010/01/20/opinion/20friedman.html?_r=0. 15 December 2013.

[14] Best, Richard A, Jr and Alfred Cumming. *Congressional Research Service.* 5 December 2007. http://www.fas.org/sgp/crs/intel/RL34270.pdf. 20 December 2013.

[15] Smith, James M. *Airpower Journal.* n.d.
http://www.airpower.maxwell.af.mil/airchronicles/apj/apj98/fal98/smith.html . 21 December 2013.

[16] U.S. Government Printing Office. *PREPARING FOR THE 21ST CENTURY: AN APPRAISAL OF U.S. INTELLIGENCE.* 1 March 1996. http://www.gpo.gov/fdsys/pkg/GPO-INTELLIGENCE/pdf/GPO-INTELLIGENCE-12.pdf. 21 December 2013.

[17] U.S. Government Printing Office. *The Commission on the Intelligence Capabilities of the United States Regarding Weapons of Mass Destruction.* 31 March 2005. http://www.gpo.gov/fdsys/pkg/GPO-WMD/pdf/GPO-WMD.pdf. 21 December 2013.

[18] Ibid.

[19] Doyle, Arthur Conan. *The Complete Sherlock Holmes.* Garden City: Double Day, 1930.

[20] Ibid.

[21] Ibid.

[22] Ibid.

[23] *European Commission.* n.d. http://ec.europa.eu/digital-agenda/futurium/en/content/can-twitter-predict-future-pentagon-says-maybe. 28 December 2013.

[24] C-SPAN. 10 April 2001. http://c-spanvideo.org/program/TheSupremeC. 21 December 2013.

[25] Kurtz, Howard. *Washington Post.* 20 September 2004.
http://www.washingtonpost.com/wp-dyn/articles/A34153-2004Sep19.html. 24 December 2013.

[26] Nixon, Richard. *Leaders.* New York: Warner Books Inc., 1982.

[27] Ibid.

[28] Ibid.

[29] Nixon, Richard. *Seize The Moment: America's Challenge In A One-Superpower World.* New York: Simon & Schuster, 1992.
[30] Fensom, Anthony. *The Diplomat.* 8 January 2013. http://thediplomat.com/2013/01/americas-economy-still-1-for-now/. 24 December 2013.
[31] PBS. *Lt. Gen. Arthur MacArthur, Jr. (1845 - 1912)* . n.d. http://www.pbs.org/wgbh/amex/macarthur/peopleevents/pandeAMEX107.html. 21 December 2013.
[32] Rovere, Richard H and Arthur, Jr. Schlesinger. *General MacArthur and President Truman: The Struggle for Control of American Foreign Policy.* New Brunswick: Transaction Publishers, 1992.
[33] PBS. *American Experience.* n.d. http://www.pbs.org/wgbh/amex/macarthur/peopleevents/pandeAMEX110.html. 24 December 2013.
[34] Ayyildiz, Judy. *Ataturk Society of America.* n.d. http://www.ataturksociety.org/speech_details.asp?id=58. 24 December 2013.

Chapter 7 End Notes

1 Bennett, William J. *Why We Fight.* Washington: Regnery, 2003.
[2] Madison, James. *Federalist 41.* n.d. http://www.constitution.org/fed/federa41.htm. 10 November 2013.
[3] *The Mariners Museum.* n.d. http://www.marinersmuseum.org/sites/micro/usnavy/04/04a.htm. 13 November 2013.
[4] Gettleman, Jeffrey. *New York Times.* 11 April 2009. http://www.nytimes.com/2009/04/12/weekinreview/12gettleman.html?_r=0. 13 November 2013.
[5] Pew Research Religion & Public Life Project. *Pew Forum.* 27 January 2011. http://www.pewforum.org/2011/01/27/the-future-of-the-global-muslim-population/. 14 November 2013.
[6] Sarker, Abraham. *Understand My Muslim People.* Newberg: Barclay Press, 2004.
[7] Zakaria, Fareed. *The Future of Freedom: Illiberal Democracy at Home and Abroad (Revised Edition).* New York: W.W. Norton & Company, 2007.
[8] Reddy, Sudeep. *Wall Street Journal.* 17 April 2013. http://blogs.wsj.com/economics/2013/04/17/where-the-worlds-poorest-people-live/. 13 November 2013.

[9] Baker, Peter. *New York Times.* 2 July 2013. http://www.nytimes.com/2013/07/03/world/africa/bush-a-fond-presence-in-africa-for-work-during-and-since-his-presidency.html?_r=0. 14 November 2013.
[10] Robinson, Eugene. *Washington Post.* 26 July 2012. http://articles.washingtonpost.com/2012-07-26/opinions/35487798_1_african-countries-pepfar-antiretroviral-treatment. 13 November 2013.
[11] Reddy, Sudeep. *Wall Street Journal.* 17 April 2013. http://blogs.wsj.com/economics/2013/04/17/where-the-worlds-poorest-people-live/. 13 November 2013.
[12] Pew Research Religion & Life Project. *Pew Forum.* 15 April 2010. http://www.pewforum.org/2010/04/15/traditional-african-religious-beliefs-and-practices-islam-and-christianity-in-sub-saharan-africa/. 13 November 2013.
[13] Avlon, John. *Daily Beast.* 13 September 2011. http://www.thedailybeast.com/articles/2011/09/13/irshad-manji-faithful-dissent-against-radical-islam.html. 14 November 2013.
[14] Pew Research Religion & Public Life Project. *Pew Forum.* 30 April 2013. http://www.pewforum.org/2013/04/30/the-worlds-muslims-religion-politics-society-beliefs-about-sharia/. 14 November 2013.
[15] Pew Research Global Attitudes Project. *Pew Global.* 10 September 2013. http://www.pewglobal.org/2013/09/10/muslim-publics-share-concerns-about-extremist-groups/. 14 November 2013.
[6] Ibid.
[17] Zakaria, Fareed. *Washington Post.* 27 May 2008. http://newsweek.washingtonpost.com/postglobal/fareed_zakaria/2008/05/the_only_thing_we_have_to_fear.html. 15 November 2013.
[18] AFP. 26 May 2013. http://www.google.com/hostednews/afp/article/ALeqM5j3T_NqxOSD-dCPTsIk6JWo_ixXcw?docId=CNG.345f824dea2ecdf955e9644d2d0ed9f4.881. 15 November 2013.
[19] Pew Research Center. *Pew Research.* 7 June 2013. http://www.pewresearch.org/fact-tank/2013/06/07/as-it-fights-in-syria-hezbollah-seen-unfavorably-in-region/. 15 November 2013.
[20] *Daily Motion.* n.d. http://www.dailymotion.com/video/xx7gp7_pure-history-features-the-cult-of-the-suicide-bomber_shortfilms. 14 November 2013.
[21] Totten, Michael J. *Commentary.* 29 December 2009. http://www.commentarymagazine.com/2009/12/29/the-iranian-regimes-battle-of-karbala/. 14 November 2013.

[22] Jupp, Michael. *New York Times.* 19 December 1988. http://www.nytimes.com/1988/12/19/opinion/l-child-soldier-treaty-has-wide-support-697888.html?src=pm. 14 November 2013.

[23] Kuntzel, Matthias. *Articles by Matthias Kuntzel.* 30 July 2006. http://www.matthiaskuentzel.de/contents/ahmadinejads-world. 14 November 2013.

[24] *United Human Rights Council.* n.d. http://www.unitedhumanrights.org/genocide/genocide-in-sudan.htm. 14 November 2013.

[25] United Nations. *United Nations Security Council.* 30 July 2004. http://www.un.org/en/ga/search/view_doc.asp?symbol=S/RES/1556(2004). 14 November 2013.

[26] United Nations. *United Nations Security Council.* 18 September 2004. http://www.un.org/News/Press/docs/2004/sc8191.doc.htm. 15 November 2013.

[27] United Nations. *United Nations Security Council.* 29 March 2005. http://www.un.org/News/Press/docs/2005/sc8346.doc.htm. 2013 November 2013.

[28] The World Bank. 26 December 2012. http://www.worldbank.org/en/news/feature/2012/12/26/indonesia-reconstruction-chapter-ends-eight-years-after-the-tsunami. 14 November 2013.

[29] *USA Today.* 12 November 2013. http://www.usatoday.com/story/opinion/2013/11/12/the-philippines-typhoon-haiyan-2004-tsunami-indonesia-editorials-debates/3511421/. 14 November 2013.

[30] Frum, David. *The Right Man: The Surprise Presidency of George W. Bush.* New York: Random House, 2003.

[31] Lewis, Bernard. *The Atlantic.* 1 September 1990. http://www.theatlantic.com/magazine/archive/1990/09/the-roots-of-muslim-rage/304643/. 14 November 2013.

[32] Ibid.

[33] Ibid.

[34] U.S. Government Printing Office. July 2004. http://www.gpo.gov/fdsys/pkg/GPO-911REPORT/pdf/GPO-911REPORT.pdf. 27 August 2013.

[35] Habeck, Mary. *Heritage Foundation.* 8 November 2004. http://www.heritage.org/research/lecture/jihadist-strategies-in-the-war-on-terrorism. 13 November 2013.

[36] Ibrahim, Raymond. *The Al-Qaeda Reader.* New York: Broadway Books, 2007.

[37] Ibid.

[38] http://www.theguardian.com/uk/2005/jul/19/iraq.july7. 30 August 2014.

[39] *BBC News:* 12 Februar,y 2003. http://news.bbc.co.uk/2/hi/middle_east/2751019.stm. 15 November 2013.

[40] Sarwar, Muhammad. *The Holy Quran: Arabic Text and English Translation (6th Edition).* April 2011. http://www.theislamicseminary.org/quran.html. 15 November 2013.

[41] Teitelbaum, Joshua. *Jerusalem Center for Public Affairs.* 27 August 2008. http://jcpa.org/text/ahmadinejad2-words.pdf. 15 November 2013.

[42] RealClearPolitics.com, 23 September 2012. http://www.realclearpolitics.com/video/2012/09/23/bill_maher_on_islam_all_religions_are_not_alike.html. 13 November 2012.

[43] Maher, Bill. *Wikiquote.* 12 November 2013. http://en.wikiquote.org/wiki/Bill_Maher. 13 November 2013.

[44] Schlesinger Jr., Arthur. *Los Angeles Times.* 12 March 2000. http://articles.latimes.com/2000/mar/12/books/bk-7842/3. 15 November 2013.

[45] Wallace, Henry. *TeachingAmericanHistory.org.* 27 March 1947. http://teachingamericanhistory.org/library/index.asp?document=852. 15 November 2013.

[46] Clinton, Bill. *My Life.* New York: Alfred A. Knopf, 2004.

[47] Kaufman, Robert G. *Henry M. Jackson: A Life Time in Politics.* Seattle: University of Washington Press, 2000.

[48] Mitgang, Herbert. *New York Times.* 15 November 2013. http://www.nytimes.com/1989/04/15/books/books-of-the-times-fulbright-has-the-last-laugh-on-many-critics.html. 15 April 1989.

[49] Kennedy, John F. *John F. Kennedy Presidential Library and Museum.* 20 January 1961. http://www.jfklibrary.org/Asset-Viewer/BqXIEM9F4024ntFl7SVAjA.aspx. 15 November 2013.

[50] Binder, David. *New York Times.* 3 January 1988. http://www.nytimes.com/1988/01/03/books/in-short-nonfiction-770088.html. 13 November 2013.

[51] de Borchgrave, Arnaud. *Washington Times.* 13 January 2004. http://www.washingtontimes.com/news/2004/jan/13/20040113-085236-5919r/?page=all#pagebreak. 13 November 2013.

[52] Pacepa, Ion Mihai. *Red Horizons: the 2nd Book. The True Story of Nicolae and Elena Ceaușescu's Crimes, Lifestyle, and Corruption.* Washington: Regnery Gateway, 1990.

[53] Pew Research Global Attitudes Project. *Pew Global.* 13 November 2013. http://www.pewglobal.org/2013/06/04/the-global-divide-on-homosexuality/. 4 June 2013.

[54] Woodward, Bob. *Shadow: Five Presidents and The Legacy of Watergate.* New York : Simon & Schuster, 1999.

[55] Hana, Adel. *USA Today.* 11 February 2004. http://usatoday30.usatoday.com/news/world/2004-02-11-arafat-wife_x.htm. 15 November 2013.

[56] Vardi, Nathan. *Forbes.* 17 March 2003. http://www.forbes.com/forbes/2003/0317/049.html. 15 November 2013.

[57] Robbins, Liz. *New York Times.* 17 February 2009. http://www.nytimes.com/2009/02/18/nyregion/18behead.html. 15 November 2013.

[58] Nomani, Asra Q. *Daily Beast.* 23 February 2009. http://www.thedailybeast.com/articles/2009/02/23/deadly-family-secrets.html. 15 November 2013.

[59] Gandy, Kim. *National Organization of Women.* 20 February 2009. http://www.now.org/news/note/022009.html. 15 November 2013.

[60] Alami, Aida. *New York Times.* 15 November 2013. http://www.nytimes.com/2013/04/11/world/middleeast/morocco-slow-to-enforce-laws-on-womens-rights.html. 10 April 2013.

[61] Page, Susan. *USA Today.* 22 April 2008. http://usatoday30.usatoday.com/news/washington/2008-04-21-bushrating_N.htm. 15 November 2013.

[62] Woodward, Bob. *State of Denial: Bush at War, Part III.* New York: Simon & Schuster, 2006.

[63] Woodward, Bob. *Plan of Attack.* New York: Simon & Schuster, 2004.

[64] Almog, Doron. *Jerusalem Center for Public Affairs.* 23 December 2004. http://www.jcpa.org/brief/brief004-12.htm. 15 November 2013.

[65] *Jewish Virtual Library.* n.d. http://www.jewishvirtuallibrary.org/jsource/Peace/osloterr.html. 15 November 2013.

[66] Benmelech, Efraim and Claude Berrebi. "Human Capital and the Productivity of Suicide Bombers." *Journal of Economic Perspectives—Volume 21, Number 3* (Summer of 2007): 223-238.

http://www.kellogg.northwestern.edu/faculty/benmelech/html/BenmelechPapers/Human_Capital_Suicide_Bombers.pdf.

[67] Byman, Daniel. "Do Targeted Killings Work?" *Foreign Affairs* (2006): 95-111.
http://www12.georgetown.edu/sfs/cpass/Articles/BymanTargetedKillings.pdf.

[68] *Reuters.* 2 May 2011.
http://www.reuters.com/article/2011/05/02/binladen-palestinians-hamas-idUSLDE74110O20110502. 15 November 2013.

[69] Topousis, Tom. *New York Post.* 19 June 2010.
http://nypost.com/2010/06/19/imam-terror-error/#ixzz0rJTKPGE6. 15 November 2013.

[70] *CNN.* 8 September 2010.
http://transcripts.cnn.com/TRANSCRIPTS/1009/08/lkl.01.html. 15 November 2013.

Chapter 8 End Notes

1 U.S. Senate Select Committee on Intelligence. *U.S. Intelligence Community's Prewar Intelligence Assessments on Iraq.* 9 July 2004.
http://www.intelligence.senate.gov/108301.pdf. 25 November 2013.

[2] *CNN Larry King Live Transcripts.* 22 July 2003.
http://transcripts.cnn.com/TRANSCRIPTS/0307/22/lkl.00.html. 5 December 2013.

[3] *CNN.* 8 June 2006.
http://www.cnn.com/2006/WORLD/meast/06/08/berg.interview/. 5 December 2013.

[4] Broder, David and Dan Balz. *Washington Post.* 16 July 2006.
http://www.washingtonpost.com/wp-dyn/content/article/2006/07/15/AR2006071500610.html. 10 December 2013.

[5] Ross, Elizabeth. *Christian Science Monitor.* 7 December 1992.
http://www.csmonitor.com/1992/1207/07082.html. 8 December 2013.

[6] Taubman, Philip. *The Partnership: Five Cold Warriors and Their Quest to Ban the Bomb.* New York : Harper Collins, 2012.

[7] Baker, James. *The Politics of Diplomacy: Revolution, War & Peace, 1989-1992.* New York: G.P. Putnam's Sons, 1995.

[8] *Arms Control Association.* July 2008. http://www.armscontrol.org/node/3289. 8 December 2013.

[9] Baker, Peter. *New York Times.* 3 December 2012. http://www.nytimes.com/2012/12/04/world/europe/obama-calls-on-russia- to-renew-weapons-pact.html?_r=0. 2013 December 2013.

[10] Bresolin, Justin. *The Center for Arms Control and Nonproliferation.* July 2003. http://armscontrolcenter.org/publications/factsheets/fact_sheet_the_cooperat ive_threat_reduction_program/. 8 December 2012.

[11] Frankel, Glenn. *Washington Post.* 17 September 1990. http://www.washingtonpost.com/wp-srv/inatl/longterm/iraq/stories/wartech091790.htm. 8 December 2013.

[12] *CNN Transcript: David Kay at Senate hearing.* 28 January 2004. http://www.cnn.com/2004/US/01/28/kay.transcript/. 5 December 2013.

[13] National Archives. *Executive Orders.* n.d. http://www.archives.gov/federal-register/codification/executive-order/12333.html. 5 December 2013.

[14] Branigin, William and Joby Warrick. *Washington Post.* 18 May 2004. http://www.washingtonpost.com/wp-dyn/articles/A33082-2004May17.html. 5 December 2013.

[15] *Huffington Post.* 1 September 2013. http://www.huffingtonpost.com/2013/09/01/what-is-sarin_n_3853044.html. 5 December 2013.

[16] CNN. 7 October 2004. http://www.cnn.com/2004/WORLD/meast/10/06/iraq.wmd.report/. 10 December 2013.

[17] Coll, Steve. *Iraq Foundation.* 3 November 3. http://www.iraqfoundation.org/news/2003/knov/3_hussein.html. 10 December 2013.

[18] CNN. 3 October 2003. http://www.cnn.com/2003/ALLPOLITICS/10/02/kay.report/. 10 December 2013.

[19] Feith, Douglas. *War and Decision.* New York : Harper Collins, 2008.

[20] Ibid.

[21] *Jewish Telegraph Agency.* 26 September 2002. http://www.jta.org/2002/09/26/archive/what-israelis-talk-about-when-they-use-the-word-matzav. 8 December 2013.

[22] Frum, David and Richard Perle. *An End To Evil: How To Win The War On Terror.* New York: Random House, 2004.

[23] Fabian, Jordan. *The Hill.* 4 May 2010. http://thehill.com/blogs/blog-briefing-room/news/95967-lieberman-wants-to-strip-citizenship-of-americans-who-join-foreign-terror-orgs. 10 December 2013.
[24] Benson, Guy. *Town Hall.* 13 October 2011. http://townhall.com/tipsheet/guybenson/2011/10/13/lieberman,_brown_introduce_legislation_to_strip_traitors_of_us_citizenship. 10 December 2013.
[25] Painter, William L. *Congressional Research Service.* 23 September 2013. http://www.fas.org/sgp/crs/homesec/R42985.pdf. 9 December 2013.
[26] Roig-Franzia, Manuel. *Washington Post.* 22 April 2005. http://www.washingtonpost.com/wp-dyn/articles/A7210-2005Apr21.html. 9 December 2013.
[27] *Australia Group.* July 2007. http://www.australiagroup.net/en/agb_july2007.pdf. 9 December 2013.
[28] *Organisation for the Prohibition of Chemical Weapons.* n.d. http://www.opcw.org/news-publications/publications/facts-and-figures/. 10 December 2013.
[29] Spencer, Richard. *Telegraph.* 29 October 2013. http://www.telegraph.co.uk/news/worldnews/middleeast/syria/10411375/Syr ia-inspectors-find-1300-tons-of-chemical-weapons.html. 10 December 2013.
[30] Lütticke, Marcus. *DW.* 11 October 2013. http://www.dw.de/opcw-leads-fight-against-chemical-weapons/a-17077312. 10 December 2013.
[31] *Nuclear Threat Initiative.* February 2013. http://www.nti.org/country-profiles/russia/chemical/. 10 December 2013.
[32] Griffin, Drew and Kathleen Johnston. *CNN.* 14 October 2013. http://www.cnn.com/2013/10/11/us/u-s-chemical-weapons/. 10 December 2013.
[33] Arms Control Association. September 2013. http://www.armscontrol.org/factsheets/LibyaChronology. 10 December 2013
[34] Arms Control Association. April 2013. http://www.armscontrol.org/factsheets/northkoreaprofile. 10 December 2013.
[35] Federal Bureau of Investigation. *Public Intelligence.* 14 October 2008. http://info.publicintelligence.net/FBIdomesticcbrn.pdf. 10 December 2013.
[36] Federal Bureau of Investigation. 17 April 2013. http://www.fbi.gov/news/pressrel/press-releases/fbi-response-to-reports-of-suspicious-letters-received-at-mail-facilities. 10 December 2013.
[37] *Jewish Telegraph Agency* . 21 April 1987. http://www.jta.org/1987/04/22/archive/karl-linnas-deported. 10 December 2013.

[38] Levin, Brian. *Huffington Post.* 19 April 2013. http://www.huffingtonpost.com/brian-levin-jd/radicalization-dzhokar-tamerlan-tsarnaev_b_3116466.html. 10 December 2013.

[39] Federal Bureau of Investigation (FBI). n.d. http://www.fbi.gov/stats-services/publications/terrorism-2002-2005/terror02_05#terror_05sum. 10 December 2013.

[40] Loftin, Clifton, et al. "Effects of restrictive licensing of handguns on homicide and suicide in the District of Columbia." *New England Journal of Medicine* (1991): 1615-1620. http://www.nejm.org/doi/pdf/10.1056/NEJM199112053252305.

[41] Gilmore, Janet. *Eureka Alert.* 16 February 2007. http://www.eurekalert.org/pub_releases/2007-02/uoc--nrr021207.php. 10 December 2013.

[42] McGreal, Chris. *Guardian.* 21 August 2011. http://www.theguardian.com/world/2011/aug/21/america-serious-crime-rate-plunging. 10 December 2013.

[43] Connolly, Matt. *The Examiner,* 10 December 2012. http://washingtonexaminer.com/d.c.-murders-fall-below-triple-digits-first-time-since-1963/article/2515584. 10 December 2013. <http://washingtonexaminer.com/d.c.-murders-fall-below-triple-digits-first-time-since-1963/article/2515584>.

[44] *BBC.* 24 November 2006. http://news.bbc.co.uk/2/hi/uk/6180682.stm. 10 December 2013.

[45] O'Reilly, Bill. *Whose Looking Out For You.* New York: Random House, 2003.

[46] Kocieniewski, David. *New York Times.* 17 September 2002. http://www.nytimes.com/2002/09/17/nyregion/challenger-to-torricelli-attacks-curbs-on-the-cia.html. 10 December 2013.

Chapter 9 End Notes

Perry, Mark J. *American Enterprise Institute.* 26 June 2013. http://www.aei-ideas.org/2013/06/federal-regulations-have-lowered-gdp-growth-by-2-per-year/. 3 January 2014.

[2] Gattuso, James. *Heritage Foundation.* 22 September 2010. http://blog.heritage.org/2010/09/22/red-tape-rises-again-cost-of-regulation-reaches-1-75-trillion/. 3 January 2014.

[3] Crews, Clyde Wayne and Ryan Young. *Competitive Enterprise Institute.* 5 June 2013. http://cei.org/op-eds-articles/twenty-years-non-stop-regulation. 3 January 2014.
[4] Whoriskey, Peter. *Washington Post.* 21 August 2012. http://www.washingtonpost.com/business/economy/regulations-an-economic-burden-to-manufacturers-report-says/2012/08/20/3aa4501a-eb01-11e1-9ddc-340d5efb1e9c_story.html. 3 January 2014.
[5] Norquist, Grover. *Human Events.* 7 February 2007. http://www.humanevents.com/2007/02/07/bush-budget-curbs-spending-growth/. 3 January 2014.
[6] Shaikh, Saad and James Leonard-Amodeo. *National Center for Biotechnology Information.* n.d. http://www.ncbi.nlm.nih.gov/pmc/articles/PMC1079389/. 3 January 2014.
[7] Pry, Peter. *Newsmax.* 28 August 2012. http://www.newsmax.com/Newsfront/roscoe-bartlett-emp-762/2012/08/28/id/450008. 4 January 2014.
[8] Alliluyeva, Svetlana. *Twenty Letters To A Friend.* New York: Harper & Row, 1967.
[9] Woolsey, R. James and Peter Vincent Pry. *Wall Street Journal.* 21 May 2013. http://online.wsj.com/news/articles/SB10001424127887324482504578455451910706908. 4 January 2014.
[10] Cooper, Henry. *American Center for Democracy.* 31 December 2013. http://acdemocracy.org/threat-from-the-gulf-of-mexico/#sthash.gZipZpdK.dpbs. 4 January 2014.
[11] Harris, Sam. *Sam Harris Blog.* 19 June 2013. http://www.samharris.org/blog/item/islam-and-the-misuses-of-ecstasy. 4 January 2014.
[12] Harris, Sam. *Sam Harris Blog.* 18 September 2006. http://www.samharris.org/site/full_text/the-end-of-liberalism/1. 4 January 2014.
[13] Albright, Madeleine. *Madam Secretary* . New York: Miramax Books, 2003.
[14] Ibid.
[15] Carter, Ashton B and William J. Perry. *Washington Post.* 22 June 2006. http://www.washingtonpost.com/wp-dyn/content/article/2006/06/21/AR2006062101518.html. 4 January 2014.
[16] Lovett, Richard A. *National Geographic News.* 2 March 2011. http://news.nationalgeographic.com/news/2011/03/110302-solar-flares-sun-storms-earth-danger-carrington-event-science/. 4 January 2014.

[17] Vergano, Dan. *USA Today*. 27 October 2010. http://usatoday30.usatoday.com/tech/science/2010-10-26-emp_N.htm. 4 January 2014.

[18] Wald, Matthew L. *New York Times*. 14 March 2012. http://www.nytimes.com/2012/03/15/business/energy-environment/electric-industry-runs-transformer-replacement-test.html. 5 January 2014.

[19] ABB. 4 October 2012. http://www.abb.us/cawp/seitp202/9a9f00ef6e90dd00c1257a7e0042e142.aspx. 5 January 2014.

[20] *Space Daily*. 5 April 2012. http://www.spacedaily.com/reports/US_DHS_Tests_Rapid_Recovery_Transformers_999.html. 5 January 2014.

[21] Cacas, Max. *Armed Forces Communications and Electronics Association (AFCEA)*. 1 June 2013. http://www.afcea.org/content/?q=node/11116. 5 January 2014.

[22] EIS Council. *Center for Security Policy*. August 2013. http://www.centerforsecuritypolicy.org/wp-content/uploads/2013/08/Catastrophic-Effect-of-an-EMP-Attack-or-Severe-Solar-Storm-5-13.pdf. 4 January 2014.

[23] Kaplan, Jeremy A. Fox News. 18 June 2013. http://www.foxnews.com/science/2013/06/18/shield-act-to-protect-from-solar-catastrophes-electromagnetic-pulses/. 4 January 2014.

[24] *Library of Congress*. n.d. http://thomas.loc.gov/cgi-bin/query/F?c113:1:./temp/~c113UObblF:e4660:. 4 January 2014.

[25] Gingrich, Newt. *Heritage Foundation*. 6 August 2009. http://www.heritage.org/research/reports/2009/08/maintaining-americas-safety-to-build-our-prosperity-and-freedom. 4 January 2014.

[26] Ibid.

[27] *Essential New York City Guide*. n.d. http://www.essential-new-york-city-guide.com/empire-state-building-facts.html. 4 January 2014.

[28] PBS. *Timeline: World Trade Center (1942-2002)*. n.d. http://www.pbs.org/wgbh/americanexperience/features/timeline/newyork/. 4 January 2014.

[29] Bagli, Charles V. *New York Times*. 17 September 2006. http://www.nytimes.com/2006/09/17/nyregion/nyregionspecial3/17freedom.html?pagewanted=all&_r=0. 4 January 2014.

[30] Suddath, Claire. *Time*. 10 September 2011. http://content.time.com/time/printout/0,8816,2092503,00.html. 4 January 2014.

[31] Rice, Christian. *Competitive Enterprise Institute.* 16 April 2013. http://www.openmarket.org/2013/04/16/lessons-on-regulatory-reform-the-brac-acts/. 5 January 2014.

[32] Putnam, Robert. *Bowling Alone: The Collapse and Revival of American Community.* New York: Simon & Schuster, 2000.

[33] Zakaria, Fareed. *Fareed Zakaria.* 3 March 2011. http://fareedzakaria.com/2011/03/03/are-americas-best-days-behind-us/. 4 January 2014.

[34] Norquist, Grover. *Leave Us Alone: Getting the Governments Hands Off Our Money, Our Guns, Our Lives.* New York: Harper Collins, 2008.

[35] General Accounting Office. February 2009. http://www.gao.gov/new.items/d09193.pdf. 5 January 2014.

[36] Will, George. *Restoration* . New York: Free Press, 1992.

[37] Ibid.

[38] Ibid.

[39] Ibid.

[40] Center for Responsive Politics. *Open Secrets.* n.d. http://www.opensecrets.org/bigpicture/reelect.php. 5 January 2014.

[41] Cooper, Michael. *New York Times.* 31 December 2002. http://www.nytimes.com/2002/12/31/nyregion/mayor-signs-law-to-ban-smoking-soon-at-most-bars.html. 6 January 2014.

[42] Clark, Amy. *CBS News.* 12 May 2006. http://www.cbsnews.com/news/school-cell-phone-ban-causes-uproar/. 6 January 2014.

[43] *NBC News.* 5 December 2006. http://www.nbcnews.com/id/16051436/#.Usp4Yfk_tu4. 6 January 2014.

[44] Kolbert, Elizabeth. *New Yorker.* 7 May 2007. http://www.newyorker.com/talk/comment/2007/05/07/070507taco_talk_kolbert. 7 January 2014.

[45] Honan, Edith. *Reuters.* 22 May 2007. http://www.reuters.com/article/2007/05/22/newyork-cabs-idUSN2250396520070522. 7 January 2014.

[46] Rivera, Ray. *New York Times.* 25 October 2007. http://www.nytimes.com/2007/10/25/nyregion/25calories.html?_r=0. 7 January 2014.

[47] *CBS News.* 23 October 2008. http://www.cbsnews.com/news/nyc-mayor-bloomberg-wins-term-limit-fight/. 7 January 2014.

[48] Myers, Steven Lee. *New York Times.* 3 November 1993. http://www.nytimes.com/1993/11/03/nyregion/new-yorkers-approve-limit-of-2-terms-for-city-officials.html. 7 January 2014.

[49] Hernandez, Javier C. *New York Times.* 3 November 2010. http://www.nytimes.com/2010/11/03/nyregion/03limits.html. 7 January 2014.

[50] Dunlap, David W. *New York Times.* 24 May 2009. http://www.nytimes.com/2009/05/25/nyregion/25bway.html. 7 January 2014.

[51] Chan, Sewell. *New York Times.* 28 October 2009. http://cityroom.blogs.nytimes.com/2009/10/28/ban-on-tobacco-flavored-products-becomes-city-law/. 7 January 2014.

[52] Ossad, Jordana. *CNN.* 24 May 2011. http://www.cnn.com/2011/US/05/23/new.york.smoking.ban/. 7 January 2014.

[53] Grynbaum, Michael H and Marjorie Connelly. *New York Times.* 23 August 2012. http://www.nytimes.com/2012/08/23/nyregion/most-new-yorkers-oppose-bloombergs-soda-ban.html. 7 January 2014.

[54] Wiessner, Daniel. *Reuters.* 17 October 2013. http://www.reuters.com/article/2013/10/17/us-nycsodaban-appeal-idUSBRE99G0T620131017. 7 January 2014.

[55] Chasmar, Jessica. *Washington Times.* 3 April 2013. http://www.washingtontimes.com/news/2013/apr/3/bill-maher-jimmy-kimmel-bloombergs-soda-ban-gives-/. 7 January 2014.

[56] Campanile, Carl. *New York Post.* 6 March 2013. http://nypost.com/2013/03/06/mayor-bloombergs-new-health-crusade-too-loud-earbuds/. 8 January 2014.

[57] *CNN.* 19 November 2013. http://www.cnn.com/2013/11/19/us/new-york-city-tobacco-age-law/. 8 January 2014.

[58] Stier, Jeff. *New York Post.* 16 December 2013. http://nypost.com/2013/12/16/bloomberg-trying-to-ban-e-cigarettes-is-silly/. 8 January 2014.

[59] Deprez, Esmé E. *Bloomberg.* 18 March 2013. http://www.bloomberg.com/news/2013-03-18/bloomberg-seeks-to-ban-cigarette-displays-in-new-york-s-stores.html. 8 January 2014.

[60] Chaban, Matt. *Crain's New York Business.* 13 June 2013. http://www.crainsnewyork.com/article/20130613/REAL_ESTATE/130619925. 8 January 2014.

[61] Flegenheimer, Matt. *New York Times*. 9 October 2013. http://www.nytimes.com/2013/10/09/nyregion/judge-blocks-new-york-city-plan-for-taxi-of-tomorrow.html?_r=0. 8 January 2014.

[62] Chayes, Matthew and Matt Clark. *Newsday*. 27 October 2013. http://www.newsday.com/news/new-york/analysis-cab-industry-donors-going-strong-for-de-blasio-1.6329782. 8 January 2014.

[63] City of New York. *Office of Mayor*. 10 October 2013. http://www1.nyc.gov/office-of-the-mayor/news/329-13/mayor-bloomberg-commissioner-sadik-khan-citywide-expansion-neighborhood-slow-zones-to. 8 January 2014.

[64] City of New York. Office of Mayor. 10 December 2013. http://www1.nyc.gov/office-of-the-mayor/news/395-13/mayor-bloomberg-buildings-commissioner-limandri-new-legislation-limit-age-of. 8 January 2014.

[65] City of New York. Office of Mayor. 17 December 2013. http://www1.nyc.gov/office-of-the-mayor/news/413-13/mayor-bloomberg-signs-legislation-prohibiting-posting-signs-city-owned-grassy-areas. 8 January 2014.

[66] News 12 Bronx. 20 December 2013. http://bronx.news12.com/news/city-council-passes-record-number-of-bills-in-final-legislative-session-of-2013-1.6647652. 8 January 2014.

[67] Alexander, Paul. *Huffington Post*. 22 April 2013. http://www.huffingtonpost.com/paul-alexander/will-the-styrofoam-cup-su_b_3108636.html. 8 January 2014.

[68] Gregory, Kia. *New York Times*. 20 December 2013. http://www.nytimes.com/2013/12/20/nyregion/new-york-council-votes-to-ban-foam-food-containers-and-to-curb-e-cigarette-smoking.html. 8 January 2014.

[69] Woolfolk, John. *San Jose Mercury News*. 27 August 2013. http://www.mercurynews.com/politics-government/ci_23958062/san-jose-approves-foam-food-container-ban. 8 January 2014.

[70] Daneman, Matthew. *USA Today*. 21 December 2013. http://www.usatoday.com/story/news/nation/2013/12/21/polystyrene-foam-ban/4141835/. 8 January 2014.

[71] Mulgrew, Michael. 15 April 2010. *Huffington Post*. 13 November 2011. <http://www.huffingtonpost.com/michael-mulgrew/closing-the-rubber-rooms_b_539745.html>.

[72] Medina, Jennifer. *New York Times*. 15 April 2010. http://www.nytimes.com/2010/04/16/nyregion/16rubber.html?_r=0. 8 January 2014.

[73] Brill, Steven. *Class Warfare: Inside the Fight to Fix America's Schools.* New York: Simon & Schuster, 2011.
[74] Ibid.
[75] Empire Center. *Triborough Trouble.* 11 January 2012. http://www.empirecenter.org/special-reports/2012/01/triboroughtrouble011112.cfm. 8 January 2014.
[76] Martinez, Barbara. *Wall Street Journal.* 1 July 2010. http://online.wsj.com/news/articles/SB10001424052748704334604575339142634105522. 8 January 2014.
[77] Brill, Steven. *Class Warfare: Inside the Fight to Fix America's Schools.* New York: Simon & Schuster, 2011.
[78] Martinez, Barbara. *Wall Street Journal.* 1 July 2010. http://online.wsj.com/news/articles/SB10001424052748704334604575339142634105522. 8 January 2014.
[79] Brill, Steven. *New Yorker.* 31 August 2009. http://www.newyorker.com/reporting/2009/08/31/090831fa_fact_brill. 8 January 2014.
[80] City of New York. Department of Education. n.d. http://schools.nyc.gov/AboutUs/default.htm. 8 January 2014.
[81] Lestch, Corinne and Ben Chapman. *New York Daily News.* 4 June 2013. http://www.nydailynews.com/new-york/nyc-education-budget-grows-25-billion-article-1.1363335. 8 January 2014.
[82] Moe, Terry M. *Hoover Institute.* 13 July 2011. http://www.hoover.org/publications/hoover-digest/article/84076. 8 January 2014.
[83] *Teachers Union Exposed.* n.d. http://teachersunionexposed.com/protecting.cfm. 8 January 2014.
[84] Hoover, Margaret. *American Individualism: How a New Generation of Conservatives Can Save the Republican Party.* New York: Crown Forum, 2011.
[85] Sink, Justin. *The Hill.* 21 November 2012. http://thehill.com/blogs/blog-briefing-room/news/269035-christie-approval-rating-up-nearly-20-percent-after-sandy. 10 January 2014.
[86] DePalma, Anthony. *New Jersey Monthly.* 13 June 2011. http://njmonthly.com/articles/lifestyle/stepping-up-communicaiton-in-post-911-new-jersey.html. 10 January 2014.
[87] New Jersey Department of Health and Senior Services. *Terrorism and Public Health Emergency Preparedness and Response Plan.* October 2002. http://www.state.nj.us/health/er/documents/erplan.pdf. 10 January 2014.

[88] McLaughlin, Seth. *Washington Times*. 29 October 2013. http://www.washingtontimes.com/news/2013/oct/29/chris-christie-superstorm-sandy-new-jersey/. 10 January 2014.

[89] Greenfieldboyce, Nell. *NPR*. 9 October 2013. http://www.npr.org/blogs/health/2013/10/11/230957188/why-scientists-held-back-details-on-a-unique-botulinum-toxin. 10 January 2014.

[90] Spalding, Matthew and Trent England. *Heritage Foundaton*. 10 February 2011. http://www.heritage.org/research/reports/2011/02/article-v-congress-conventions-and-constitutional-amendments. 10 January 2014.

[91] Shea, Christopher. *Wall Street Journal*. 2 November 2011. http://blogs.wsj.com/ideas-market/2011/11/02/time-for-a-constitutional-convention/. 10 January 2014.

[92] Greenspan, Alan. *The Map and the Territory: Risk, Human Nature, and the Future of Forecasting*. New York: Penguin Press, 2013.

[93] Ibid.

[94] Cassidy, John. *New Yorker*. 29 October 2013. http://www.newyorker.com/online/blogs/johncassidy/2013/10/alan-greenspan-rediscovers-keynes-sort-of.html. 10 January 2014.

[95] Ariely, Dan. *Harvard Business Review*, July 2009. http://hbr.org/2009/07/the-end-of-rational-economics/ar/1. 10 January 2014.

[96] Davidson, Dan. *Federal Times*. 11 November 2002. http://www.thecre.com/pdf/20021111_fedtimes-tozzi.pdf. 10 January 2014.

[97] Boudreaux, Donald J. *Wall Street Journal*, 23 April 2013. http://online.wsj.com/news/articles/SB10001424127887324105204578384850872793208. 10 January 2014.

[98] Ibid.

[99] The Avalon Project at Yale Law School. *Thomas Jefferson First Inaugural Address*. n.d. http://avalon.law.yale.edu/19th_century/jefinau1.asp. 10 January 2014.

[100] Sloman, Steve. *American Scientist*. 2012. http://www.americanscientist.org/bookshelf/pub/the-battle-between-intuition-and-deliberation. 11 January 2014.

Chapter 10 End Notes

1 MacArthur, Douglas. *Reminiscences*. New York: McGraw-Hill, 1964.

[2] Manchester, William. *American Caesar: Douglas MacArthur 1880-1964.* New York: Back Bay Books/ Little, Brown and Company, 2008. http://books.google.com/books?id=iuA-ZOCpTfIC&pg=PT161&dq=Don't+be+foolish+douglas;+you+and+the+budget+must+get+together+on+this&hl=en&sa=X&ei=Myt6Uq3_EbPIsATLyILoCA&ved=0CDUQ6AEwAQ#v=onepage&q=Don't%20be%20foolish%20douglas%3B%20you%20and%20the%20budget%.

[3] Grafton, John. *Great Speeches: Franklin Delano Roosevelt.* Mineola: Dover Publications, Inc., 1999.

[4] Samuelson, Robert. *RealClearPolitics.* 5 September 2013. http://www.realclearpolitics.com/articles/2013/09/05/the_war_weary_myth_119832.html. 25 October 2013.

[5] *Office of Management and Budget Historical Tables.* n.d. http://www.whitehouse.gov/sites/default/files/omb/budget/fy2013/assets/hist.pdf. 25 October 2013.

[6] Eberstadt, Nicholas. *A Nation of Takers: America's Entitlement Epidemic.* West Conshohocken: Templeton Press, 2012.

[7] Cary, Mary Kate. *U.S. News and World Report.* 19 December 2012. http://www.usnews.com/opinion/articles/2012/12/19/the-shocking-truth-on-entitlements. 25 October 2013.

[8] Sherman, Arloc, Robert Greenstein and Kathy Ruffing. *Center on Budget and Policy Priorities.* 10 February 2012. http://www.cbpp.org/cms/?fa=view&id=3677. 25 October 2013.

[9] Hobbs, Frank and Nicole Stoops. *U.S. Census Bureau.* n.d. http://www.census.gov/prod/2002pubs/censr-4.pdf. 25 October 2013.

[10] Johnson, Paul. *A History of the American People.* New York: Harper Collins, 1997.

[11] England, Gordon. *New York Times*, 15 July 2011. http://www.nytimes.com/2011/07/15/opinion/15England.html?_r=0. 28 October 2013.

[12] Higham, Scott, Kimberly Kindy and Dan Keating. *Washington Post*, 18 December 2010. http://www.washingtonpost.com/politics/senate-panel-ban-on-stock-for-appointees-but-not-itself-seen-as-double-standard/2012/02/06/gIQAGA6euQ_story.html. 28 October 2013.

[13] Gates, Robert. *U.S. Department of Defense.* 3 May 2010. http://www.defense.gov/speeches/speech.aspx?speechid=1460. 1 November 2013.

[14] Coburn, Tom A. *Debt Bomb.* Nashville: Thomas Nelson, 2012.

[15] Ibid.

[16] Liu, Korbin and Kenneth G. Manton. *U.S. Department of Health and Human Services*. February 1988. http://aspe.hhs.gov/daltcp/reports/pps.htm. 1 November 2013.

[17] Daggett, Stephen. *Congressional Research Service*. 12 August 2010. http://www.fas.org/sgp/crs/natsec/efficiency.pdf. 29 October 2013.

[18] National Commission on Fiscal Responsibility and Reform. *National Commission on Fiscal Responsibility and Reform*. 10 November 2010. http://www.fiscalcommission.gov/sites/fiscalcommission.gov/files/documents/Illustrative_List_11.10.2010.pdf. 29 October 2013.

[19] Coburn, Tom. *U.S. Senator Tom Coburn*. July 2011. http://www.coburn.senate.gov/public//index.cfm?a=Files.Serve&File_id=92a11aeb-a484-45d4-b02a-83071603accf. 29 October 2013.

[20] Rosenberg, Alyssa. *Government Executive*. 3 September 2009. http://www.govexec.com/oversight/2009/09/agencies-cut-back-on-travel/29896/. 1 November 2013.

[21] Freeman, Ben. *Third Way*. June 2013. http://www.thirdway.org/publications/713. 3 November 2013.

[22] Ziezulewicz, Geoff and John Vandiver. *Stars and Stripes*. 24 March 2011. http://www.stripes.com/news/gates-memo-includes-cuts-to-102-flag-general-officer-positions-1.138794. 3 November 2013.

[23] Freeman, Ben. *Third Way*. June 2013. http://www.thirdway.org/publications/713. 3 November 2013.

[24] *Fabius Maximus*. 10 September 2012. http://fabiusmaximus.com/2012/09/10/american-military-force-changed-43153/. 3 November 2013.

[25] Baddin, Jed. *American Spectator*. 20 February 2012. http://spectator.org/archives/2012/02/20/tar-and-feathers-for-ray-mabus/. 3 November 2013.

[26] Bell, Steve, et al. *Bipartisan Policy Center*. 11 October 2013. http://bipartisanpolicy.org/library/report/merely-stupid-dangerous-sequester%E2%80%99s-effects-national-and-economic-security. 3 November 2013.

[27] Lane, Charles. *Washington Post*, 25 March 2013. http://articles.washingtonpost.com/2013-03-25/opinions/38008249_1_working-age-retirees-tricare-military-health. 3 November 2013.

[28] Roy, Avik. *Forbes*. 12 March 2012. http://www.forbes.com/sites/aroy/2012/03/12/how-health-care-spending-strains-the-u-s-military/. 3 November 2013.

[29] *General Accounting Office (GAO).* March 2011. http://www.gao.gov/new.items/d11318sp.pdf. 3 November 2013.

[30] Coburn, Tom. *U.S. Senator Tom Coburn.* July 2011. http://www.coburn.senate.gov/public//index.cfm?a=Files.Serve&File_id=92a11aeb-a484-45d4-b02a-83071603accf. 29 October 2013.

[31] Congressional Budget Office. March 2011. http://www.cbo.gov/sites/default/files/cbofiles/ftpdocs/120xx/doc12085/03-10-reducingthedeficit.pdf. 4 November 2013.

[32] Roy, Avik. *Forbes.* 12 March 2012. http://www.forbes.com/sites/aroy/2012/03/12/how-health-care-spending-strains-the-u-s-military/. 3 November 2013.

[33] *Veterans of Modern Warfare (VMW).* n.d. http://www.vmwusa.org/index.php/healthcareservices/hcarticles/47-health/1079-va-care-end-eyed-for-13-million-vets. 4 November 2013.

[34] Will, George. *Washington Post,* 26 October 2012. http://articles.washingtonpost.com/2012-10-26/opinions/35501609_1_disability-romney-federal-transfer-payments. 4 November 2013.

[35] Roy, Avik. *Forbes*, 22 August 2011. http://www.forbes.com/sites/theapothecary/2011/08/22/hospital-monopolies-the-biggest-driver-of-health-costs-that-nobody-talks-about/. 4 November 2013.

[36] Roy, Avik. *National Review*, 2 June 2010. http://www.nationalreview.com/agenda/56277/how-socialized-medicine-harms-veterans/avik-roy. 4 November 2013.

[37] Oswald, Rachel. *Nuclear Threat Initiative.* 11 May 2012. http://www.nti.org/gsn/article/nato-should-use-summit-address-us-tactical-nukes-europe-experts-say/. 6 November 2013.

[38] Fradkin, Hillel and Lewis Libby. *Hudson Institute.* 25 June 2013. https://www.hudson.org/index.cfm?fuseaction=publication_details&id=9638. 18 January 2014.

[39] Ignatius, David. *Washington Post.* 16 October 2013. http://www.washingtonpost.com/opinions/david-ignatius-turkey-blows-israels-cover-for-iranian-spy-ring/2013/10/16/7d9c1eb2-3686-11e3-be86-6aeaa439845b_story.html. 6 November 2013.

[40] Morrison, Wayne M. *Congressional Research Service.* 14 January 2014. http://www.fas.org/sgp/crs/row/RL33536.pdf. 18 January 2014

[41] Ibid.

[42] Bradsher, Keith. *New York Times.* 19 May 2007. http://www.nytimes.com/2007/05/19/business/worldbusiness/19yuan.html?pagewanted=print&_r=0. 5 November 2013.

[43] *Wall Street Journal.* 7 August 2013. http://blogs.wsj.com/moneybeat/2013/08/07/yuan-touches-record-high-against-dollar/. 5 November 2013.

[44] Kissinger, Henry. *Does America Need A Foreign Policy?* New York: Simon & Schuster, 2001.

[45] Rinehart, Ian E, Steven A Hildreth and Susan V. Lawrence. 24 June 2013. *Congressional Research Service.* http://www.fas.org/sgp/crs/nuke/R43116.pdf. 6 November 2013.

[46] Barnes, Julian E, Nathan Hodge and Jeremy Page. *Wall Street Journal.* 4 January 2012. http://online.wsj.com/news/articles/SB10001424052970204397704577074631582060996. 6 November 2013.

[47] Office of the Secretary of Defense. "Annual Report to Congress: Military and Security Involving the People's Republic of China." n.d. http://www.defense.gov/pubs/2013_china_report_final.pdf. 6 November 2013.

[48] Blanchard, Ben and John Ruwitch. *Reuters.* 5 March 2013. http://www.reuters.com/article/2013/03/05/us-china-parliament-defence-idUSBRE92403620130305. 6 November 2013.

[49] 19 August 2011. *Politifact.com.* http://www.politifact.com/truth-o-meter/statements/2011/aug/19/jon-huntsman/jon-huntsman-says-internet-use-china-forum-discon/. 6 November 2013.

[50] Zakaria, Fareed. *The Post-American World.* New York: W.W. Norton, 2008.

[51] Pomfret, John. 27 July 2008. *Washington Post.* http://articles.washingtonpost.com/2008-07-27/opinions/36920178_1_china-people-s-republic-hardscrabble-countryside. 6 November 2013.

[52] Tatlow, Didi Kirsten. *New York Times.* 10 September 2012._ http://www.nytimes.com/2012/09/11/business/global/rise-in-chinas-aging-poses-challenge-to-beijing.html?pagewanted=all. 6 November 2013.